Psychoanalysis from the Ii

In the face of considerable scepticism over the function and effectiveness of psychoanalysis, Lena Ehrlich demonstrates how analysis is unique in its potential to transform patients at an emotionally cellular level by helping them access and process long-standing conflicts and traumatic experiences.

Using detailed clinical vignettes, the author illustrates that when analysts practice from the inside out, i.e. consider that external obstacles to initiating and deepening an analysis inevitably reflect analysts' fears of their internal world and of intimacy, they become better able to speak to patients' long-term suffering.

This book, free from psychoanalytic jargon, stands out in its ability to help readers feel more effective, confident, and optimistic about practicing psychoanalysis by providing insights and recommendations about beginning and deepening analysis and sustaining oneself as an analyst over time. It will appeal to both beginners and experienced analysts, as well as supervisors, educators, and those interested in the workings of their minds and in building more intimate relationships.

Lena Theodorou Ehrlich is a Training and Supervising Analyst at the Michigan Psychoanalytic Institute, and a Clinical Supervisor in the Department of Psychiatry, University of Michigan Medical School. In addition to maintaining a lively practice of psychoanalysis, psychotherapy and supervision for 30 years, she is widely recognized for her original contributions to the literature on beginning and deepening analysis and building and maintaining a psychoanalytic practice. Born and raised in Greece, she is a trilingual immigrant, a wife, mother, and avid traveler.

"Through her sensitive clinical practice, Lena Ehrlich shows how the psychoanalytic process begins and deepens in the analyst's mind and explores our resistances to letting it come to life and grow. Her writing has strengthened my own identity and practice as psychoanalyst. It has also informed our research in the Working Party on Initiating Psychoanalysis of the European Psychoanalytic Federation; in turn, our findings have confirmed those from her fine clinical practice. Even on the difficult topic of teleanalysis she is well-informed, cogent and thought-provoking. It is a real treat to have her work collected in this book, which will be a must for all psychoanalysts."

—**Bernard Reith**, President of the Swiss Psychoanalytical Society

"In lucid prose, Lena Ehrlich conveys the multitudinous ways an analyst develops her capacities to face her own conflicts, resistances, and to tolerate her own affect and intense countertransference reactions. Simultaneously, she shows us her belief in her patients' capacities to grow and change. These two developments within herself combine to create the conditions for the development of a deep, intimate analytic process to evolve. Her openness in facing her own struggle to form an analytic identity provides a model of self-scrutiny that should be inspiring to all clinicians and especially for young analysts."

—**Judy L. Kantrowitz**, Training and supervising analyst,
Boston Psychoanalytic Society and Institute

"Based on extensive experience and written with uncommon clarity, this timely book demonstrates convincingly that psychoanalysis, despite its troubled history and many current challenges, 'has the potential to transform us at an emotionally cellular level, helping us be present and sturdy inside ourselves and better able to connect with and love others.'"

—**Howard B. Levine**, MD, Editor-in-Chief, The
Routledge W. R. Bion Studies Series

Psychoanalysis from the Inside Out

Developing and Sustaining an Analytic Identity and Practice

Lena Theodorou Ehrlich

Routledge
Taylor & Francis Group

LONDON AND NEW YORK

First published 2020
by Routledge
2 Park Square, Milton Park, Abingdon, Oxon OX14 4RN

and by Routledge
52 Vanderbilt Avenue, New York, NY 10017

Routledge is an imprint of the Taylor & Francis Group, an informa business

British Library Cataloguing-in-Publication Data
A catalogue record for this book is available from the British Library

Library of Congress Cataloging-in-Publication Data
A catalog record has been requested for this book

ISBN: 978-0-367-50516-5 (hbk)
ISBN: 978-0-367-50519-6 (pbk)
ISBN: 978-1-003-05019-3 (ebk)

Typeset in Times New Roman
by Taylor & Francis Books

Contents

In memory of my mother, Elektra, whose name captured the vibrancy of her spirit

To my husband, Joshua, and my children, Anna and Alexi

Acknowledgments

I'm delighted to be writing these acknowledgments because I can envision the completion of this project and it gives me the chance to take stock of my good fortune of having the kind of support that makes writing a book possible. I've been blessed with generous and inspiring supervisors, mentors, and colleagues. As a patient, I've also been fortunate to have found analysts who believed strongly in psychoanalysis and whose ongoing internal presence contributes to my capacity to function as an analyst.

Coming of age analytically at the Michigan Psychoanalytic Institute and Society, a psychoanalytic organization with many members who practice analysis, has also been critical to my developing the vision that practicing analysis is possible and to acquiring the skills and fortitude to do it. The MPI/MPS community has provided a sturdy, nurturing professional home for me. I'm grateful to my hardworking colleagues for contributing immeasurable time and effort to sustain it as a generative, welcoming, and analysis-friendly institution.

Both my national and local study groups have been integral to my strengthening my sense of myself as an analyst and continuing to develop my skills. I'm thankful to the members of my national cohort, Group for the Study of Psychoanalytic Process, for preparing, presenting, and energetically discussing more hours of detailed quality analytic process at a time than in any other professional setting I've been in. I have found that having such direct access to senior analysts' work provides more opportunities for experiential learning second only to being in or practicing analysis. My local study group members are my monthly companions who listen closely to analytic process, which we take turns presenting. Listening to their work and their input provides me with courage and inspiration and continuously stretches my ability to listen and intervene.

I'm deeply grateful to my patients for entrusting me with their profoundest fears and most intimate wishes and for permitting me to stay with them closely enough, intensively enough, and long enough to be of help. Each one in his or her own unique way has contributed to who I am as an analyst, a writer, and a person. This book, literally, would not be possible without them. I also feel very thankful for my supervisees and consultees who share their analytic journeys with me and provide me with opportunities to keep learning.

Many people assisted me directly with this project. I'm indebted to my friends and colleagues Drs. Aisha Abbasi, William Bernstein, Dale Boesky, Harvey Falit, Margaret Ann Hanly, Nancy Kulish, Howard Levine, Channing Lipson, Jerry Melchiode, Shelley Orgel, Dwarky Rao, Sally Rosenberg, and Arden Rothstein for their careful reading and invaluable feedback on earlier versions of chapters in this book. I'm also appreciative of Salman Akhtar's help in reviewing and offering suggestions for my initial proposal and directing me to a receptive publisher. Last but not least, I'm greatly appreciative of my sister-in-law of 34 years and published author, Esther Ehrlich, who served as a wise and diligent copy editor and helped give this book its final form.

Some claim that choosing a life partner is the most consequential decision a person makes. That's certainly true for me. Joshua Ehrlich, my life partner, has been the harbor from which all my travels—intellectual, emotional, and visiting wildlife around the world—have been made possible. His love, lucidity, editing skills, and generosity are evident throughout this book. I'm also deeply grateful for my adult children, Anna and Alexi, and their partners, Dirk and Becca, who have been steadfast in their belief in me and in their vision that this project, too, will end satisfactorily someday. Their loving presence in my life profoundly sustains me.

In closing, I'm immeasurably grateful to E. who helped me find A. within me and refind aspects of myself and psychoanalysis.

Chapter 1 is based on "The Analyst's Reluctance to Begin a New Analysis", *Journal of the American Psychoanalytic Association*, 52: 1075–1093. (2004) Used with permission of SAGE Publications, Inc. doi: 10.1177/00030651040520040501.

Chapter 2 is based on "Analysis Begins in the Analyst's Mind: Conceptual and Technical Considerations on Recommending Analysis", *Journal of the American Psychoanalytic Association*, 61: 1077–1107. (2013) Used with permission of SAGE Publications, Inc. doi: 10.1177/0003065113511988.

Chapter 3 is based on "Finding Control Cases and Maintaining Immersion: Challenges and Opportunities", *Journal of the American Psychoanalytic Association*, 64: 983–1012. (2016) Used with permission of SAGE Publications, Inc. doi: 10.1177/0003065116671306.

Chapter 4 is based on "The Analyst's Ambivalence About Continuing and Deepening an Analysis", *Journal of the American Psychoanalytic Association*, 58: 515–532. (2010) Used with permission of SAGE Publications, Inc. doi: 10.1177/000306651103748615116688460.

Chapter 5 is based on "Teleanalysis: Slippery Slope or Rich Opportunity?", *Journal of the American Psychoanalytic Association*, 67: 249–279. (2017) Used with permission of SAGE Publications, Inc. doi: 10.1177/0003065119847170.

Introduction: Why practice psychoanalysis?

The New Yorker cartoons, a remaining bastion for psychoanalysis in popular culture, offer a window into the public's view of the analyst at work. Perhaps you've seen the cartoon, which shows an exasperated patient turning around to look at his impassive male analyst and asking "Are we there yet?" or the cartoon with an apprehensive patient relaying his chiropractor's warning to his middle-aged male analyst that lying on a couch is the worst possible position for a person's back, or the one that portrays patient and analyst having fallen asleep on the job? Although a few cartoons offer sympathetic portrayals of analysis, many depict emotionally distant male analysts conducting never-ending, ineffective treatments with beleaguered patients—a vision of analysis as an archaic, self-indulgent, exploitative undertaking. I find some merit in these popular views of psychoanalysis. Aspects of psychoanalytic theory are, indeed, obsolete; analysis has been and can be practiced inadequately and exploitatively, and it's an expensive, time-consuming treatment, ill-suited to the expediency our fast-paced contemporary life requires.

In addition to navigating negative public opinions, contemporary analysts must contend with many challenging realities within the field of psychoanalysis, including the multitude of competing theories of the mind and of therapeutic action, the lack of consensus among analysts about which therapeutic elements lead to the best outcomes for which patients, and even a lack of agreement as to what good outcomes look like. Added to these considerations, many psycho-analysts bear the burden of being affiliated with fractured psychoanalytic organizations and practicing among colleagues who have been traumatized by analysis and feel cynical or hopeless.

Analysts also face daunting demands in the consulting room. Most analysts I know practice analysis with the conscious intention of helping each patient with what's most difficult for that patient to feel and know. Yet, what we've come to understand about our participation is that, in the process of helping each patient with what's most difficult in the patient, we inevitably experience states of mind that are hard to identify, bear, and make sense of in ourselves. While these distressing states of mind—ours and our patients—compel us to continue to do psychological work, they can also repel us from analyzing.

Some analysts stop practicing analysis altogether and shift to other undertakings. The rest of us continue to practice but with various levels of engagement and sense of satisfaction. Some of us register that we're dissatisfied and emotionally disengaged; many of us don't. I've seen this conscious or unconscious emotional disengagement take different forms. I've seen it manifested in analysts' pessimistic attitudes about our capacity to help or our patients' capacity to be helped, our going-through-the-motions participation, and in some instances, our narcissistically motivated misusing or abusing our patients.

At this point, you'd be justified in asking yourself: Given its considerable risks, demands, and failings, why would I practice psychoanalysis at all? How can I help myself or, in my role as educator, help my analytic students develop and sustain the interest, determination, and commitment to continue to practice psychoanalysis, given the adverse pressure from outside and within the psychoanalytic world and the formidable strains of the daily clinical work and my internal life?

The present collection of essays, born out of my experiences with psychoanalysis as a candidate, patient, graduate analyst, teacher, supervisor, and Candidate Progression Chair, is intended as a response to these and other pressing questions about psychoanalytic identity and practice. Having sustained a robust analytic and supervisory practice in a small city with a high concentration of qualified mental health professionals for 30 years, I share my understanding of how analysts can find, develop, and nurture our capacity to practice analytically and how we can engage patients and deepen that engagement. I convey my experience that psychoanalysis can be beneficial, even life-sustaining, that maintaining a psychoanalytic practice is possible, and that analysis begins and deepens in the analyst's mind. Most critically, I illuminate how by identifying and focusing on the internal variables that facilitate and prevent analysts from initiating, deepening, and helping patients end their analysis—practicing from the inside out—we become better able to respond to patients' needs for intensive treatment.

While acknowledging the merits of some criticisms about psychoanalysis, I offer an alternative perspective. I claim that, when practiced well enough, the contemporary practice of psychoanalysis can not only be helpful and feasible but has the potential to be more effective than ever. I demonstrate that, despite its limitations and dangers of misuse, psychoanalysis, now more than ever, offers a relationship and a process that has the potential to transform us at an emotionally cellular level, helping us be present and sturdy inside ourselves and better able to connect with and love others.

Why now more than ever? Listening closely, and often failing to listen closely, behind the couch for longer than a century has taught us much about how the human mind and relationships work. We've developed greater insights into the nature and functions of unconscious fantasy, infantile sexuality, defenses, countertransference, affect tolerance, attachment, conflict, trauma, self-states, narcissistic vulnerability, facilitating environments, and psychic retreats. We now possess more experience and a greater, more refined understanding of the mani-festations and effects of inhibitions, guilt, and dissociation. We also have a better appreciation of the vulnerability of the analyst's role and our inadvertent parti-cipation in the analytic process, which helps us listen closer, understand better, and intervene more effectively.

I have a long-standing interest in identifying what allows analysts to remain committed to searching for emotional truth and intimacy. Like many analysts I know well, my passion for psychoanalysis can be traced back to when I was a child and looking to understand and manage difficult emotions in myself and toward important adults around me. Although, of course, I didn't explicitly know it at the time, my many thoughts, questions, and feelings about my parents' divorce and remarriage to each other, the loss of a beloved nanny, the birth of my brother, and the behavior and moods of the adults in my life, moved me to search for answers and relief. Novels served as my first psychoanalytic textbooks. I was interested in identifying how others felt and finding clues to how they managed their feelings. I functioned as an amateur psychoanalyst long before I signed up for formal training.

Given my passion for reading, it was fitting that my formal introduction to psychoanalysis also took place through the written word. As a young adoles-cent, I discovered Freud (1900). When his classic book, *The Interpretation of Dreams*, appeared on our coffee table it served as my first reading in psycho-analysis. My mother, a dynamic Greek woman whose drive and curiosity didn't match the place and time of her birth, had wanted to become a psychologist. As a young woman, she'd tried to pursue her ambition and, since psychology wasn't taught in Greece, even went as far as applying and securing an accep-tance to a psychology program at an English university. As family lore has it, on the eve of my mother's departure and while inspecting his only child's packed suitcases, her protective Greek father had a change of heart. Evoking the perils awaiting a young woman alone in a foreign city, my grandfather called off my mother's trip. Though her plans were thwarted, her interest in psychology remained strong.

Years later, when she'd become a young mother, her earlier interest found expression in her entering psychoanalysis with the first Greek analyst, Dr. Kouretas, who had just returned from Paris freshly analyzed by Marie Bona-parte. Though I didn't learn the history of her frustrated ambition to study psychology until I was an adult, my mother's strong desire to make sense of her own and others' feelings and later her love for psychoanalysis and for her analyst were palpable while I was growing up; they were among her many gifts to me. It would be an oversimplification to suggest that what motivated me to become an analyst was to fulfill my mother's dreams, or surpass her, or become the object of her oedipal love, like her analyst had been. But it would not be off the mark to suggest that each of these motivations contributed to my own strong interest to become a psychoanalyst.

Later, in formally becoming a psychoanalyst, my long-standing pursuit of understanding and articulating feelings found a welcoming port. I felt at home being taught that feelings were not facts but there were facts within the feelings. I felt sustained and affirmed to be surrounded by colleagues who believed that disturbing thoughts and feelings were not bad, shameful, or wrong but had history and meaning. I felt inspired to discover that feelings could be used to deconstruct and reconstruct one's past to find a less distorted, kinder version of oneself and better capacity to love and feel loved.

During training and the beginning of my career as an analyst, I became enthralled by my profession. I thought that psychoanalysis was *the* antidote for emotional suffering because it provided answers to all of life's difficulties for everyone. It took me some time to recognize that this kind of idealization contained both my genuine love and appreciation for analysis and analysts but also my attempts to cover what I found deficient and disappointing in psychoanalytic theory, in practice, in my own analysis, and in myself.

I felt propelled to write this book for two main reasons. First, as a psychoanalyst, I'm determined to identify obstacles that prevent analysts from practicing more and better analysis. Second, as someone who has benefited from analysis as a patient, I want analysis to continue to be available for those who need it. Therefore, I'm interested in countering the tendency I see in myself and other analysts to attribute hesitancy about recommending and practicing analysis to patients' lack of interest in intensive treatment. Although anecdotal reports suggest that fewer patients now enter treatment explicitly requesting analysis than they did when psychoanalysis was in vogue, I've observed that as many prospective patients as ever continue to present in analysts' and candidates' offices suffering from deep-rooted and often crippling emotional difficulties that call for the depth of understanding that is uniquely psychoanalytic. Because the quality of many human lives depends on receiving the intensive psychological help that only psychoanalysts are trained to provide, analysts must continue to offer psychoanalysis and strive to identify the conditions that allow us to assist our patients in benefiting the most from their analysis.

What has enabled me to continue to practice analysis past graduation has not been just my enthusiasm but my continued effort to let myself know the perils of psychoanalysis and my fears of initiating and practicing it. I've relied as much on my confidence in its usefulness as on identifying and analyzing my reservations about its efficacy. Therefore, I also write to highlight the demands of practicing psychoanalysis and to explore their influence on our capacity to engage and practice analytically.

One of the many ways that I sustain myself is by reading the writing of other analysts, who I imagine in their consulting room, intently working to find a way to help others with their daily suffering. Their courage, resolve, and dedication has motivated and nurtured me. From readers' responses to my writing, I've also found that my speaking about the challenges and the opportunities in the work has been helpful to others. I've been told by colleagues that reading my view that analysis begins and deepens in the analyst's mind encourages them to look for and reflect upon their fears of analyzing, which often results in their becoming better able to engage with their patients.

My writing represents one analyst's effort to communicate her way of becoming and continuing to become an analyst. I articulate what makes it possible for me to practice analytically in the hope that you can find what might better sustain you in your analytic practice. I also write because, in addition to my motivation to help other analysts, expressing my struggles as an analyst assists me in my continuous effort to face them. I offer my thoughts and experience with the hope that they will provide a counterpoint to the bitterness, discouragement, and externalization of difficulty in analytic writings on one hand and a cavalier, rigid, idealized, perfectionistic view of analysis on the other.

Over the years of practicing and witnessing others learn to practice psychoanalysis, I've come to recognize that rich and meaningful training experiences constitute necessary but not sufficient conditions for maintaining an analytic mind and identity. I've observed that analysts vary in our capacity to sustain the confidence and desire to practice analysis. Even those of us who have continued to practice post-graduation are interested in which variables facilitate and which impede our capacity to practice analysis. This book is written for you whether you are an analyst in training, a graduate analyst who wants to continue to practice and teach psychoanalysis or a human being who strives to savor more of the richness and complexity of relationships and your inner life.

The chapters that follow reflect my thinking and experience over the course of the last 30 years. In reading my work, you might notice differences in both content and style between chapters that I wrote more recently and ones that I wrote at an earlier time. Some changes I explicitly articulate, others remain implicit. My commitment to non-externalization has remained steady and passionate while my appreciation of the demands of practicing, the limitations of psychoanalysis and its misuses, and the importance of the analyst's mind in facilitating analysis at each stage has increased. You might also notice that while I persist in valuing free association and articulating meaning, I've become progressively more aware that understanding alone is not deeply transformative. I've come to better appreciate the curative effects of good-enough interpersonal experiences while in psychoanalysis—experiences of being listened to closely enough, kindly enough, with enough genuine interest and care, and clear thoughtful boundaries.

How can analysts find, develop, and sustain past graduation the confidence and desire to practice analysis? What makes it feasible for analysts to maintain optimism that analysis will help our patients in the face of our own and our patients' realistic and unrealistic fears? How can we facilitate the beginning and deepening of an analysis? What exactly *is* deepening? How can we help our candidates find cases and practice as much analysis as they want? What are the analytic merits of Skype and telephone analysis? Under what conditions can teleanalysis be useful? What can analysts gain from consultation? With detailed clinical material, I'll address these and many more questions essential to contemporary analytic practice.

References

Freud, S. (1900). *The Interpretation of Dreams*. Standard Edition, Volume IV, The Hogarth Press and the Institute of Psychoanalysis, London.

Part One

Finding Ourselves as Analysts

Chapter 1

The analyst's reluctance to begin a new analysis

At present in the United States we practice less analysis per analyst than ever before. The last full report (Brauer and Brauer 1996) from a survey conducted by the Committee on Psychoanalytic Practice of the American Psychoanalytic Association presents the following findings: the number of patients in analysis per analyst has been steadily diminishing over the last twenty-five years, at a rate of roughly one per cent a year. At the time of the last survey, certified or active members who had patients in analysis saw on average three analytic cases. The reported morale and level of satisfaction of those who practiced less analysis was low in comparison to that of those practicing more analysis. Troubled by these findings, psychoanalysts have been searching for an explanation of why psychoanalysis is practiced less. Widely accepted reasons include the public's negative attitude toward psychoanalysis, the current socioeconomic climate, and the public's expectation of a quick cure.

While useful to consider at the organizational level, these realities can't of themselves fully illuminate the factors affecting the *individual* analyst's practice. The analyst's interest, experience, confidence, energy level, skill, unconscious conflicts, personality style, social and professional affiliations, locale, attitude, and conviction are among the many variables that can affect an analyst's practice. My primary interest in what follows is to explore how one variable, the analyst's reluctance to begin an analysis, affects analytic practice. I don't intend to negate the role of external realities; instead I suggest that analysts can use adverse external realities to obscure this reluctance.

Psychoanalytic training, demanding as it sometimes was, helpfully cushioned me from fully realizing the implications of being an analyst. During training, my anxiety about analytic work was mediated by the support that an analyst-in-training receives as a candidate (Kantrowitz et al. 1989). My analysis and work in close supervision tempered some of my conflicts and insecurities about practicing independently, provided narcissistic support, afforded me the illusion of sharing the responsibility for the work, and offered me a fantasy of protection. I immersed myself in studying and practicing analysis and focused on becoming an analyst. The more I experienced the healing possibilities of the method, the more unwavering I became in my commitment to practicing analysis, or so I thought. While in training, I'd been able to find analytic patients easily and speedily in order to fulfill the requirements of my institute. I had one low-fee, one moderate-fee, and one full-fee patient. Nonetheless, as I approached graduation, I began to question whether it would be possible to develop an analytic practice. I listened anxiously to reports that the number of patients in analysis was decreasing. I worried about rumors that there were no patients willing to engage in a time-consuming, expensive, and out-of-favor endeavor—at least not with a beginning analyst.

For a few months after my graduation, I thought my worry was justified by external reality. Gradually, however, I realized that I was failing to take into account my own experience: I'd been able to find analytic patients in the recent past (I'd begun my last control case within the last year). I then started to question whether the obstacle was indeed patient availability. Reassessing my practice, I realized that during the initial consultations with several patients who might benefit from more intensive work I'd accepted too readily that they were unavailable for analysis. This puzzled me further. Reluctantly, I turned my attention to the possibility that, despite my conscious eagerness to practice as an analyst, I was hesitant to recommend and engage in analysis.

The analyst's reluctance

Starting with Freud (1912a, 1912b, 1913), analysts have portrayed analytic beginnings as predictable, grounded in reasonable considerations, and leading to objectively determined recommendations. Efforts to determine analyzability (Bachrach 1990; Erle and Goldberg 2003) and proper beginning technique (Lichtenberg and Auchincloss 1989; Busch 1995) dominated these discussions. This emphasis reflected the prevailing assumptions of the time that treatment outcome depends primarily on the patient's ability to participate in the analytic process (Kantrowitz 1993) and the analyst's capacity to apply correct technique. Analysts' participation was portrayed as technically neutral, comparable, and uniform (Bachrach 1983).

In recent years, we've expanded our understanding of analytic process to include not only the patient's conflicts and resistances but also the analyst's inadvertent participation. Boesky (1990), in a seminal paper on psychoanalytic process, discusses the analyst's unconscious contribution to the patient's resistance: "If there can be no analysis without resistance by the patient, then it is equally true that there can be no treatment conducted by any analyst without counter-resistance or countertransference, sooner or later" (p. 573). Smith (1993) writes about the analyst's reluctance to engage in analytic work as a manifestation of resistance to self-analysis. He proposes that all analysts in the course of their work face, and at the same time avoid facing, our own character difficulties. As the patient resists engagement, so too does the analyst.

Given my present task, the central questions are: How do the analyst's counter-resistances manifest themselves at the beginning of treatment? And, more specifically, how do they bear on the analyst's recommendations?

Jacobs (1988) is among the few analysts who have identified "internal factors" in the analyst as a critical variable affecting the practice of analysis. As chair of the American Psychoanalytic Association's Committee on Psychoanalytic Practice, he suggested, based on information collected from seventy-one analysts from several institutes, including training analysts, senior non-training analysts, and recent graduates, that the number of referrals didn't determine the size of an analyst's practice. According to Jacobs, the way the analyst conducted the consultation and the opening phase of treatment was more decisive. Jacobs concluded his report by stressing "that internal factors operating in the analyst seem to be as important as such external conditions as the state of the economy, the intellectual climate, the kind of insurance coverage available and the prevailing attitude toward analysis in any given locale. Not surprisingly, ambivalence toward recommending analysis to patients is not uncommon in analysts. What feeds this ambivalence is not clear at this point and in any case is an issue beyond the scope of this report" (pp. 101–102).

Some writers have suggested that the analyst's ambivalence is a reaction to the intense affect generated in the analytic situation. Friedman (1988) speaks to powerful feelings engendered by the therapeutic situation and to the discomfort that is a constant companion to clinical work. He suggests that therapists don't acknowledge that they "function in a sea of trouble" or that treatment is "an uncivil, threatening, even brutal struggle, instigated by gently reflective intellectuals dedicated to delicate speculations" (p. 6). Elaborating on Friedman's ideas, Greenberg (2002) suggests that analysts at work are in a constant state of tension between our natural inclination to respond to the patient in a personal and unreflective manner and our professional inclination to analyze.

In an address to the Board on Professional Standards, Orgel (1989) also attended to the turmoil of analysis and the defensiveness that it evokes. He referred specifically to the emotional challenge of practicing as an analyst while simultaneously wishing not to analyze. Orgel described having witnessed analysts and candidates who, in parallel with their patients, defend against "terrifying and/or forbidden drives" by resisting doing analysis. In another contribution, Orgel (1990) relates this resistance to doing analysis to analysts' unrecognized feelings toward their own analysts. He suggests that analysts must become well acquainted with their idealizations and aggression regarding their training analysts in order to function effectively as analysts. "I have speculated that some candidates' difficulty in keeping patients, and their anxiety about losing them, are the results of unanalyzed fears of losing or destroying their training analysts, displaced into their patients" (p. 735). Orgel further maintains that some analysts' lack of conviction about the therapeutic value of analysis reflects disappointment in aspects of their training analysis.

Observing the analyst's reluctance, Gabbard (2003) proposes that the analyst's love of analysis is continuously in jeopardy because of a countervailing unconscious hatred of it. As a result of that hatred, he suggests, we might be too quick to abandon the analytic method and impulsively resort to harmful actions; often the hatred is linked, in part, to envy of the patient for receiving the intensive and undivided analytic attention that we unconsciously crave.

Many authors address specifically the analyst's anxiety and defensiveness at the beginning of treatment. Referring to the initial phase, Friedman (1988) proposes that the tension that characterizes treatment can be witnessed most dramatically at the beginning. Yet, he observes, therapists tend to consider beginnings as less tumultuous than the rest of the treatment. Orgel (1989) suggests that not recommending analysis, or not analyzing resistance in the months following a recommendation, can be a manifestation of the analyst's defense against aggression: "An underside of our therapeutic ambitions" can be seen in "contrary wishes—not to cure, not to help, not to understand, but to overthrow and defeat, sadistic wishes which are both satisfied and defended against by failing in the therapeutic task" (p. 534).

Poland (2001) speaks to the fear that attends analytic work and how it affects his every analytic beginning: "So my career-long eagerness to have a new analytic patient is now accompanied by a hesitant fear, a small reluctance to start a new analysis. For as much as I want to do my work, as much as I enjoy doing my work, as much as I believe that the likelihood of success justifies the pains ahead, still there is something else I also know. And that is that whatever else happens this new analysis is going to go into areas I don't want to enter, into fears I would rather keep hidden away."

Ogden (1992) examines the sense of danger and fear associated with initial consultation sessions. Like Poland, he attributes this feeling to the anticipation of becoming aware of his and his patient's inner life. Ogden suggests that beginning analysts misapprehend their own fear. While consciously they worry that patients will leave, unconsciously they're afraid that patients will stay. Chused (in Jordan 2002) discusses how uncertainty influences analytic work. She focuses on how her doubts about whether she'd been helpful to a small number of patients—who claimed they weren't helped—make her fearful about the value of analysis. Bernstein (1990) is another who explores this uncertainty. He describes analysts who recommend analysis tentatively and in a manner that reveals their reservations about their motives for recommending analysis or about its usefulness. Bernstein suggests that analysts often manifest their reluctance by failing to interpret patients' resistances following a recommendation for analysis.

Bassen (1989) suggests that recommendations for analysis made during psychotherapy aren't as simple or non-conflictual as they often appear. She regards such recommendations as possible enactments of transference-countertransference wishes or fears mobilized in the therapy. Similar considerations, she suggests, might apply to the recommendation process at the beginning of treatment.

Of all analysts, Rothstein has written most extensively about the analyst's reluctance during the consultation phase. He proposes that the analyst's emphasis on analyzability (1994, 1998) and diagnosis (2002) can serve a defensive function. If taken at face value, this focus can obscure useful transference-countertransference manifestations. Rothstein (1998) proposes that "there are many patients who are particularly disturbing to analysts both during the consultation and/or in the course of their analyses. It is not uncommon for analysts to respond to their own disturbances by deciding the patient is not suitable for standard analysis ..." (p. 541). Rothstein considers the analyst's optimistic attitude (about a patient's capacity to work analytically and benefit from analysis) and conviction (about the usefulness of analysis) as critical variables affecting whether a patient will accept the analyst's recommendation for analysis (1994) and stresses how little able we are to predict at the outset who can benefit from analysis (1994, 1998). He recommends that most patients who consult an analyst should be considered analysands and be seen in a trial analysis.

Rothstein maintains that analysts don't consider or recommend analysis as often as it's indicated, either because patients don't fit some strict criterion about analyzability or because they're disturbing to the analyst. He considers the analyst's inhibition, pessimism, and lack of conviction to be the result of a misguided educational focus (a focus on the selection of patients who will respond primarily to interpretation of conflict and a focus on outcome) or the result of conflict evoked by a particular patient. Rothstein postulates that the analyst's attitude and sense of conviction about the therapeutic value of analysis is determined to a great extent by an "unconscious bias" for or against analysis.

Whether referring to a "hesitant fear" to begin a new analysis (Poland) or "wishes not to cure, not to help, not to understand" (Orgel) or a fear that the patient *will* stay in treatment (Ogden), several analysts have explored the analyst's reluctance to analyze. Ogden implies that beginners are particularly unaware of their hesitancy to start an analysis. Orgel, however, suggests that students and graduate analysts can be identical in their lack of awareness and hesitancy. Many analysts propose that analysts' reluctance is related to their fear of affects (Gabbard, Ogden, Orgel, Poland, Rothstein). Some authors view the analysts' reluctance as a momentary hesitation to begin (Ogden, Poland), while others suggest that it interferes with its actual beginning (Jacobs, Orgel, Rothstein). Several authors point to a lack of certainty about the efficacy of analysis as a critical variable affecting the manner in which analysts deal with recommendations for analysis (Bernstein, Chused, Jacobs, Rothstein).

To my knowledge, no detailed clinical contribution has demonstrated in detail the analyst's reluctance as it manifests itself during the consultation or the opening phases of a treatment. In what follows, I offer detailed clinical material from my work with two patients who eventually settled into productive psychoanalyses. I focus specifically on the initial phase of treatment: the consultation with Mr. A and the early psychotherapy with Ms. B. I examine my developing awareness of my reluctance to engage these patients deeply, which bore directly on my recommendations for psychoanalysis. I describe the various manifestations of my reluctance, my understanding of its sources, and its effect on the work. In the discussion that follows, I examine how my own findings and understanding add to existing views on the analyst's reluctance to begin an analysis.

Clinical material

Mr. A

Mr. A, a senior at a local college, left a message on my answering machine saying that he was hoping to see me before he graduated and left town in nine weeks. When we spoke by phone, he repeated his wish to see me but asked if it made sense for us to meet since he was leaving so soon. Hesitantly, I replied that he must have had reasons to call me and therefore it might make sense for us to meet and talk things over in person. Although in his phone message he had sounded definite about when he was scheduled to leave, it turned out that he was less clear. He was to leave sometime after graduation, travel in Europe with a friend for the summer, and work as a waiter in New York in the fall. Because of Mr. A's plans to leave in the near future, we initially met on a weekly basis, with no clear goals or plans for treatment.

Mr. A, twenty-one, had spent the last years in high school and his years in college using alcohol and drugs daily, had been in physically abusive relationships, and had been involved in two serious car accidents. Although adequate, his academic performance didn't match his intellectual abilities or ambition. His career choice and plans for the future were unclear, with various and contradictory aspirations. During these first few weeks, Mr. A complained vaguely of not feeling good about himself and of being unable to find satisfying love relationships, although he'd had several lasting friendships.

In what was to have been our last session, he announced that his upcoming summer plans had fallen through because his traveling companion was no longer available. Instead, he would now be looking for another companion. I asked if he'd considered staying and continuing the inner travel that he'd started. He responded that it hadn't occurred to him because this was the time of life to travel, experience other cultures, meet different people, and experiment.

Despite stating various objections, Mr. A postponed his departure yet again, this time until the end of the summer. At that time, we increased to twice-a-week therapy. I saw it as my task to work with him in a short-term way to facilitate a referral to another analyst in another state once he settled down. As the end of the summer approached, symptoms that had vanished shortly after he started treatment now reappeared. I related these symptoms to his plans to end therapy and asked again if he would consider staying and working in an open-ended, intensive way on the unhappiness that had plagued him for years. Visibly relieved yet manifestly noncommittal, Mr. A, during the next weeks, made arrangements to stay. Within a few weeks, he had increased to five times a week and began using the couch.

My private response to Mr. A's first telephone message had been to question whether it made sense to meet with him, given that he was about to leave town. My second response was to think of my contact with him as "just a consultation." At the time, I considered these responses to be realistic reactions to his situation. A turning point came for Mr. A when his travel plans were canceled. By that time, five weeks into an extended consultation, he had been responding to treatment with significant symptomatic relief. He showed dramatic improvement in his mood and energy level, and stopped daily drug use for the first time in years. Despite this, I didn't consider recommending more intensive treatment. One could argue that Mr. A wasn't ready to consider analysis and that I'd responded empathically to him. However, regardless of *his* readiness, *I* wasn't ready because I didn't, even privately, consider recommending analysis, despite obvious indications. What's most striking about this is that I *consciously* was determined to practice as much analysis as possible.

Initially, I took at face value Mr. A's intention to leave soon and his lack of interest in committing to long-term treatment—at least in our locale. I experienced him as unavailable for analysis and questioned the wisdom of beginning with him when what he appeared to need most was a chance to experiment and exercise his independence. In retrospect, I privileged what I saw as his developmental needs, viewing his plans for out-of-town study and overseas exploration as consistent with those needs. As an immigrant myself, this defensive inclination was particularly compelling to me. Inviting him to stay, but not in analysis, was my compromise of the moment.

It wasn't until Mr. A became symptomatic in anticipation of ending his "short-term" treatment and leaving town that I was able to clearly recognize the potential value of analysis for him and was able to recommend it. I finally could give proper weight to his considerable, long-standing pain and his equally significant and chronic inability to use his ample resources to his advantage in the present or to plan for his future.

Typical of several young adults that I treat in the college city where I practice, Mr. A was transient to the area. Yet, he called on me with very real difficulties that had marked his life in important ways and were likely to derail or adversely affect his future. Although the decision was ultimately his, I was responsible for delineating his choices and providing a strong recommendation. Inadvertently, I had initially backed away from offering him the optimal treatment. That this young man engaged in five-times-a-week analysis was as much the result of my overcoming my own resistance as of him overcoming his. Had I not recognized my reluctance and recommended analysis, Mr. A, given his counterdependence and insecurity, wouldn't have remained in treatment. One can view the reluctant beginning of this analysis in terms of transference and countertransference. From the outset, Mr. A and I enacted his difficulties. From the initial phone call, he conveyed that he was only temporarily available. Partly out of insecurity and fear of rejection, Mr. A had waited to call me until just a few weeks before moving out of town permanently. In a similar manner, I responded with the self-protective thought that it was just a consultation, proactively limiting my hopes for a longer involvement with him. During the first call, when he asked for my reassurance, I, in turn, felt reluctant to reassure him.

By declaring his provisional availability, Mr. A attempted to hide needs and yearnings that he considered shameful. Throughout his childhood and particularly during adolescence, Mr. A characteristically had dealt with rejection by making himself only fleetingly available and by being the first to leave. In his manifest independence, he concealed fierce counter-dependence. In part because of my own fears of dependence and needful-ness (especially at a time when I felt I *needed* another analytic patient), I identified with Mr. A's wish to leave. I thereby overlooked *his* needs and implicitly agreed with him that travel and education were more important than addressing his long-standing pain. Defending against my fears of dependency and yearning, which were mobilized by his looming departure, I denied that I wanted to work with him. Instead, I thought, I was "generously" preparing him to see another analyst. We'd joined together in denying needs and yearnings.

Anticipating that Mr. A was going to leave, I took at face value his plans and underestimated his motivation for intensive treatment. My anticipation of his leaving reflected, in part, my ambivalence about working with him in analysis: at some level I wanted him to leave. Only when I could recognize this could I function more effectively as his analyst. Specifically, I could facilitate the beginning of the analysis: give proper weight to his conflicts and distress; withstand his passive-into-active style of engaging; maintain confidence in the work and in *my* ability to be of help to him; and tolerate the inherent ambiguity in considering recommen-dations to a young adult. It was then that I found it within myself to assume responsibility for my judgment and to trust I was addressing the best inter-ests of the patient.

When Mr. A became symptomatic on the eve of his departure, I finally was able to recognize my reluctance and to see through his denial. Only then was I able to extend to him an invitation for analysis. As he had been ready before I was, Mr. A promptly accepted. He's now in a productive analysis, which he's funding by working. In addition, he's taking classes at night in preparation for applying to graduate school

Ms. B

An engineer in her thirties, Ms. B had ended several previous treatments prematurely and unhappily. The mother of two young children, whom she both adored and unconsciously wanted to destroy, Ms. B sought treatment because of her flickering recognition that she was at risk of hurting them and/ or herself. She experienced her children as extremely demanding and attended to them in a masochistic way that increased her rage.

Although desperate for help, Ms. B was too afraid of criticism and too full of guilt and shame to hope that she could find it. She seemed in great distress, yet she also appeared indifferent and guarded. During the initial consultation, Ms. B made it clear that she had very low expectations for our work and referred frequently to her failed treatments. Given the nature and history of her difficulties and my experience of her during our meetings, I concluded that she could benefit from analysis and recommended to her that she attend as many sessions per week as she could. Although I hadn't specified the number of times she should attend and hadn't referred to "analysis" while making my recommendation, she countered that she wasn't interested in a "five-times-a-week analysis." We began with a three-times-a-week psychotherapy.

Hearing through her rejection of analysis her frightened interest in more engagement, I listened for the fears that prevented her from coming as often as she wanted. In the first few weeks of the therapy, Ms. B revealed her worries that she'd fail as a patient; that she'd be found to be defective and beyond repair; and that she'd expose herself as inexplicably and indefensibly evil. Identifying these worries and particularly relating them to her reluctance to come more often, she resignedly accepted a fourth appointment. Still, she reiterated a refusal to consider a fifth session and lie on the couch, a stance she experienced as preserving her autonomy.

Ms. B reacted to the increased frequency with a reduction in her symptoms. Her rage toward her children and her sense of despair abated, and she began to speak about herself with some small measure of trust and a tentative sense of connection. Yet she continued to have intense, wearisome, even at times alarming (to both of us) reactions to interruptions of any kind to our work. Witnessing Ms. B's distress, I continued to believe that she wanted to come more often and that she was reacting with distress to not doing so. I also thought that her coming more often would allow us to address her conflicts more effectively. I felt frustrated by her reluctance. During this time, I consciously felt that I wanted to work with her, and I was pleased to have another analytic patient.

For about four months, I was convinced that the obstacles to more intensive engagement came from Ms. B. Then an interaction led me to reconsider this. One day, noticing that Ms. B had looked at the couch, I invited her to share her thoughts. She responded that she knew people who used the couch, but she couldn't imagine using it herself because she would fall asleep. She then asked me why people use the couch. I found myself responding with a clumsy explanation without any attempt to ask her for her thoughts, to address her fears, and without extending to her the obvious open-ended invitation to use the couch anytime she felt ready.

Reflecting on my response to her inquiry about the couch, I realized that despite my recommendation I had serious reservations about getting genuinely and deeply involved with Ms. B. Indeed, I recognized, I was unsure whether I wanted Ms. B to come more often after all. I knew that I had been feeling apprehensive about her narcissistic vulnerability and accompanying rage, her potential for regression, and her propensity for abrupt and unhappy leavings. I also knew that I feared she'd hurt herself or her children. Yet until I reflected on the meaning of our exchange about the couch, I hadn't recognized how reluctant I felt about experiencing the intensity of those feelings in our relationship.

My fearfulness also reflected an identification with Ms. B's fear of attachment. Like her, I worried about precipitous endings to therapy and being hurt. In my unwelcoming response to her inquiry, I also was identifying with Ms. B's dismissiveness and aloofness, her characteristic ways of dealing with her deep fears of being left or feeling unwanted.

I recognized gradually that my focus on the fifth session had been a smoke screen for my reluctance to genuinely engage with Ms. B. My ostensible eagerness was a defense against my hidden reluctance. I was reluctant to bear her shattering sense of being inconsequential, insignificant, and powerless; to really know her profound shame and sense of inferiority; to experience my fears of being dismissed summarily; and my own wishes to dismiss her. Scared of her pain, I insisted on more contact, rather than truly encouraging her immersion.

This struggle wasn't just my response to fear of feelings or uncertainty about the work ahead and my capacity to do it. It was also a meaningful enactment between us. We have since come to learn that my initial conflictual engagement with Ms. B corresponds to a view of her mother as a self-centered, frightened, and controlling woman whose dread of attachment was manifested in a tyrannical, authoritarian, and depriving way of parenting. Reluctant to begin with Ms. B, I focused on the form rather than the essence of our analytic engagement and enacted a sadomasochistic struggle. In that struggle, control and distance substituted for engagement and understanding. Becoming aware of my reluctance, I became freer to move toward her on her terms and to extend to her a more genuine, less conflicted invitation to begin analytic work.

Discussion

These two cases highlight several important issues regarding the analyst's reluctance. The case of Mr. A raises questions about the analyses of young adults. Because of their unique developmental tasks, young adults present special challenges to analysts regarding recommendations for analysis. Young adults competing, and at times compelling, choices test an analyst's belief in the value of psychoanalysis, as opposed to the value of education, travel, or other endeavors. Abend (1987) concludes that analysts have to live with uncertainty when recommending analysis to young adults: "Hard and fast criteria do not exist, and it is possible that the degree to which the analyst believes in the special value of psychoanalytic treatment ... may determine what he advises as much as any other single factor" (p. 34).

Although these considerations are most obvious with young adults, I've concluded from my work with Ms. B and other patients that they're relevant with analysands of any age. Most patients arrive with personal circumstances or reasons, with some basis in reality, about why they shouldn't or can't be in analysis. The challenge of arriving at a recommendation is increased by the analyst's awareness that analysis is an expensive, time-consuming, and emotionally demanding treatment without a guaranteed outcome. Yet most analysts also know it's true that psychoanalysis, even with all its limitations, remains a discontented person's best opportunity for a more fulfilled life. In agreement with Rothstein, I've come to think that if analysts don't privilege this point of view with a given patient, they should seriously consider that they're reluctant to analyze that patient.

In my view, as analysts we can't consider our doubts about the value of psychoanalysis or our capacity to practice it without considering the influence of our training analysis. Although often alluded to, the ongoing influence of the analyst's personal analysis hasn't been fully acknowledged in our literature (Grusky 1999). I speculate that we haven't explored this topic more fully in part because of the expectation that a training analysis should leave no psychic residue—a remnant of the belief in the perfectly analyzed analyst whose conflicts and transferences will dissolve at the end of the analysis.

Addressing the clear need for more knowledge in this area, Smith (2001) gives evidence of analysts' ongoing internal relationship with our training analyst and how it manifests itself in our work. Smith suggests that "the analyst's identifications and idealizations modify over time but, never fully given up, remain as compromised responses to both the analyst's and the patient's conflicts in a dynamic reciprocal relationship with the patient's inner life" (p. 809). As noted earlier, Orgel (2000) has explored the influence of the training analysis and suggested that analysts' lingering disappointment in our training analysis is one source of our lack of conviction about analysis.

Based on my work with Mr. A and Ms. B, I'd add that another source of some of our lack of conviction about the usefulness of analysis can be found in competitive feelings toward our own analyst. Analysts can express this competitiveness by denying the therapeutic value of our training analysis or the effectiveness of our analyst. We can also express rivalry with the training analyst in our work. For me, functioning as an analyst stimulated competitive/aggressive strivings toward my own analyst. In turn, my conflicts over those wishes fueled my reluctance to engage with these two patients. Specifically, by temporarily retreating from practicing as an analyst, I defended against wanting to be the better analyst. For example, I was fearful that both Mr. A and Ms. B were going to leave. My worry that they would leave was also a wish: if they left, I would never be as successful as my analyst.

My uncertainty about the value of analysis not only reflected my aggression toward my analyst. It was also a defense against my love and gratitude. Thus, my fear/wish that my patients would leave was also a defense against my awareness of loving feelings. If my prospective analytic patients left, I would not have to practice as an analyst and be in touch with how much my analyst had helped me, nor with the attendant sadness over the end of my analysis.

Although questioning any strong inclination within me has become second nature in the course of my daily work as an analyst, I was particularly resistant to questioning my seeming eagerness to practice analysis. I suggest that one obstacle that blocks our considering our reluctance to begin an analysis is the idealization of our wish to analyze. Abend (1986) reminds us that, despite our intellectual understanding that analytic ability is a dynamic function, we're still prone to "unconscious narcissistic fantasies of perfection" and to "unrealistic and unrealizable ideals" (p. 565). Analysts resist recognizing our conflictual contribution in the course of the analysis. It follows that we don't recognize or anticipate our "resistance" at the beginning of an analysis. Despite what we know about the dynamic nature of psychic functioning, we often want to see the wish to begin an analysis as invariant. Although psychoanalysts have increasingly recognized and explored the tension and turmoil of analysis, Friedman (1988) has noted that many analysts still view the beginning of treatment as isolated from the irrational forces that govern the rest of the analysis. Similarly, the recommendation for analysis is often considered to be an "objectively" motivated act (Bassen 1989).

Based on my own experience recommending analysis, I concur with the view that the recommendation for analysis is from the outset infused with realistic and infantile wishes and fears from both therapeutic partners. This understanding has allowed me to consider how I might match or complement, with my own ambivalence, a patient's seeming unavailability or unwillingness to commit to analysis. To elaborate on Bassen's view of a recommendation for analysis during psychotherapy as an enactment, I believe it useful to consider that *not making* a recommendation for analysis during psychotherapy can also be an enactment, a manifestation of cocreated resistance. This is seen in my work with Mr. A, where not making a timely recommendation was an enactment of conflicts about dependency fears and wishes.

As my clinical material demonstrates, the analyst's reluctance can influence analytic practice. At present, the extent of its influence isn't clear. However, from my own work, from reading clinical accounts in the literature, from listening to cases presented in various professional forums, and from anecdotal reports, I've concluded that reluctance to engage in analysis affects analytic practice more frequently than is recognized. As is true during the course of an analysis, our reluctance at the beginning can significantly influence our attitude and performance. However, analysts' reluctance in the beginning, when the relationship with the patient is most tenuous, can more easily contribute to the premature end of a potentially useful, and often much-needed treatment. My reluctance to consider or recommend analysis for Mr. A and Ms. B and my subsequent recognition of that reluctance affected—though in opposite ways—the quality of my clinical work and the nature of my clinical practice.

Analysts' reluctance to begin an analysis is not new; one of its earlier manifestations has been a defensive focus on analyzability. However, because a less overt demand for psychoanalysis exists today than in past decades, psychoanalysts can more easily obscure our reluctance to analyze by citing patient scarcity. Given the reality of an atmosphere adverse to psychoanalysis, analysts can more readily rationalize our own reluctance to begin an analysis.

Concluding remarks

I've explored how the reluctance to begin a new analysis influences the individual analyst's thinking and practice and considered the analyst's reluctance from different vantage points: as a response to intense affects mobilized by the consultation, as part of a cocreated enactment, and as a manifestation of the analyst's conflicts. Analysts can use the compelling reality of an environment adverse to long-term treatments to rationalize our reluctance to engage patients in analysis. This reluctance to begin an analysis appears to be an underestimated factor in explaining why analysis is not practiced more.

One of the many paradoxes that characterize our "impossible profession" is that we're reluctant to practice it. Although we might not wish it to be so, the reluctance to begin analysis, like counter-resistance at any time during an analysis, appears ubiquitous. Whether it will become an interference or an aid to beginning depends in part on our capacity to anticipate it in our consultations and to recognize how it manifests itself in relation to a specific patient. I've found it is clinically useful to anticipate that my hesitancy to analyze will manifest itself with each new patient and to consider, also with each patient, how I play a part in their resistance to beginnings.

References

Abend, S. (1986). Countertransference, empathy, and the analytic ideal: The impact of life stresses on analytic capability. *Psychoanalytic Quarterly*, 55: 563–575.

Abend, S. (1987). Evaluating young adults for analysis. *Psychoanalytic Inquiry*, 7: 31–38.

Bachrach, H. (1983). On the concept of analyzability. *Psychoanalytic Quarterly*, 52: 180–203.

Bachrach, H. (1990). The analyst's thinking and attitude at the beginning of analysis: The influence of research data at the beginning of an analysis. In *On Beginning an Analysis*, ed. T. Jacobs & A. Rothstein. Madison, CT: International Universities Press, pp. 83–100.

Bassen, C. (1989). Transference-countertransference enactment in the recommendation to convert psychotherapy to psychoanalysis. *International Journal of Psycho-Analysis*, 16: 79–92.

Bernstein, S. (1990). Motivation for psychoanalysis and the transition from psychotherapy. *Psychoanalytic Inquiry*, 10: 21–42.

Boesky, D. (1990). The psychoanalytic process and its components. *Psychoanalytic Quarterly*, 59: 550–584.

Brauer, L.D., & Brauer, S.L. (1996). *Basic report about members who are graduates of institutes: Survey of psychoanalytic practice.* Committee on Psychoanalytic Practice, American Psychoanalytic Association.

Busch, F. (1995). Beginning a psychoanalytic treatment: Establishing an analytic frame. *Journal of the American Psychoanalytic Association*, 43: 449–468.

Erle, J.B. & Goldberg, D.A. (2003). The course of 253 analyses from selection to outcome. *Journal of the American Psychoanalytic Association*, 51: 257–294.

Freud, S. (1912a). *The dynamics of transference.* Standard Edition 12: 97–108.

Freud, S. (1912b). *Recommendations to physicians practicing psychoanalysis.* Standard Edition 12: 109–120.

Freud, S. (1913). *On beginning the treatment.* Standard Edition 12: 123–144.

Friedman, L. (1988). *The Anatomy of Psychotherapy.* Hillsdale, NJ: Analytic Press.

Gabbard, G.O. (2003). Miscarriages of psychoanalytic treatment with suicidal patients. *International Journal of Psycho-Analysis*, 84: 249–263.

Greenberg, J. (2002). Psychoanalytic goals, therapeutic action, and the analyst's tension. *Psychoanalytic Quarterly*, 71: 651–678.

Grusky, Z. (1999). Conviction and conversion: The role of shared fantasies about analysis. *Psychoanalytic Quarterly*, 68: 401–430.

Jacobs, T. (1988). Unpublished report to the Executive Council by the Committee on Psychoanalytic Practice. Montreal, Canada.

Jordan, L. (2002). Panel report: The analyst's uncertainty and fear. *Journal of the American Psychoanalytic Association*, 50: 989–993.

Kantrowitz, J. (1993). The uniqueness of the patient-analyst pair: Approaches for elucidating the analyst's role. *International Journal of Psycho-Analysis*, 74: 893–904.

Kantrowitz, J., Katz, A., Greenman, D., Morris, H., Paolitto, F., Sashin, J., & Solomon, L. (1989). The patient-analyst match and the outcome of psychoanalysis: A pilot study. *Journal of the American Psychoanalytic Association*, 37: 893–919.

Lichtenberg, J. & Auchincloss, E. (1989). Panel report: The opening phase of psychoanalysis. *Journal of the American Psychoanalytic Association*, 37: 199–214.

Ogden, T. (1992). Comments on transference and countertransference in the initial analytic meeting. *Psychoanalytic Inquiry*, 12: 225–247.

Orgel, S. (1989). Address to the Board on Professional Standards. *Journal of the American Psychoanalytic Association*, 37: 531–541.

Orgel, S. (1990). The future of psychoanalysis. *Psychoanalytic Quarterly*, 59: 1–20.

Orgel, S. (2000). Thoughts on termination. *Journal of the American Psychoanalytic Association*, 48: 719–738.

Poland, W. (2001). The analyst's fear. Paper presented at panel "The Analyst's Fear and Uncertainty," American Psychoanalytic Association, New Orleans, May 5.

Rothstein, A. (1994). A perspective on doing a consultation and making the recommendation of analysis to a prospective analysand. *Psychoanalytic Quarterly*, 63: 680–695.

Rothstein, A. (1998). *Psychoanalytic Technique and the Creation of Analytic Patients.* Madison, CT: International Universities Press.

Rothstein, A. (2002). Reflections on the creative aspects of psychoanalytic diagnosing. *Psychoanalytic Quarterly*, 71: 301–326.

Smith, H. (1993). Engagements in the analytic work. *Psychoanalytic Inquiry*, 13: 425–454.

Smith, H. (2001). Hearing voices: The fate of the analyst's identifications. *Journal of the American Psychoanalytic Association*, 49: 781–812.

Chapter 2

Analysis begins in the analyst's mind

Conceptual and technical considerations on recommending analysis

Conceptual considerations

Whether immobilized by fear, haunted by grief, or persecuted by guilt and self-hatred, many people have inner lives that prevent them from living fully, or even continuing to live, without intensive psychological help. From personal and supervisory experience, I've concluded that analysis or intensive therapy can benefit some patients more than any other treatment. This chapter is born out of the recognition that even though analysis is practiced less, has proven to have more modest results than were claimed for it when it was idealized, and is an expensive, difficult, and inconvenient treatment, it remains, at least for now, the best chance for help for those who desperately need it.

I think it's critical for patients who need analysis that analysts[1] share our thinking and experiences and identify the conditions that facilitate beginning analytic treatment. This sharing can help us contain the fear and uncertainty that is an essential part of psychoanalytic work and can embolden us, and our younger colleagues, to recommend intensive treatment when needed and continue to engage deeply with ourselves and our patients.[2]

In the first chapter, I explored barriers that analysts, including myself, encounter that can impede our recommending and practicing analysis (Ehrlich 2004, 2010). Here I'll broaden my focus and examine the frame of mind of the analyst that facilitates the beginning of analysis. I'll examine the ways analysts think about our function, our patients, and the therapeutic process that allow us to recommend and practice intensive therapy or analysis despite the profound challenges inherent in practicing analysis and an adverse and even antagonistic cultural, professional, and socioeconomic climate. First, I'll discuss my thesis that analysis begins in the mind of the analyst. I'll then focus on technical considerations in recommending analysis, describing how I translate my analytic frame of mind into specific interventions that mediate the patient's deeper engagement. Finally, I'll provide a detailed clinical example to illustrate how my analytic mindset informed my participation in the initial phase of a treatment with a patient who engaged in useful psychoanalytic work.

In my own work and in observing the work of others, I've concluded that the analyst must do a great deal of internal work every step of the way—from the initial contact with a prospective patient to the time the patient actually begins analysis—in order for an analysis to begin. In other words, a helpful analysis begins in the mind of the analyst.[3] It is the analyst's emotional engagement and capacity to think psychologically about the patient during the consultation that launches the therapeutic process within which the patient can begin to have greater access to her own mind and capacity for psychological mindedness. What I'm suggesting here about the beginning therapeutic process resonates with the developmental perspectives offered by both Winnicott and Bion. Winnicott (1960) compellingly describes how the infant's ability to develop "a separate personal self" depends in great part on the mother's care and capacity for awareness and empathy. The mother's emotional investment and abilities guide her to respond in a good-enough way to her baby's needs and temperament. Bion (1959, 1962) similarly suggests that it takes the mother's mind and her capacity to feel and process her child's feelings to allow the child to begin to have his own mind—to perceive himself, the mother, and the world in a realistic way. Bion suggests that it's the mother's ability to receive and mentally process the infant's incomprehensible experiences in the form of normal projective identifications that allows the child to develop the capacity to eventually tolerate and emotionally understand his inner experience, especially his distress. Bion extends this idea, suggesting that two minds are needed to think and feel one's most disturbing thoughts at any age (Ogden 2008).

To illuminate the nature of the analyst's engagement and capacities for psychological work during the consultation and the beginning of treatment, I've identified six distinctive yet interrelated aspects of the analyst's internal work. All six are requisite to facilitate the patient's engagement in the analytic process: (1) Being receptive to the patient's need for intensive treatment (2) Identifying and imagining the patient's strengths and potential (3) Envisioning the patient in analysis with oneself (4) Generating a realistic sense of confidence that analysis is the most useful treatment for this patient (5) Recognizing the patient's *wish* for analysis (6) Considering as analytic data the patient's and one's own reservations about analysis.[4]

Being receptive to the patient's need for intensive treatment

Even though most prospective analytic patients come to analysts asking for help, nearly all enter the initial consultation minimizing their need for help and protecting themselves from knowing the disturbing meanings and full measure of their pain and difficulties. In order to recommend intensive treatment or analysis for patients who need it and can benefit from it, the clinician must create a psychological space in her own mind that allows her to appreciate the patient's profound need for intensive help.

Analysis therefore begins with a process in which the analyst finds a way through her patient's and her own defenses to connect with and imagine the meaning and degree of the patient's pain—in its rawest form possible. As part of this process, the analyst must work to recognize her tendency, parallel to the patient's, to deny, minimize, or externalize evidence of the patient's deeper needs, fears, and traumas.

Additionally, to be in a position to offer intensive help, the analyst must let herself unflinchingly recognize the full impact of inner conflicts and traumatic experiences on the patient's life: how long the patient has suffered, the many ways this suffering has affected and continues to affect his or her life, and how, despite profound hesitations and fears about change, the patient feels desperate for help. Only by being awash in the patient's pain, and recognizing how limiting and wasteful a patient's symptoms can be, can the analyst recognize the need for—and convincingly recommend—a treatment as demanding as analysis.

Extending Winnicott's evocative idea that "there is no such thing as a baby" (meaning that the baby cannot exist apart from the mother's care), Ogden (1994) suggested that there is no such thing as an analysand. Ogden emphasizes the interdependence of subject and object in both the mother-infant and the analyst-analysand dyad. My emphasis here is different. Although patient and analyst (like infant and mother) affect and change the other from the outset, I suggest that the analyst's receptivity, awareness, and empathy are disproportionately consequential in the beginning analytic process, just as the mother's are in her child's infancy. Because of the distorting impact of defenses, particularly in the beginning of treatment, patients often are unable to conceive or articulate the nature and meaning of their pain and often cannot imagine how relief is possible. Many patients depend, therefore, on the analyst's mind to lead the way in registering the extent and nature of their emotional difficulties and in offering a vision of how they can be helped.

The recommendation for analysis signals to the patient, for the most part preconsciously, that the analyst is receptive to registering the patient's difficulties and is willing to lend her psychological capacities in the service of the patient's emotional well-being. In turn, this awareness of the analyst's availability allows the patient to begin to perceive and tolerate her feelings and consider their meaning. The analyst's willingness and capacity to register the patient's trouble launches a back-and-forth process between the analyst's mind and the patient's mind that, over time, allows the patient to develop or exercise the capacities necessary to access her most disturbing thoughts and feelings, and their meaning.

Identifying and imagining the patient's strengths and potential

Because of conflict or trauma, many patients view themselves as inadequate, unworthy, unlovable, destructive, or bad, among many other negative views. For patients I think might benefit from analysis, I've observed that I can't engage them in treatment unless I can move beyond their negative view of themselves, beyond their sense of hopelessness and helplessness and "find" the resiliency, creativity, and strength hiding within their defensive adaptation.

In my experience, I'm not able to recommend intensive treatment, even when indicated, until I can imagine the patient as capable of participating in and benefiting from analysis and envision what that benefit might look like once her inhibitions are no longer needed and her strengths and ego capacities become more usable to her. I see it as my analytic task to "hold" the image of the patient's potential until the patient becomes psychologically capable of perceiving and appreciating her latent abilities on her own. Being able to recognize and keep in mind the patient's strengths, potential, and sense of goodness is an essential part of my analytic mindset throughout every treatment, but especially in the beginning. Imagining aspects of the patient that she isn't yet in a position to perceive instigates a helpful cycle of engagement: my view of her capabilities affects my patient's view of herself and her capacity to engage with herself and with me, which in turn affects my view of her and so on.

Envisioning the patient in analysis with oneself

Our patients invariably convey in the initial meetings—through accounts of their history and through interactions with the analyst—a preview of things to come in the transference-countertransference.[5] In other words, during the consultation the analyst has many opportunities to come in contact, often preconsciously, with the patient's unconscious fantasies of the dangers lurking in relationships, including the analytic relationship. During the initial meetings the patient depends on the analyst to withstand this dark vision of destructive relationships and imagine being able to bear it and help transform it in the future.[6]

In addition to containing the patient's warnings about how bad things could get, the analyst, in order to recommend analysis, must tolerate the risk of investing in a relationship the patient might turn down. For analysis to begin, the patient depends on the analyst to unilaterally invest in the relationship, to want to know and connect with the patient before the patient is consciously aware of a similar need. Thus, the analyst must bear the insecurity and vulnerability that goes along with proposing an intensely intimate relationship *before* knowing how the other will respond.

As I'll discuss later, the analyst's invitation takes on many meanings for the patient. Among these, it signals to the patient that the analyst is willing to withstand the terrors inherent in the patient's internal world. The analyst's invitation for analysis offers the patient a glimmer of hope that the analytic relationship might help her feel safer and less destructive. The analyst's investment in knowing the patient, and in helping the two of them begin a back-and-forth process between their minds, can eventually allow the patient to engage more intimately with the analyst and to tolerate, transform, and integrate disturbing aspects of herself and her objects.

Other analysts also view this relational component of the analyst's beginning mindset as essential. Arnold Rothstein (2010) speaks of a "trusting" model of consultation that centers on "the analyst's attitude and subjectivity and privileges countertransference" (p. 787). He reports that in his experience the most effective way of helping a patient enter analysis is "creating" or "collaboratively developing" an analysand (p. 788)—that is, analyst and analysand together exploring, during the consultation and a trial period of analysis, whether they can work together.

I agree with Rothstein that the analyst's attitude and awareness of her subjectivity and countertransference are critical in helping a patient enter analysis. I would add that the analyst's imaginative capacities that allow her to generate an internal view of herself as the patient's analyst and envision an intimate and useful analytic collaboration are prerequisite to an eventual actual collaboration.

Levine (2010) speaks to the analyst's imaginative capacity and its vital role in beginning an analysis. He suggests that internally creating a view of oneself as an analyst "with and for that patient" is fundamental to the patient's accepting a recommendation for analysis. Levine offers that for patients who don't have the capacity to mentalize, the analyst's capacity to imagine, feel, and look for meaning in relation to the patient has a transformative effect: the analyst's capacity allows the patient to develop an ability to be in analysis that previously didn't exist.

Given that all emotional suffering has unconscious roots, patients arrive at the consultation lacking in varying degree the capacity to appreciate the depth of their own pain, to empathize with themselves, or to seek the meaning of their symptoms. Extending Levine's idea, then, I suggest that the analyst's capacity to imagine, empathically feel, and look for meaning has a transformative effect on *all* patients, even those capable of mentalizing. The analyst's creative and empathic capacity allows *all* prospective analysands to develop the ability to be in analysis.

Generating a realistic sense of confidence that analysis is the most useful treatment for this patient

I've found from my own practice and in consulting with other analysts that to recommend analysis to a specific patient, an analyst must feel confident that analytic help is the best available option for the patient at that time. Unless an analyst believes that analysis is the best choice for a prospective patient, he won't invite the patient to undertake it. Or, if the analyst does, he or she won't invite the patient with enough confidence and conviction that the patient will accept the invitation. Unless the analyst invites a patient to be in analysis, and does so with genuine conviction, there won't be an analysis.[7]

For patients who need it, I think of analysis as the only treatment available that provides the kind of access to the recesses of patients' minds that's necessary to help them reclaim aspects of themselves that have been lost to unconscious conflict and/or trauma. Meeting as frequently as possible gives these patients and me the best opportunity to listen to and understand their suffering in the closest, most profound, and most useful way possible. In my experience, it takes two people to understand and help one, and the more often these two people meet, the greater the opportunity for creating the trust, continuity, and connection necessary to address what troubles the patient. Despite external and internal pressures for quick and easy results, I strive not to deny how much time and effort it takes for characterological change to occur. Recommending intensive treatment isn't recommending what is expedient or comfortable but what the analyst thinks is necessary for the patient's well-being.

At the same time, as analysts, we know that to arrive at a realistic sense of confidence in analysis, we must attend not only to the benefits of analysis but to its costs and inherent limitations, even dangers. Analysis is an emotionally demanding, lengthy, and costly treatment. Although we can imagine the potential benefits of analysis for a given patient, what can in fact be accomplished can't be known until the analysis is completed, and sometimes until long after. Additionally, the analyst must live with the knowledge that analysis will not cure the patient of her human condition; analysis will not undo her traumas, eliminate all her conflicts, or leave her pain free (Chused 2012).

Further, despite my generally optimistic attitude toward analysis, I grapple with what I recognize as the perils inherent in analysis, how the rigors of the work have the potential of leading analysts to regress to stances of omnipotence, idealization, self-interest, or disengagement (Hirsch 2008). In considering the usefulness of analysis, I also struggle with the knowledge that the privacy of analytic work and patients' inherent dependency on analysts as helpers can serve as fertile ground for unexamined enactments that can be hurtful and damaging to the patient and his or her family. To arrive at a realistic sense of analysis and not defensively overvalue or underappreciate it, I work within myself to find personal meaning in my disappointing or even hurtful experiences of analysis, as both analyst and patient. Consequently, my confidence in analytic work is not fixed, but dynamic—with every prospective patient, in each consultation, throughout each analysis.

Recognizing the patient's wish for analysis

I'm often asked how I manage to convince patients to sign on to analysis. The question implies a disjuncture between my wish to meet with patients at an analytic frequency and the patients' wishes to be seen less frequently. Given the assumption of a disjuncture, the question implies that the only way to get patients into analysis is to maneuver them to my position from theirs.

As analysts, we strive to be aware of our patients' fear of their inner lives and of relationships. Our focus on our patients' fear, I think, leads us at times to overlook their wish for emotional truth and intimacy. Although all patients fear analysis, my experience over the years has shown me that many who consult with me come to my office already preconsciously wishing to be known by me and to connect with me in the deepest way possible. What prevents them from engaging with me as intensively as they need to are the same unconscious dilemmas and fears that brought them to treatment in the first place. In many cases, therefore, I don't see a disjuncture between my wish for my patient to be in analysis and what I've come to recognize is my patient's wish.

In the beginning, as throughout a treatment, I don't see my task as convincing the patient to come more frequently. Instead I try to help the patient with worries that interfere with getting what she needs and wishes in her relationships, including the relationship with me. In order to help a prospective patient, I must work within my mind to recognize the longings (for safety, recognition, understanding, intimacy, connection, etc.) that lie hidden behind her fear. Whether we work out a daily frequency or not, my having invited her to work intensively signals my patient that I have a sense of how deep and conflictual her longings are and that I'm prepared to acknowledge and feel her desires until they feel less dangerous or shameful and she can experience them herself. My invitation becomes a subtext to our work at any frequency and allows my patient to feel more hope about my capacity to understand her and my readiness to help.

Considering as analytic data the patient's and one's own reservations about engaging in analysis

Finally, for me one of the important elements of engaging a patient who needs analysis has been discovering and rediscovering my own fears about doing analysis. As I've written before, I've found from my own experience and from listening to accounts of others' analytic work that ambivalence about doing analytic work is ubiquitous. Given that there can be no analysis without the analyst's recommending it, I've concluded that my own fears at times pose a greater obstacle to beginning than do the patient's. Rothstein's pioneer writing in this area has influenced me, and his recommendation to analysts to privilege self-analytic inquiry into their experience of patients as disturbing has been valuable advice for engaging with patients analytically. Levine (2010) writes beautifully about this as well.

Technical considerations

I'll now describe how my analytic mindset guides my participation in a consultation and facilitates the patient's engagement. I'll then move on to the specific issue of recommending analysis. When a prospective patient contacts me, I suggest that we meet for a consultation, typically two to three appointments, in order for her to tell me about herself. If it's agreeable to her, we set up times to meet. At the end of the consultation, I share with her my understanding of what she's struggling with and what she's hoping to achieve. I also offer my recommendation about how best to proceed. If feasible, I try to have the consultation appointments as close together as possible, preferably on consecutive days. Doing so allows for continuity and a chance for the patient to get a feeling for what several sessions a week can offer. This way the patient can begin to *experience* rather than just imagine the potential benefits of daily analytic meetings.

From the first moment of the initial phone contact with a patient, I search for meaning in everything the prospective patient presents and in everything I think and feel in relation to him or her. I'm particularly attentive to any sign of discomfort our encounter engenders, in my patient or me, even if minor. I work to register and articulate to myself my reservations about working with this patient and how I might be identifying with the patient's defenses and rationalizations. This awareness often increases my capacity to imagine more fully the pain and disturbance that bring the patient to treatment but aren't consciously available to her.

Reith (2010), reporting on a ten-year study on initial psychoanalytic interviews, writes that the most robust finding about analytic process in initial interviews was the power of unconscious or preconscious transference-countertransference dynamics: "Whether or not the analyst and/or the patient became consciously aware of them at the time, the unconscious transference and countertransference dynamics could be so potent, and their effect on both protagonists (as well as on others later on in the investigative process) so destabilizing, that we have found Bion's (1979) idea of an unconscious emotional 'storm' that arises whenever two persons meet, to be a particularly apt way of describing them" (p. 70). I believe that the analyst's anticipation of the storm within herself, and her openness to it, allows her to be more receptive to its often subtle manifestations during the consultation. By registering and making sense of her difficult feelings in relation to the patient, the analyst can begin to understand the patient's turmoil.

During the consultation, I try to ascertain which aspects of the patient's difficulties relate to problems that are "internal, longstanding and portable" (Bernstein 2000). I also assess her level of motivation to change. I want to know what solutions she's tried and how they've worked out. I'm especially interested in any history of past treatments and her history of relationships. If I can find a specific example, and I believe it will be compelling, I point out to the patient how a feature of her response to me during the consultation parallels a dilemma or difficulty she has outside the consultation room. Doing so provides an opportunity to demonstrate to a prospective patient how analysis works, to demystify the process, and for me to get a preliminary sense of how the patient will respond if analysis proceeds.

Given the crucial importance of studying analytic beginnings for our practices and the future of our profession, it's noteworthy that comparatively little has been written about the dynamics of the initial sessions and even less on how and what exactly analysts recommend. Notable exceptions can be found in the work of Ogden (1992), Busch (1995), Schlesinger (2005), and Wille (2012), who persuasively describe the richness and dynamic complexity of the initial sessions. A recent international collection of papers on launching analysis assembled by the Working Party on Initiating Psychoanalysis of the European Federation, *Initiating Psychoanalysis* (Reith et al. 2012), includes contributions from diverse theoretical perspectives on the dynamics of initial interviews. Although this collection usefully describes the complexity and intensity of the initial sessions and the analyst's frame of mind, it doesn't focus on the technical aspects of recommending analysis. For technical considerations regarding the recommendation of analysis and the resistances that typically follow, the writings I've found most useful are Brenner (1990), Busch (1995), Hall (1998), Bernstein (1990, 2000), Rothstein (1994, 1995, 2010), and Levine (2010). [8]

While what we actually say to a patient at any time, including the recommendation, depends on our beginning understanding of that patient's difficulties and experience of self and others, I still believe it's useful for analysts to share with each other our characteristic ways of recommending. Further, though every authentic analytic moment is unique and what I say, how I say it, or when I say it varies depending on each patient and each individual interaction, I've found that there are certain important elements that I include in my recommendation when I've concluded that analysis is the treatment of choice. I try to convey to the patient my understanding of her life goals and the obstacles she has encountered in her efforts to reach them, as well as my understanding of her attempts to help herself. I offer her my view of possible options for how to proceed: to wait and see if time will help, to try again some of the solutions she's tried before, to try medication or short-term therapy, etc. I share with the patient my estimation of the advantages and disadvantages of each option. I then offer my recommendation that we meet with the goal of understanding the reasons she's been unable to achieve some of what she wants. I add that we can accomplish this by listening together to her thoughts and feelings and trying to understand them. Depending on how the patient responds to the first part of my recommendation, I offer the second part, which is the conditions necessary if the kind of treatment I'm proposing is to work. I suggest that we meet as often as possible, preferably daily and in an open-ended way, until we decide that we have accomplished our goals.[9]

What about patients who need analysis but aren't ready to consider a recommendation for daily meetings, even if they're suitable? I see it as my professional responsibility to recommend what I think the patient needs. At the same time, however, it's neither helpful nor empathic to make a recommendation the patient can't make use of. If I think a patient needs analysis but isn't ready to hear this, I don't suggest daily meetings. Instead I recommend that she come as frequently as she can arrange. In some cases, when I feel strongly that a patient needs higher frequency immediately, I explain my thinking and suggest that she come at least three times a week from the outset.

There are various ways of recommending analysis. Rothstein (2010), like Freud, recommends a trial of analysis: "Recommending a trial of analysis derives from my belief that for most prospective analysands the analyst cannot know, without a trial, with whom she/he can successfully collaborate. For this reason, I often say to a patient: we can give it a try and we will know in three to six months if it is for you" (p. 789). Although I agree with Rothstein's notion that we can't predict the outcome of any relationship, including analysis, I don't think of the initial stages of analysis as a trial, nor do I frame it that way to a patient. Instead I proceed with the assumption that we can work out a rich, constructive analytic relationship. When I think back to the beginning of every analysis I've engaged in, I recognize that thinking about a particular beginning as a "trial" was an indication that there was something in that consultation that was especially disturbing to me. In other words, thinking of the beginning as a trial was a signal of my reservations about proceeding and of engaging more fully with that patient.

After I recommend analysis, I listen for what my recommendation has meant to the patient. I assume that the recommendation acquires multiple meanings but listen for the meaning most accessible to the patient at any given time. To the patient the recommendation might signify punishment, criticism, seduction, being chosen, an invitation for regression, an offer of help, or being understood, among many other meanings. It is inevitably a seduction, gratifying and scary, both a compliment and an insult. I work to understand these fears about the idea of analysis and then, if possible, help the patient recognize how her trepidation about analysis relates to fears that brought her to seek a consultation in the first place.

What about patients who receive but don't accept the analyst's invitation to be in analysis? Rothstein offers to see such patients on their terms only if they *explicitly* agree to work to understand the obstacles to their accepting what he believes are the optimal conditions for their treatment. I differ from Rothstein in that I accept the patient's preference for less-than-optimal conditions as a starting point *without* making an explicit contract with the patient to explore his reservations further. If the patient decides he can't proceed at an analytic frequency and suggests a lesser frequency, I accept it. I do, however, tell the patient that although I understand that this is what's possible at this time, I hope that together we can discover what stands in the way of his being able to come more frequently and that possibly he'll feel differently as our work progresses.

I have found that even if patients turn down my offer of analysis, once the recommendation has been made, and as long as they're in treatment with me, they continue to wrestle with their wishes and fears about engaging more deeply. Thus, regardless of whether we make an explicit contract, we inevitably encounter and explore their reservations. When I look back at the treatments I've been engaged in, I see that exploration of the patient's fears has often led to an analysis, but that sometimes it hasn't. Whatever frequency a patient chooses, my recommendation for daily meetings remains on the table and serves as a residue for the patient's associations. When I hear allusions to frequency in the patient's associations, I address them only if they're close to the surface of the patient's awareness. I attend first to the patient's resistance to the awareness of thinking about it by asking if he's considered adding a session. I then interpret the fear that's contained in the patient's reservations about increased frequency.

What do we look for in patients' thoughts that alerts us to the possibility that they might be ready to intensify their treatment? Among possible indicators are allusions to frequency (often in displacement to activities other than therapy), complaints about time, increased frustration with symptoms, and my own impatience and dissatisfaction with the existing frequency. I also listen for patients' increased sense of trust and comfort in the treatment and their wish for deeper engagement.

I've had the repeated experience that patients ask for additional appointments in indirect ways. For example, I have found that when patients ask to reschedule on a day we're not meeting, it often turns out that they're actually considering adding a session but are afraid to know it or ask for it. For one patient, seeking to reschedule was a way to find out indirectly whether I was available and willing to meet with him more intensively. Afraid of wanting something he might not be able to have, he needed to be assured that I was available before even letting himself know that he wanted more.

I have found that Rothstein's technique of asking patients to agree explicitly to examine the obstacles to beginning analysis runs the risk of fostering externalization. In other words, patients might perceive the wish for analysis as coming from only the analyst, not the patient. By not asking for an explicit contract, analysts increase the possibility that patients will experience conflicts about beginning analysis as internal: patients want analysis and, simultaneously, are afraid of it. When patients experience their conflicts as internal, we have a better chance of understanding their many fears about engagement, whether they enter analysis or not.

Given the expense of a several-times-weekly treatment, I'm often asked how my patients can afford my fee. I began my practice many years ago with the assumption that the frequency of treatment would be determined by the patient's finances. I've found that to be true in some cases but not all. Although finances might determine frequency at the beginning, I've found that if analysis is helpful, patients often become increasingly capable of supporting the treatment they need. I have many examples of patients who began treatment unable to afford daily sessions. As they progressed—felt less inhibited, for example, or less guilty—they were able to find a way to pay for additional sessions.

I've found it essential in order to maintain my analytic equilibrium not to feel underpaid. At the same time, I don't want to feel that the patient is paying more than she can afford, at the expense of maintaining a reasonable lifestyle. As with many matters in analysis, interactions involving money (such as, setting, negotiating, and collecting fees) present many opportunities for helping the patient understand and integrate disturbing feelings such as greed, entitlement, guilt, and longing to be taken care of. However, interactions involving money can also lead to destructive enactments such as analysts taking advantage of patients by overcharging them or enticing them into analysis by undercharging them, ending low-fee treatments prematurely, or turning patients into annuities (Hirsch 2008).

Interactions around fees highlight the tension between the analyst's self-interest and desire and the patient's interest. This is a tension that bears on the analyst's recommendation for analysis. To explore this topic in depth goes beyond my scope here. Nonetheless, I'll share a few thoughts at this point and will address it later in my clinical example.

Doing analysis at a daily frequency is deeply gratifying to me. It's also how I make a living. How, then, do I distinguish whether my wish to see a patient more frequently is primarily in my patient's interest or is primarily serving mine?[10] I've found that this question remains in my mind from the consultation until the end of any treatment and constitutes an ongoing tension. This internal tension increases or decreases depending on many factors (e.g. my assessment of the patient's needs, my assessment of the usefulness of the analysis for the patient, my confidence in my skills or the healing power of the analytic process, the state of my practice, whether exploitation is prominent in the patient's dynamics and therefore is being evoked between us). I'm less worried that I'm inadvertently privileging my own interests when I'm clear in my mind that the patient needs the analysis and will likely benefit from it and that no other treatment will likely help her reach her goals. I'm tenser when the patient's dynamics are such that she's prone to being exploited, and when I'm especially ambivalent about engaging with this patient. I believe the worry about exploiting patients is a necessary burden that each analyst carries throughout each analysis. I recognize that my awareness of my capacity to privilege my interest over a patient's does not guarantee that I won't unconsciously act it out. Though there are no easy assurances that we won't inadvertently exploit patients, there are several measures that we can take to decrease the chances of destructive enactments; these measures include self-analysis, reanalysis, frequent peer consultation, and working firmly within the ethical standards of our profession.

Finally, it might be useful to address my diagnostic criteria for recommending analysis. This topic merits its own chapter, so I'll discuss it only briefly here. I don't think that every patient who consults with me needs and would benefit from an analysis. I see patients on a once or twice-a-week basis who benefit from treatment. I recommend analysis at the outset when the patient's emotional difficulties are long-standing and particularly entrenched and/or disrupt the patient's life in profound ways; when her treatment goals are ambitious quality-of-life goals; and when I think that the patient will benefit from analysis and that no other treatment will help the patient achieve his or her goals. In trying to decide whether to recommend analysis, I have several considerations during the consultation: the patient's level of suffering and its duration, the primary ways the patient deals with that suffering, the quality of his or her current relationships, his or her capacity for work and for rest and pleasure, the kind of help the patient has sought in the past and how it worked out, and whether I have a sense that I can relate to the patient's pain and can work with this person. I wish I could say that my criteria always have served as accurate predictors of outcome, but that hasn't been the case. One of the people that I've been able to help the least, in my opinion, was an obsessively defended woman with a neurotic character structure who I thought would benefit greatly from analysis. Despite both of our efforts, though she made some changes in her life, she remained quite limited in her capacity to make emotional contact with others and retained many of her symptoms. On the other hand, I think about a young man who told me during the consultation that he sold and used drugs daily. He'd been involved in drug-related violent altercations and two car accidents. I was wary, but I thought he needed the intensity of an analysis. During his treatment, we were able to engage in a rich, close, and deeply meaningful analytic process. Over eight years, he got to know himself better and empathize with himself, to use his many talents and inner resources to create an intimate relationship with a loving mate, and to enter a highly competitive and demanding profession.

Some analysts believe that patients in the neurotic range benefit most from analysis. My experience has been that less neurotically put-together people benefit from analysis just as much. I've found that intensive work is as necessary to addressing the effects of trauma and early developmental disruptions as to understanding profound guilt. I've treated two critically suicidal patients in analysis: one who became suicidal after the sudden death of a spouse during the analysis and another who suffered from chronic suicidal fantasies and had made suicidal gestures. Seeing them daily was vital, in all the senses of the word, in keeping a connection with them and trying to help them with the depth of their pain and despair, and even, at times, their psychotic states of mind.

Clinical example

Ms. B. was referred to me by her divorce attorney. My initial impression was of a strikingly beautiful woman in her thirties who carried herself with an air of self-assurance tinged with aloofness. Ms. B. had recently separated from her third husband, Jonathan, who was also her business partner. Cautiously she disclosed that Jonathan had caught her having an affair. Although the affair had ended, and her husband still wanted the marriage, she couldn't decide whether to remain married. Unhappy with Jonathan and yearning for independence, Ms. B. wanted the divorce. At the same time, doubting her capacity to support herself and their three young children, she felt incapable of proceeding with it. Ms. B. thought her husband had been doing all the "heavy lifting" in their accounting firm and that she was "just the bookkeeper." She believed that without him she was "nothing" and would be left with nothing. Ms. B. felt desperately caught. She experienced deep affection for her husband and greatly admired his business acumen, his confidence, and his love of life. However, she also saw him as judgmental, domineering, and self-involved, even oblivious to others. She felt lost without him but suffocated by his presence.

Ms. B. grew up the middle child in an Eastern European immigrant family with seven children born a year apart. During her childhood, while her mother worked during the day and went to school in the evenings, Ms. B. had a large share of the responsibility for cooking, cleaning, and taking care of her younger siblings. She described her mother as self-involved and unavailable but praised her father for being interested and loving. In quick succession, her father had acquired and lost several businesses. Because of the father's business troubles, the family had at times experienced great financial hardship. During those times they had furniture repossessed, lived with the threat of losing their home, and worried about their next meal.

Apprehensive about relationships and new to therapy, Ms. B. came to see me thinking that we'd meet briefly, and I would help her decide whether to divorce. I experienced palpably her pressure for answers and her urgency to arrive at a quick decision concerning her marriage. Given that she was in the midst of a life crisis, I considered privately whether short-term or couples' therapy might be the treatment of choice for her. As I thought about her treatment needs, I wrestled with many considerations. During the consultation it had become apparent to me that Ms. B. was deeply unhappy with herself and dissatisfied with most aspects of her life (her relationships, her work, her sense of herself) and had been so as far back as she could remember. In addition, I thought, although she wanted to know whether to continue her third marriage, Ms. B. couldn't make an informed decision until she understood more about herself and her motivations. Given the long-standing nature of her difficulties and the fact that she didn't want to work on her marriage, I decided not to recommend short-term treatment or couples' therapy. As I grappled with whether she could make use of an analysis, I registered my observation that Ms. B. responded to the consultation quickly by seeming less depressed, more hopeful, and less urgent. This initial reaction gave me an optimistic sense about her ability to engage in and benefit from intensive treatment with me.

At the end of the second session, as I imagined myself recommending analysis, I became aware of some additional doubts. Given Ms. B.'s naiveté about therapy, I thought to myself that she might be scared of the analytic frequency or the open-endedness inherent in an analysis. I also wondered if, as a businesswoman, she was too practical and focused on clear cost-benefit considerations to undertake analysis, an uncertain venture from a business perspective. Would she think that I was out of my mind to suggest frequent meetings?

Before my third meeting with Ms. B., I reconsidered my reasons for recommending intensive treatment. I thought about how Ms. B. had told me of her hopes for her future: to have a close and loving relationship with a man without turmoil and drama, to take good care of her beloved children, to achieve financial independence and stability, and to feel good about herself. Although I registered that despite her presentation she experienced herself as helpless and brittle, I also saw a different version of Ms. B.: a determined, resourceful, capable, and likable woman. Also, though she looked self-composed and self-assured, I sensed much uncertainty, fear, and private suffering. I envisioned that analysis would help her become better able to use and appreciate her strengths, become kinder to herself about her vulnerabilities and more aware and understanding of her self-destructiveness and unconscious rage. Given her account of her history, my contact with her and with her deep pain, and my analytic experience, I reestablished in my mind that Ms. B.'s capacity to achieve her ambitious goals depended on her resolving deep, long-standing conflicts about intimacy and success, and appreciating the effects of early deprivation and disruptions in her experience of herself and the world around her.

Letting myself think back to our initial meetings, I was able to recognize several unpleasant feelings in relation to Ms. B., feelings that I'd barely registered before. I recalled that I reacted to her poise and aloofness with some unease and had passing thoughts throughout the first meetings that either she was so well put together that she might not need an analysis after all or, alternatively, that she might be difficult to reach. I also recognized that I responded to her mention of having had an affair with apprehension and concerns about her propensity for acting out and possible impulse control problems. I also felt uneasy about a theme of exploitation and misuse in her description of relationships and my prediction that once in analysis this unpleasant emotional climate would sooner or later infuse our relating. In addition, I noticed that I was reacting to her appearance with barely registered discomfort, a mixture of admiration and slight anxiety. In retrospect, these relatively tame feelings foreshadowed the emotional storms to come a few months into the analysis.

Despite not knowing the meaning of my uneasy feelings at the time, recognizing my anxiety and thinking that it had meaning freed me enough to proceed. At the end of our third meeting, after explaining my sense of her difficulties and my understanding of her goals and reviewing treatment options with her, I recommended that Ms. B. come as often as possible, optimally daily, and stay in treatment as long as she would need. Not directly responding to the recommended frequency but referring to the demands on her time, given her work and her parenting responsibilities, Ms. B. decided she could manage two times a week. I agreed to start on those terms.

In the next days, I realized that I had mixed feelings about starting therapy with Ms. B. I felt disappointed that we could not start more intensively. At the same time, I noticed a sense of relief that she had decided to proceed slowly. This relief was another signal to me that I had more worries in relation to her than I was consciously aware of.

In the first weeks of treatment, Ms. B. alternated between eagerly looking for immediate solutions and appearing inhibited and ill at ease. During this time, she focused on a list of the pros and cons of pursuing a divorce. When not attending to this concern, she spoke of worrying that she didn't have anything important to talk about and that perhaps the twice-a-week schedule was "too much." I felt, and worked to contain, great pressure to be useful and provide her with parenting advice and answers about her marriage. When she looked painfully self-conscious, I felt an equal amount of pressure to put her at ease and reassure her that I was interested in what she had to say. I felt a sense of urgency to engage her and had the perception that she was about to flee.

When I was able to recognize these reactions to her as signs of my anxiety, I began to consider its meaning. Realizing that I was identifying with Ms. B., I was able to register more clearly the extent of *her* anxiety and the pressure she seemed to feel to provide me with what *I* wanted. After I shared these impressions with her, Ms. B. was able to speak directly about her discomfort during the sessions and described how she searched her mind in vain for what she imagined an interesting patient would talk about. Slowly she recognized that this was a familiar worry, a long-standing distressing feeling that who she was would not be interesting enough to others, that she didn't have what it took to hold someone's interest for long. Together we began to discover that Ms. B. considered herself responsible for not having received the attention and interest that she needed from the important others in her life, most recently her husband.

By looking closer at her thoughts during her self-conscious silences, Ms. B. and I discovered how disparaging she anticipated me to be. Little by little, we came to understand that seeing me as a harsh critic reflected her own self-criticisms, and she began to recognize that she was an unforgiving judge of herself. As she became a bit less worried about *my* judgment, Ms. B.'s self-consciousness eased some and she shared more freely her thoughts and feelings. I noticed that at the end of sessions she made passing remarks about how she had more left to say or how fast the time had passed. Or, at the beginning of sessions, she would comment on how long it seemed since our last meeting. I heard these remarks as an indication of her wish to have more time. I sensed that Ms. B. was beginning to find the twice-a-week meetings frustrating. With several areas of concern on the table, I also started to feel that we needed more time together to allow us to go beyond the surface. I asked Ms. B. whether she had considered adding a session. She replied that, although it had occurred to her, she was concerned about lack of time and finances, especially about how her finances might change if she proceeded with a divorce. When, after exploring it further, it turned out that it was unclear to her whether her finances would be an issue in the future, I offered that her concerns about money at this time might also reflect some other worry related to adding a session.

At this juncture, I found that I had to tolerate and grapple with my concerns about my motivation. Given the uncertainty about her marriage and her finances, I wondered if it was prudent for her to increase. Why was I encouraging her? Was it primarily self-interest? In considering my motivations, I privately reviewed my reasons for recommending analysis and looked at the progress we had made. I had recommended analysis because her long history of failed relationships, work dissatisfaction, and disturbing feelings about herself indicated long-standing, multilayered conflict around intimacy and success, and possibly trauma. From experience I knew that short-term measures couldn't address the layers and complexity of her difficulties. I concluded that although she was using the twice-a-week meetings well and we were moving along in our understanding of her by beginning to identify her fears and wishes, for our work to deepen she needed increased frequency. My additional knowledge about her (her profound insecurity, her sense of deprivation, and the harshness of her judgment toward herself) further supported my rationale for recommending analysis. Ms. B.'s increased capacity to think freely and psychologically as a result of being listened to analytically supported my assessment that she could make good use of intensive work.

As she imagined adding a session, Ms. B. experienced a new wave of apprehension about how I might perceive her. She spoke of worrying that coming more often would make her "deficiencies," which she worked so hard to hide, more obvious. She worried about not being able to speak intelligently or make sense of her thoughts. Other than her looks, Ms. B. disclosed, she believed she had nothing to offer. She felt she wasn't well-educated, well-traveled, or particularly bright. I observed her dilemma that although she was aware of wanting more help with these very disturbing feelings, she worried that increasing her sessions would make her feel worse. I shared with her that I understood that she felt painfully deficient regardless of how frequently we met but having more time together would allow us a better chance of understanding this disturbing feeling that led her to keep her distance in relationships. Soon thereafter, Ms. B. added a third session.

With the increase in frequency serving the dual function of giving us more time to explore her feelings and of reassuring her of my interest, Ms. B. brought more of herself into her sessions. She began to examine her feelings about her marriage in a deeper way and to consider her motivations for having married and for staying married. She understood that in her husband she looked for someone who could provide her with the comfort and security she lacked as a child.

Sorrowfully, Ms. B. recalled feeling deprived and alone as a child in a home where there was never enough: food, attention, or affection. She identified a similar feeling within her marriage. With much regret, Ms. B. slowly realized how she and her husband had made an unspoken agreement to remain distant. In the early years of the marriage, when they were building their business, he traveled all week and came home only on weekends. She recalled how relieved she felt when he was leaving again at the end of the weekend and how apprehensive she'd felt just before he was due to come home.

As we explored her memories further, she began to reconsider: perhaps what she feared most were his departures, not his arrivals. She recalled the time when he first began his travel and how she missed him when he was away for days at a time, month after month. Knowing that it was a necessary sacrifice for the future of their business, she tried to ignore her building anger and resentment and pretended, even to herself, not to need his presence or his help. Ms. B. and I came to see that trying to ignore her distress and need for help and relying on herself had been her characteristic way of coping with deprivation since she was a child.

After noticing that she appeared more distant and guarded on Mondays and in sessions after an off-day, I suggested to Ms. B. that a similar process might have been taking place between us: she had been bracing herself to not feel that she wanted or needed help. Ms. B. confirmed that often on days we didn't meet she questioned her need for treatment and thought she might be better off meditating or doing yoga.

Thinking that meeting more often would allow us to help her better tolerate her longings and become acquainted with her defenses against them, I shared my thought with her that adding a session might be helpful at this time. I also suggested that, as with her husband, her fear of relying on others might be keeping her from recognizing her wish for more help. Ms. B. revealed that she'd been thinking about adding another session. Yet she felt worried that it was an indication that she was too dependent on others and feared that were she to come more often, she would become too dependent on me. Some months into the treatment, after realizing that her fear of dependency was another old, recurrent worry that she was trying to manage by staying distant and aloof, she added a fourth session and started to use the couch.

She felt as if she had been "made to do it," as if she had submitted to my will. I found myself irritated by Ms. B.'s view of me as forcing her and considered it her projection. Over the next sessions, as I thought about my irritation, I gradually realized that she wasn't simply projecting but was also picking up accurately that indeed I *wanted* her on the couch. I then recognized that I was invested in her continuing to use it. I resolved that although it could be useful for the analysis for her to lie on the couch, it would be even more useful to explore her conflict about it. This reminder helped me become less invested in her remaining on the couch and allowed me to help her further explore her feelings.

In response to my invitation to tell me more about her feeling that she *had* to continue to lie on the couch, over a number of sessions we recognized that she was importing an old and familiar experience in relationships, feeling forced and having no options. At the same time, lying on the couch evoked Ms. B.'s fears of a lack of connection or engagement. Not being able to see me, she expressed fears that she would lose touch with me or, alternatively, that I'd get lost in my own thoughts, lose track of her, and neglect her.

I think, in part, because I had mentioned in my initial recommendation that five times a week was the best treatment for her, Ms. B. soon began to allude to a fifth session. I say "in part" because I expected that wanting more contact would have come up sooner or later regardless of whether I had mentioned it. She first introduced the topic by referring to her wish to be a better tennis player and concluding that for her to play tennis well it was important to play five times a week. Although she wasn't aware of these reactions, she nevertheless anticipated Tuesday, her weekday off, with sadness or aloofness and showed visible relief when we resumed on Wednesday. At this juncture too, I registered my own disinclination to raise the issue with her. I wondered to myself if four times a week was good enough and whether it was my therapeutic zeal that was motivating me to want to raise the issue of a fifth session, rather than a consideration of Ms. B.'s best interest. I privately questioned if, by adding a fifth hour, Ms. B. would be overextending herself. Yet thinking back on my experience with other patients and examples from the work of colleagues, I determined that, if it was possible, the fifth hour would increase Ms. B.'s opportunity to consider her disturbing feelings and thereby her chances of coming to terms with them. When I thought about it further, I realized that my own fears of increased involvement with her had led me to think about limiting our contact rather than picking up on *her* interest, exploring it with her, and recognizing her autonomy to decide how she wanted to proceed. In addition to considering my own motivations, I thought about whether Ms. B. was ready to go deeper and, if so, how to give her the chance to explore the issue without pushing her beyond where she was.

When I shared with Ms. B. that her alluding to the importance of frequency in getting a job well done led me to wonder if she had given any thought to coming a fifth time, she responded that indeed she had been imagining what coming every day might be like. However, she felt concerned about her propensity to be self-indulgent and often didn't allow herself to have what she wanted to counter that trend. Ms. B. recognized that five sessions felt like a privilege: allowing herself to have the most of what she could have. Yet the recognition that she wanted to come a fifth time brought with it fears of losing control and wanting even more, worries that she would lose her autonomy and her capacity to think for herself, and concerns that she would exhaust all her resources or me. I believe because she was aware by now, eight months into the treatment, of the benefits of time and continuity, Ms. B., despite her fears, asked for a fifth hour.

During the analysis, I gradually understood some of the sources of my initial apprehension. In retrospect, this apprehension was an indication of the unconscious storms that Ms. B. and I were immersed in but couldn't fully register. As we began to work together, we came to experience more directly and fully the stormy transferential and countertransferential feelings that were preconscious during the consultation and to begin to understand their meanings. Shortly after Ms. B. began daily sessions, and I believe because she felt safer and more contained, she disclosed a "secret." In a circuitous and halting manner, she described a period of weeks, in December of the year before she came for the consultation, when she felt increasingly depressed and overwhelmed. With thoughts of killing herself by overdosing on her husband's sleeping pills, she called the police for help and was hospitalized for three days. I felt alarmed by her disclosure and worried that I'd underestimated her level of disturbance. Was she indeed more troubled than I'd allowed myself to know? What was I getting myself into? Reeling, I reached in my mind for the thought that the timing of her disclosure, as well as the feelings that she engendered in me, had meaning. I managed to suggest to her that being in analysis five days a week might be very frightening to her, for reasons that we had yet to understand.

Ms. B. hesitantly acknowledged that she had been feeling terrified that the frequency of our meetings would reveal her "craziness," which most of the time she kept under wraps. She further disclosed that she felt scared of the unpredictable outbursts of rage or despair she had occasionally experienced since she was an adolescent. Ms. B. worried that the more time we spent together, the more opportunity there was for her to experience, and for me to learn, the extent of her mental trouble. She anticipated she could become overwhelmed and would overwhelm me. I shared with Ms. B. my thinking that she must have reasons that we had yet to understand that caused her to anticipate that she would be left alone with overwhelming feelings. I further suggested that there must be some basis in her past experience that led her to worry that no one was sturdy enough or caring enough to tolerate and help her with the intensity of her feelings of powerful anger or extreme disappointment.

Not having made it clear in her initial recounting, Ms. B. described that what precipitated her hospitalization was a period of intense marital conflict culminating in an argument with her husband and his threatening to move out. Eventually we came to understand that fear of rejection and profound shame regarding her needs were some of the important reasons that Ms. B. had kept her hospitalization secret, as well as other matters she eventually disclosed, including that she was still sucking her thumb at night, that she occasionally slept wrapped around one of her children, that she had had multiple affairs.

As we continued our work, more elements of my initial apprehension became understandable. I slowly came to realize that my early sense of unease with her aloofness was the leading edge of my fear, at times terror, of feeling profoundly alone, inferior, and rejected in our relationship. I had hesitated to engage with her in analysis in part because, in identification with her counterdependent stance, I preconsciously and accurately anticipated that in getting to know her I would have to tolerate and contain feelings of dependency and neediness that would be profoundly difficult for me. Later in the analysis when she left me a phone message unilaterally changing the frequency of our meetings or in a remote and dismissive tone announced at a session that she had decided to end her analysis "by the end of the week," I understood my initial apprehension about her impulse control, as my preconscious identification with her characteristic style of preemptively rejecting others.

In the course of our work together we came to understand that Ms. B. had felt neglected by both her parents. As a young child she'd felt inadequately held and attended to by her busy and overwhelmed mother. She'd also felt "dropped" each time her mother gave birth to a younger sibling and when her mother preferred her father's company to hers. In addition, Ms. B. felt disregarded and teased by her father, who, while seemingly favoring her among his children, used her as a cover for his affairs. Ms. B.'s father often brought her along while visiting his mistresses, which included one of her elementary school teachers. As she did with all relationships, including her marriages, Ms. B. entered our relationship assuming she would be mistreated by me and imagining that her only protection against neglect or misuse was to drop me first by involving herself with others or by leaving.

Much later in the analysis, when she came to an analytic appointment with a plunging neckline or wearing skin-tight clothes or when she recounted in evocative detail and in a breathless, husky voice her most recent sexual encounter, I began to understand some of my initial reactions to Ms. B.'s appearance as a reflection of my competitive and erotic feelings toward her. My discomfort foreshadowed intensely shameful feelings of arousal and envy that I had to contain and make sense of in my interactions with Ms. B. She and I came to appreciate that from quite a young age, Ms. B. had to rely on herself and develop ways to get what she needed. We learned that having been noticed and admired for her appearance, Ms. B. used seduction to meet her needs for nurturance and affection. Having been at once underparented and overstimulated, including being sexually teased by relatives, Ms. B. conceived of relationships as mutual stimulations and offered herself sexually to others partly in the hope that she'd be taken care of. This highly sexualized mode of relating protected Ms. B. from painful feelings of helplessness, rage, unfulfilled want, and shame.

Ms. B. had felt used by both her parents, by her mother to help with younger siblings and the household and by her father to help him cover up his affairs and feel desirable and virile. Thus, she approached our relationship expecting to be used and thinking that the only way to get what she needed was to allow, or to look like she allowed me to use her. My preconscious perception of her expectation of being used by me dovetailed with and fueled my preconscious fear of exploiting her. Although we don't talk about it often, we clinicians *need* our patients for many reasons: to earn a living, to exercise our professional skills, for professional advancement, and of course for our own deep-seated emotional reasons. Our ability to keep the patient's treatment needs primary is crucial to the patient's welfare. Ms. B. was to become one of my first analytic patients post-graduation. Although I wasn't fully aware of it at the time, I felt I *needed* Ms. B.—to be a five-times-weekly analytic patient who came regularly, lay on the couch, and paid my fee—in order to prove to myself that I was a "real" analyst. Looking back, I realize that because I *needed* Ms. B. to be in analysis, I worried at a preconscious level that I'd be exploiting her by recommending analysis and increasing her frequency. I now understand these thoughts and feelings as a manifestation of my uncertainty about engaging with her more intimately. I also see them as role-responsive feelings—a response to what she evoked in me and a necessary part of relating to her and understanding her.

Is this case report an example of analysis beginning in the analyst's mind or an example of the deepening of a psychotherapy that led to an analysis? It's both. Whether Ms. B.'s analysis started at an analytic frequency or built up to it wasn't consequential for her well-being. What was crucial in helping Ms. B. with her suffering was the emotional work that I, as her analyst, had to do to deny neither her pain nor the tremendous effort that would be necessary on both our parts to provide her with the help she needed. During the consultation and the deepening period, it was crucial for this patient's life that I was able to generate and maintain, and regain when I lost it, a vision of what was needed and trust in both of us that we could help her. I've tried to illustrate that the work that took place in my mind—both my initial and my ongoing conscious and preconscious assessment that Ms. B. needed psychoanalytic assistance and my willingness to engage with her at an analytic frequency and intensity—was a prerequisite for this patient to get the help she greatly needed. I chose this case example because Ms. B. is the kind of person, given her initial presentation, life circumstances, and therapeutic naiveté, to whom an analyst might not have offered an analysis. She could easily have been seen for years at a twice-a-week frequency without her unconscious storms being fully manifested, identified, or understood. Ms. B. is a patient who could easily have just been given psychotropic medication or sent for couples' work. She would never have grown to recognize and come to terms with the depth or sources of her pain or to understand that her ways of protecting herself prolonged, even compounded, her suffering.

Concluding remarks

In this paper, I've shared my thinking and experience of the conditions that have facilitated the beginning of the analyses that I've been part of or have observed closely as a peer or supervisory consultant. I've described how I find it useful in my clinical work to consider analysis as beginning in the analyst's mind. Although patients and analysts affect and shape each other from the outset, I think it's the analyst's responsibility to initiate intensive treatment. Patients depend on the analyst to recognize their need for analysis, recommend analysis, and facilitate their engagement.

The analyst's emotional investment and capacities allow for the beginning of a back-and-forth between analyst and patient that allows the latter to engage in a useful analysis. These capacities include the ability to identify the patient's pain and fear; the capacity to envision how the patient could develop as a result of understanding conflicts and traumatic experiences; the capacity to envision working helpfully together with the patient; a realistic confidence in analysis; and an awareness that most patients want to know the truth about themselves and to engage deeply and intimately. Recognizing from the outset how much apprehension a close encounter with another's inner world can engender within me and keeping in mind that this fear is crucial in understanding the patient has been a central aspect of my development as an analyst. This recognition has enhanced my ability to listen, engage, and stay the course.

Notes

1 I am offering my ideas for analysts who wish to practice more analysis. I am *not* advocating that all analysts should practice only or mostly analysis. I know many analysts with different interests and inclinations who are very identified with psychoanalysis and genuinely satisfied with how they have applied their analytic training productively in research, education, forensics, substance abuse treatment, etc. and are not interested in doing more clinical psychoanalysis.

2 In the introduction to their collection of papers on Betty Joseph, Hargreaves and Varchevker (2004) write: "Joseph believes that the very important function of the group is found in the capacity of members to help each other to contain the anxiety, sense of frustration and professional inadequacy that the work inevitably entails and make use of the awareness of these issues to further understanding of the patient's anxiety, defensive maneuvers and sense of impasse that otherwise can prevent true psychic change" (p. 7).

3 Although for the purposes of this paper I focus on the analyst's intrapsychic work, I take it as a given that from the very first moment of contact with the patient, the analyst's inner life is affected by the patient's.

4 This is not intended as an exhaustive or prescriptive list but as a beginning effort to conceptualize the state of mind of the analyst that facilitates the beginning of analysis.

5 Ogden (1992) compellingly articulates the extent to which the patient's drama begins even before the first hour and how wishes and fears in both patient and analyst are activated and come into powerful interplay during the initial meeting.

6 In my experience, to envision herself and the patient as capable of having a productive relationship, the analyst must remain in touch with her own good experiences in relationships, including experiences of having been helped and her own capacities to be generative, helpful, and analytically effective. I believe it is also essential for the analyst not to deny her worries about her own badness or destructiveness and to work internally to locate within her experience of the patient some of what has been good in the patient's past relationships.

7 Recommending analysis is one part of the analyst's invitation. I consider addressing the inevitable fears, both the patient's and the analyst's, that follow the recommendation to be part of the invitation as well. Frank (2004) and Wille (2012) provide useful discussions of the analyst's trust in analysis.

8 Two papers by candidates, Gann (2000) and Glover (2000), also add to the literature about recommending analysis. In addition, a volume edited by Jacobs and Rothstein (1990) richly contributes to the conceptual and technical considerations on beginning analysis with an emphasis on particular subsets of patients, such as candidates, the elderly, and patients with eating disorders.

9 I want to clarify that I do not always recognize the need for analysis during the initial consultation. There have been instances when I concluded that analysis was indicated well into a treatment. Unless I am confident in my own mind that analysis is needed and will likely benefit the patient, I will not recommend it at the outset.

10 I have found discussions on the analyst's self-interest and desire by Friedman (2012), Hirsch (2008), Mendelsohn (2002), and Wilson (2003) especially useful.

References

Bernstein, S.B. (1990). Motivation for psychoanalysis and the transition from psychotherapy. *Psychoanalytic Inquiry*, 10: 242.

Bernstein, S.B. (2000). Developing a psychoanalytic practice. *Psychoanalytic Inquiry*, 20: 574–593.

Bion, W.R. (1959). Attacks on linking. *International Journal of Psychoanalysis*, 40: 308–315.

Bion, W.R. (1962). *Learning from Experience*. London: Tavistock.

Bion, W.R. (1979). Making the best of a bad job. In *Clinical Seminars and Four Papers*, ed. F. Bion. Abingdon, England: Fleetwood Press, 1987, pp. 247–257.

Brenner, C. (1990). On beginning an analysis. In *On Beginning an Analysis*, eds. T. Jacobs & A. Rothstein. Madison, CT: International Universities Press, pp. 47–55.

Busch, F. (1995). Beginning a psychoanalytic treatment: Establishing an analytic frame. *Journal of the American Psychoanalytic Association*, 43: 449–468.

Chused, J.F. (2012). The analyst's narcissism. *Journal of the American Psychoanalytic Association*, 60: 899–915.

Ehrlich, L.T. (2004). The analyst's reluctance to begin a new analysis. *Journal of the American Psychoanalytic Association*, 52: 1075–1093.

Ehrlich, L.T. (2010). The analyst's ambivalence about continuing and deepening an analysis. *Journal of the American Psychoanalytic Association*, 58: 515–532.

Frank, K.A. (2004). The analyst's trust and therapeutic action. *Psychoanalytic Quarterly*, 2: 335–378.

Friedman, L. (2012). A holist's anxiety of influence: Commentary on Kirshner. *Journal of the American Psychoanalytic Association*, 60: 1259–1279.

Gann, M.F. (2000). Making the first move: A candidate's step-by-step guide to recommending psychoanalysis. *Journal of Clinical Psychoanalysis*, 9: 9–19.

Glover, W.C. (2000). Where do analysands come from? A candidate's experience in recommending psychoanalysis. *Journal of Clinical Psychoanalysis*, 9: 21–37.

Hall, J.S. (1998). *Deepening the Treatment*. Lanham, MD: Aronson.

Hargreaves, E. & Varchevker, A. (2004). *In Pursuit of Change: The Betty Joseph Workshop*. Hove, East Sussex: Brunner-Routledge.

Hirsch, I. (2008). *Coasting in the Countertransference: Conflicts of Self-Interest between Analyst and Patient*. New York: Analytic Press.

Jacobs, T.J. & Rothstein, A. (1990). *On Beginning an Analysis*. Madison, CT: International Universities Press.

Levine, H. B. (2010). Creating analysts, creating analytic patients. *International Journal of Psychoanalysis*, 91: 1385–1404.

Mendelsohn, E. (2002). The analyst's bad-enough participation. *Psychoanalytic Dialogues*, 12: 331–358.

Ogden, T.H. (1992). Comments on transference and countertransference in the initial analytic meeting. *Psychoanalytic Inquiry*, 12: 225–247.

Ogden, T.H. (1994). The analytic third: Working with intersubjective clinical facts. *International Journal of Psychoanalysis*, 75: 3–19.

Ogden, T.H. (2008). Bion's four principles of mental functioning. *Fort Da*, 14: 11–35.

Reith, B. (2010). The specific dynamics of initial interviews: Switching the level, or opening up a meaning space? *Bulletin of the European Federation of Psycho-analysis*, 4(Suppl.): 57–80.

Reith, B., Lagerlof, S., Crick, P., Moller, M., & Skale, E. (2012). *Initiating Psychoanalysis: Perspectives*. London: Routledge.

Rothstein, A. (1994). A perspective on doing a consultation and making the recommendation of analysis to a perspective analyzand. *Psychoanalytic Quarterly*, 63: 680–695.

Rothstein, A. (1995). Psychoanalytic technique and the creation of analysands: On beginning an analysis with patients who are reluctant to pay the analyst's fee. *Psychoanalytic Quarterly*, 64: 306–325.

Rothstein, A. (2010). Psychoanalytic technique and the creation of analytic patients: An addendum. *Psychoanalytic Quarterly*, 79: 785–794.

Schlesinger, H.J. (2005). *Endings and Beginnings: On Terminating Psycho-therapy and Psychoanalysis*. New York: Analytic Press.

Wille, R. (2012). The analyst's trust in psychoanalysis and the communication of that trust in initial interviews. *Psychoanalytic Quarterly*, 81: 875–904.

Wilson, M. (2003). The analyst's desire and the problem of narcissistic resistances. *Journal of the American Psychoanalytic Association*, 51: 71–99.

Winnicott, D.W. (1960). The theory of the parent-infant relationship. *International Journal of Psychoanalysis*, 41: 585–595.

Chapter 3

Finding control cases and maintaining immersion

Turning challenges into opportunities

In Katz, Kaplan and Stromberg's national survey on motivation, obstacles, and ideas on increasing interest in psychoanalytic training, the authors quote candidates as saying:

> The field is a mess, and the institutes are in turmoil. It is hard to get cases, at least for me, as patients have not heard of analysis and I have to develop them slowly. Lots quit therapy when I bring up frequency or analysis—others quit analysis for one or the other reason. It has been tough.
>
> It's hard finding control cases and the fact that insurers do not pay for analysis makes it difficult now and makes anticipating a future practice somewhat dim.
>
> Obtaining three control cases for four-times-a-week analysis is unrealistic yet required. This delays graduation and makes training more difficult than it should be.
>
> (Katz, Kaplan, and Stromberg 2012a, p. 83)

Finding cases and maintaining immersion are challenging for most candidates. National and local survey results, authors, and anecdotal reports in the United States and worldwide suggest these challenges are common and widespread. Katz, Kaplan, and Stromberg (2012a), reporting the results of a national survey of candidates, found that "difficulty finding cases" was among the most frequently cited reasons for dissatisfaction with training among respondents (21%). Candidates expressed concern about needing patients of both genders, a certain number of cases, and a frequency of four times weekly in order to graduate. Difficulty finding cases was also among the five most highly ranked obstacles when candidates rated their perceptions of past or current obstacles to training (Katz, Kaplan, and Stromberg 2012b).

Difficulty beginning a first case was identified as problematic at the New York University Psychoanalytic Institute, where half the members of a talented second-year class couldn't progress in their training because they lacked control cases (Rothstein 2010a, 2010b).[1] In addition to candidates delaying picking up their first case, Rothstein reported a second trend: a number of advanced candidates, despite being further along in training, didn't have sufficient immersion to graduate.

What happens after graduation? Survey data from the practice patterns of graduate analysts reveal that difficulty finding cases and maintaining immersion persists, even amplifies. Cherry et al. (2004) conducted a systematic assessment of psychoanalytic practice in the early postgraduate years at the Columbia Center for Psychoanalytic Training and Research and found that "strikingly little four-times-weekly psychoanalysis is being conducted among analysts who graduated within the last fifteen years. Graduates who are not certified and have not become training analysts (78% of our sample) conduct almost no four-times-weekly analysis once their control cases terminate" (p. 861). More specifically, Cherry et al. report that analysts who aren't certified see an average of from zero to one patient at a frequency greater than twice a week and only two patients in twice-a-week treatment.

As with candidates, graduate analysts' difficulties are not uncommon or confined to one location. On the contrary, comparing immersion data of recent graduates from three institutes,[2] Kaplan et al. (2009) found that "at all three study sites, very little analysis, as defined by four-times-weekly frequency, is practiced by the majority of graduates" (p. 1172). Analyzing the data further, Kaplan et al. report that "the typical non-training analyst" sees three to four patients at a twice-a-week frequency and just one patient at a three- or four-times-a-week frequency (p. 1173).

At the Chicago Institute, Schneider et al. (2014) conducted a survey of all living graduate analysts of the last six decades. They report that 38% of the respondents "had none or only one patient in analysis" (p. 95). Yet 98% of the respondents felt that psychoanalytic training had enhanced their clinical work.

These data corroborate what many candidates and psychoanalytic educators know from daily experience: case finding and clinical immersion, although desired by clinical candidates and required for graduation, present a challenge of varying degrees for candidates. In addition, the remarkable fact that most graduate analysts in these surveys don't begin new analytic cases once their control cases terminate indicates that these problems not only persist post-graduation but increase, affecting an even greater number of analysts. It also suggests that psychoanalytic training doesn't sufficiently address the difficulty future analysts will have finding cases.

Although case finding and maintaining immersion during candidacy is a common and widespread problem that's likely to persist beyond graduation and therefore affect candidates' careers, recruitment to the profession (Katz 2012b), and the future of psychoanalysis, very little has been written specifically about how to understand it and even less about how to address it. This is so, despite the vast literature focusing on problems of psychoanalytic education.

External challenges faced by candidates

A large body of literature suggests there are fundamental unaddressed problems in our institutes and our educational system, problems that affect candidates adversely. Some authors contend that the hierarchical structure and insular nature of our training institutions do not promote independent and creative thinking and learning among candidates. Pointing specifically to the flaws and limitations of the training analyst system, they argue that it leads, at best, to idealizations that hamper an objective assessment of the usefulness of analysis (their own and their patients') and, at worst, to boundary violations and/or the emotional misuse and abuse of candidates (Kirsner 2001, 2010; Berman 2004; Casement 2005; Raubolt 2006; Kernberg 2014).

Critics of psychoanalytic education also point to the lack of clear criteria for progression, which they argue leads to "bean counting" of analytic and supervisory hours, frequency of sessions, and time spent conducting control analyses, rather than assessing candidates' analytic competency (Kernberg 1986, 2000, 2007, 2010). Responding to the call for more objective criteria for assessing analytic competence, an increasing number of contributions address progression criteria and learning objectives (Körner 2002; Tuckett 2005; Cabaniss 2008; Junkers, Tuckett, and Zachrisson 2008; Israelstam 2011; Rothstein 2017).

> Candidates are affected also by iatrogenic anxieties and suspiciousness fostered by the limits of objective evaluation given the person-related competence inherent in practicing analysis (Brodbeck 2008) and must grapple with developmental stresses and the inevitable regression and persecutory feelings that accompany a radical transformation of their identity.
>
> (Bruzzone et al. 1985; Ward, Gibson, and Miqueu-Baz 2010)

Mary Target (2001), who reviewed and distilled the criticisms contained in some 300 papers on psychoanalytic education,[3] agrees that the training has many limitations, including a tendency to infantilize students, some harsh and authoritarian teachers, and poorly taught and organized curricula. However, she concludes that such a critique "really only captures one side of the picture. It leaves out the imparting of profound understanding and skill, both through training analysis and through teaching, which have surely changed many of us *fundamentally*, in our psychoanalytic education" (p. 15). Target asks if the "chorus of criticism" stands proxy for analysts' displaced representation of dissatisfaction with their careers or psychoanalysis itself. She proposes that we think more complexly about these dissatisfactions and examine them "analytically" in order to understand this paradox.

All of us who have been in training can attest that the requirements involving control analyses are logistically and financially demanding. Most graduate analysts remember the time and cost involved in being in a training analysis, attending seminars, and analyzing three supervised cases, not to mention the challenges of making a living and preserving time for family, exercise, leisure, and recreation!

Adding to the challenges, being a candidate and finding control cases in today's world means learning new ways of thinking and being, as a clinician, in a context of ever greater theoretical and technical diversity. Candidates encounter a multitude of theoretical ideas, concepts, and technical recommendations. Concepts are usually offered in the language of specific schools and without the translation necessary for candidates to easily ascertain if or how they might correspond to concepts from other theoretical viewpoints. This theoretical and technical plurality highlights the enormous complexity of practicing as an analyst and the lack of agreement regarding the goals of psychoanalytic treatment.

Some authors, though not speaking directly to case finding and immersion, have written more specifically about the influence of analytic training on candidates' clinical work. Cabaniss and Roose (1997) suggest that candidates' difficulties in analyzing control cases are inherent in being an analyst-in-training. They suggest that candidates' freedom to set the frame and to interpret, especially patients' negative transferences, is compromised by graduation requirements, beginners' lack of confidence, and the nature of the cases themselves, which are conducted under supervision and are often low fee and seen in clinics. Similarly, Jaffe (2001) suggests that case requirements stimulate "indirect" countertransferences[4] and affect candidates' interventions. He maintains that candidates are subject to even more indirect countertransferences than graduate analysts.

Shifting the focus away from external challenges, Joshua Ehrlich (2003) emphasizes the *meaning* of training for candidates and how this meaning reveals itself in the transference-countertransference manifestations. He cautions that fixing exclusively on the impact of training on cases deprives candidates of an opportunity to explore the meaning of these manifestations and how it affects their clinical work. He further argues that the external stresses of training, though unique, parallel ongoing impingements that analysts face throughout their careers, such as pregnancy, illness, and daily events. He concludes that learning to identify and understand the influence of training on their control analyses would enhance candidates' capacity to appreciate the complex interplay of fantasy and reality in their practice as graduate analysts.

Internal challenges faced by candidates

As our profession matures and we accumulate more data about teaching and doing analysis, we've become increasingly aware of the enormous emotional demands of functioning analytically. Far from the early days of denying or underappreciating our emotional involvement, we recognize that a helpful analysis is an emotional journey that requires the analyst's deep involvement and that our distressing feelings in relation to our patients are our best guides to finding their pain and difficulties (Winnicott 1949; Heimann 1950; Racker 1957; Bion 1962; Jacobs 1973, 1991; Sandler 1976; Bollas 1979; Boesky 1990; Ogden 1992, 1994; Gabbard 1995; Smith 2000; Parsons 2006; Baranger and Baranger 2008). We now appreciate that ascertaining distress[5] within ourselves and using it analytically is our best tool for helping our patients. In other words, attending diligently to our transferential and counter-transferential feelings is essential to a useful analysis.[6] Unfortunately, we haven't applied this vital understanding sufficiently to help candidates learn how to find cases, maintain immersion, and develop an analytic identity[7] as clinical psychoanalysts.

Whether or not we're aware of it at the time, in addition to studying to become psychoanalysts, we sign up for analytic training hoping to suffer less. We seek candidacy motivated by profound needs to make sense of our disturbing feelings and symptoms and be more integrated and intimate with others. Doing emotional work is a vital need that drives us not only to be in analysis but to *do* analysis. This profound motivation explains, in part, our willingness to dedicate the enormous amount of time, energy, and money necessary to become graduate analysts.

Yet, this profound motivation to make sense of our troubled emotions is inevitably met with equally powerful fears of encountering them, which lead us to back away from ourselves and from our patients. Whether it's difficulty starting a first control case, working with a particular gender, finding our last case and moving toward graduation, or maintaining immersion, I suggest that framing these difficulties as meaningful, partly a manifestation of fear, is vital to helping candidates construct a psychoanalytic frame of mind and identity.

However, the notion that a candidate is afraid to do the work she is spending a lot of time, effort, and resources to pursue is a psychoanalytic finding that requires significant emotional effort before it can be processed and accepted. More than a hundred years of experience has taught us that ambivalence is inherent in every relationship and endeavor. Expecting that candidates will be afraid to initiate analysis means accepting one of the most profound psychoanalytic discoveries about the human mind: it protects itself from suffering. Fear of having an intimate encounter is as ubiquitous in analysis as in any other relationship. The uncomfortable paradox that candidates, while determined to engage patients, are also afraid of their feelings and of intimacy is an understanding that is intrinsic to developing and maintaining a psychoanalytic identity and analytic approach. Unless we embrace this insight and consider difficulties with our analytic functioning as symptoms with meaning that need to be understood, we will rationalize our internal difficulties as external difficulties and will not be able to find a place in our minds to think analytically and practice analysis.

I recommend that in analyzing, teaching, and supervising candidates we devote specific attention to helping candidates appreciate the value of identifying and making use of transference-countertransference dynamics as they search for control cases in general and/or as they evaluate an individual patient. More specifically, I recommend that we help candidates frame their concerns about external obstacles to initiating an analysis (e.g. graduation requirements, doubts whether a patient is suitable or an analysis is practically feasible) as possible signals of their transference-countertransference reactions to analyzing in general and to engaging intensively with particular patients. I also propose helping candidates understand that their hesitation to engage with a potential control case is a window into that patient's difficulties and the reason she needs intensive help. This will assist candidates in learning how to "find" patients in their own minds, not only to complete the training requirements but to have the option of practicing analysis post-graduation.

Embracing fear as a stimulus for growth

In my experience as a candidate, graduate analyst, supervisor, and progression chair, I've found it most fruitful to frame each obstacle to finding analytic cases and maintaining immersion as a manifestation of the analyst's unconscious or preconscious fears.[8] The candidate's analysis, control cases, and weekly supervisions provide trainees rich opportunities to recognize and engage their fears, as well as their patients'.

With every prospective control case, a candidate faces internal preconscious and unconscious pressures that affect finding cases and maintaining immersion. I will list a few:

- Unconscious or preconscious fantasies about relationships and what can happen between two people when they have a close encounter: Who will do what to whom? Fantasies of analysis as regressive, hurtful, intrusive, controlling, depriving, manipulating, overstimulating, or illicit, among many possible fantasies.
- Feelings about one's training analysis and the particular transferences toward the training analyst one is struggling with when looking for a control case. For instance, how does my training analyst feel about my becoming an analyst? How would my success or failure affect my analyst?
- Worries about the nature of one's motivations, including power, selfishness, greed, exploitation, sadism, voyeurism, etc.
- Concerns in relation to supervisors, some of which might be displaced from the training analyst: Do they have anything to teach? Can they support me? Will they be critical?
- Worries specific to a specific patient's dynamics: Is the patient too disturbed? Is the patient likely to leave prematurely? Will I be able to help/understand/survive this patient?

Every beginning analytic encounter mobilizes fears and wishes (Ogden 1992), in both patient and analyst. The difference between patient and analyst is that the analyst, if she can recognize, contain, and make use of her fears, can make space in her own mind for the patient and invite the patient to get the help she needs.

Case example: Dr. B.

Dr. B., a first-year candidate, was looking for a first case and complained to her advisor that, though eager to begin, she wasn't getting referrals for analysis from her fellow candidates or the faculty. When her advisor asked about her practice, it turned out that Dr. B. had a full-time practice of two- and three-times-weekly patients. The advisor asked if she'd considered whether one of her private patients could benefit from analysis. Dr. B. replied that she'd reviewed her caseload and concluded that none of her private patients could be in analysis because most couldn't afford it, others had schedules that wouldn't permit it, and yet others were too disturbed to benefit from it. The advisor suggested that, because analysts have fears about beginning analysis, Dr. B. might consider that her inability to think of any of her patients as suitable might relate to fears about working with them more intensively.

Dr. B. was irritated by the advisor's suggestion and skeptical regarding its validity. Yet, intrigued, she brought the advisor's suggestion to her own analysis. Dr. B. slowly noticed that she came to her analysis with an agenda and rarely spoke her mind freely. She rarely allowed herself to be curious about her analyst and mostly discussed her patients. In addition, she recognized that she limited her time with her husband and children by working long hours during the week and, when at home, retreating to TV or her computer. Slowly she began to explore the many causes of this protective need to keep her distance from others, including her worry that she would be too dependent, overwhelmed, or overwhelming or would become overexcited and lose control.

Meanwhile, Dr. B.'s supervisor suggested they take a second look at her caseload to see if they could identify a potential control case. They focused on a twice-a-week patient, Mr. Y., who felt stuck after years of psychotherapy and complained he was not getting "enough" out of his treatment. Dr. B. thought Mr. Y. needed more help but hadn't considered offering him analysis. To her supervisor's question about her reservations, Dr. B. responded that she thought Mr. Y. was in a high-demand profession that precluded his being able to attend more frequently. The supervisor encouraged Dr. B. to consider that when Mr. Y. complained about not getting enough, he might have been pre-consciously hinting that he wanted and needed more time and engagement with her to address his difficulties. The supervisor asked her what seeing him daily would be like for her if she recommended additional sessions and Mr. Y. agreed to arrange his time. As Dr. B. imagined him attending more frequently, she found herself thinking about his history of frequent geographical moves and infidelity and realized that his propensity to leave and betray others frightened her. Initially, she thought she was afraid that Mr. Y. would leave before the case could "count" and thus would delay her progression. Then she recognized that Mr. Y.'s fear of loss, betrayal, and helplessness in relation to an exciting and abandoning other resonated with her own early experience.

Thinking further about what it might be like if Mr. Y. actually accepted her invitation, Dr. B., associating to his muscular physique and his shy smile when she greeted him at the beginning of hours, realized that she felt anxious about spending more time with him. Tapping into her fear of being attracted to him, she recognized not only that this was an area left unexplored in her own analysis but was also an area where the patient needed help. Dr. B. suggested to Mr. Y. that more time was needed to understand his fearful wish to have more in relationships and invited him to attend more frequently. Mr. Y., after some exploration of his fears, was able to make the necessary changes to be able to come to treatment daily.

Discussion

With the help of her advisor, her supervisor, and her analyst, Dr. B. became aware that her various explanations for not being able to begin an analytic case were in significant part manifestations of her fears of beginning an analysis in general, and with Mr. Y. in particular. Dr. B., initially unaware of being afraid, hadn't recognized that she was invested in delaying her beginning an analysis. Instead she attributed this delay to external circumstances such as not getting referrals and not having a suitable patient in her practice. Invested in thinking that the conditions necessary for an analysis could not be met, she unconsciously failed to see that a patient in her practice needed and was ready for intensive help.

What made the beginning of this analysis possible? First, Dr. B. needed help in recognizing that her inability to identify a control case had meaning. She then needed help in her analysis to discover her transferential fears regarding intimacy. Dr. B. needed her supervisor's help in taking a second look at her patient's needs. Although she saw that Mr. Y. needed additional help, she thought he would be unwilling to attend more frequently. She mistook her fears for his unavailability. When asked to imagine him in analysis with her, she began to detect her own worries. Identifying, containing, and finding meaning in these concerns, Dr. B. was able to discover aspects of Mr. Y.'s fear of excitement, abandonment, and betrayal within herself. She could then empathize with these concerns and with his need for help.

It was useful for Dr. B. to recognize that the analyst's reservations are inevitably linked with, and illuminate, the patient's fears. Her intimate understanding of Mr. Y.'s worries in turn allowed her to address them with immediacy and emotional resonance, which increased the patient's sense of safety and hope. It's beneficial for candidates to know that any reservations on the part of the analyst, no matter how reasonable they seem, contain aspects of the analyst's fears and, in a role-responsive way, the patient's as well (Sandler 1976).

To engage a patient in analysis, candidates must establish and maintain an analytic setting, internal and external, that allows them to translate their own and their patient's obstacles/objections to analysis (time, money, frequency, etc.) into particular fears about beginning the analytic relationship (being criticized, neglected, seduced, etc.) and fears about the nature and intensity of their thoughts and feelings, such as intense shame, fear, anger, excitement, pleasure, etc. Moreover, in order to do analysis candidates must convey their analytic understanding of a patient's presenting difficulties in a way that can reach the patient emotionally. They must be able to recommend analysis and respond to the patient's response in ways that facilitate the patient's awareness of the need for treatment.

Case example: Dr. C.

Dr. C., an advanced candidate, was entering his third year of training without having found a control case. In his analysis, he spoke of long-standing insecurities about his worth and capabilities, concerns that had intensified during training. In supervision, he spoke of feeling unsure about "when, how, or to whom to make the recommendation." He wondered what words to use and whether there was information about the process of recommending that he had somehow missed. In his private practice, Dr. C. customarily offered weekly treatment to his patients unless they were in crisis.

Shortly after entering his third year, Dr. C. recommended weekly treatment to a new patient, Ms. Z., a depressed woman with a history of relational difficulties, depression, bulimia, and psychotherapy treatments that had helped her but in a limited way. After working with the patient for a few months, Dr. C. observed that Ms. Z. felt less depressed and more optimistic about herself. At that point, he recommended that she increase her frequency to "four or five" sessions a week in order to "explore her feelings in a deeper, more meaningful way." Dr. C. anticipated that Ms. Z. would turn down his offer. However, to his surprise, she readily agreed. Further, she revealed that she had found his name on the institute's website and had specifically chosen him because of his affiliation and with the hope of eventually being in analysis. Ms. Z. committed to four-weekly sessions.

As he began the analysis, Dr. C. reported feeling anxious. He worried that Ms. Z., now deprived of face-to-face contact, would find the new arrangement intolerable. He also feared that Ms. Z. would feel too regressed and unable to bear her feelings. Dr. C. hoped that he and analysis would not fail the patient. As they began the new schedule, Ms. Z. said she found lying on the couch relaxing. At the same time, however, she reported extreme fatigue and spoke of unremitting hunger and struggles with food between sessions. Ms. Z. also spoke of her mounting concern that the analysis would cause her to lose control and become "weak, ugly, lazy, and dirty." During this beginning period, the patient often canceled sessions to attend work meetings or family events. On the advice of his supervisor, Dr. C. invited Ms. Z. to consider that these cancellations might have deeper meanings. The patient spoke of her propensity to prioritize others, a tendency toward martyrdom, and a disdain of her wish to be cared for.

A year into treatment, Ms. Z. announced that one of her hours, a morning appointment, was interfering with her sleep and she had decided to reduce her sessions from four to three. Encouraged to elaborate, she claimed that the early hour had been difficult for her because she had to go directly to work without being able to reflect on difficult feelings that would come up, and this was affecting her work. Ms. Z. added that cutting back on her hours had become necessary because attending to her grandchildren was requiring more time. After reducing her sessions, the patient reported feeling overwhelmed and associated to a dream of an out-of-control truck running over a man who was lying naked in the street. Dr. C. wondered privately whether Ms. Z. experienced *him* as out of control and had felt run over by his wish that she maintain her frequency of four sessions a week.

Indeed, Dr. C. was distressed at her unilaterally dropping a session and worried that the analysis would not meet his institute's graduation requirements. He found himself angry about the progression committee's expectations regarding analytic frequency and wished he was a candidate at an institute with more flexible requirements. He felt helpless and stuck. Though feeling a pull to "make" the patient attend more frequently, he wished that she herself desired to come more often. For the next year, on good days and with the help of his supervisor, Dr. C. sustained the belief that the reduction had meaning and that, once it was understood, the patient would want to return to her old frequency. On bad days, all he could think about was the expense of the training, the patient's low fee, and the fact that at this frequency the case would not count toward graduation.

An instructor, after listening to Dr. C.'s recounting of the patient's thoughts, suggested that Ms. Z., despite claiming otherwise, was distressed by the increased distance between herself and her analyst and appeared to recognize that she needed more help than she was allowing herself. The instructor asked Dr. C. if he had considered that there might be reasons why *he* might not want her to increase? Puzzled but intrigued, Dr. C. began to examine his participation in this analysis. In his own analysis, Dr. C. realized, he had been focusing defensively on "analytic technique" and "the analytic process," avoiding how scared he felt about the intensity of Ms. Z.'s need for him and his need for her to be his analytic patient. He also began to recognize how scared he was by his love for his own analyst and by how much he longed to be with her and depend on her.

Dr. C. realized he had identified with the patient's defensive devaluing of their relationship and had failed to notice the signs of Ms. Z.'s battle against her insatiable hunger for him. Sturdier on his analytic feet now, Dr. C. spoke with the patient about her dread of what seemed to her a ravenous hunger for more contact and increased dependence, a feeling she had been trying unsuccessfully to manage by reducing her sessions. He also addressed her many fearful expectations related to being with him as often as she needed and wanted, including her fear that she would lose control of herself and run him over with her feelings. The patient responded by becoming less guarded and more engaged. Dr. C. suggested that they return to four sessions weekly in order to further explore the difficult feelings preventing her from being as intimate in relationships as she wanted. As if she'd been waiting to be asked, Ms. Z. promptly agreed.

Discussion

Although Dr. C. didn't understand it at the time, not knowing when, how, or to whom to recommend analysis wasn't the crucial impediment to his progression. For many beginning candidates like Dr. C., lack of experience and skills isn't the main obstacle to finding control cases. Candidates must discover during candidacy that initiating analysis is less about having skills and more about opening the space in one's mind to the experience of being with the patient and with the disturbance it generates, and about translating this disturbance into an understanding of the patient's beginning fears.

Thinking about inviting a patient to work closely with him evoked Dr. C.'s enduring fears of relationships generally: insecurity about his lovability, fear of being rejected, and preconscious concerns about being harmed or harming others. In his practice, he managed these fears by seeing patients once a week; in training, he managed them by focusing on coursework and delaying inviting patients into analysis until it was absolutely required for his progression. What had changed when Dr. C. recommended analysis was not the patient—she had made her first call to him needing and wanting psychoanalysis. Instead, what had evolved was the analyst's capacity to perceive her need and to find it within himself to respond to it.

Although analyst and patient became slightly less fearful of themselves and one another, and more willing to engage more intensively, their reluctance still shaped the analyst's recommendation and the patient's response. At the outset, the candidate had offered "four or five" sessions weekly, not five. Ms. Z., who like most patients was extremely attuned to the nuances of what the analyst recommends, heard and reacted to Dr. C.'s hesitation. Projecting her own fear of her neediness and also reacting to Dr. C.'s hedging, Ms. Z. interpreted his recommendation to mean he wasn't sure that he wanted five sessions. Worried he might not be able to tolerate the full intensity of her needs, Ms. Z. chose the lesser frequency. Unconsciously, she then further protected both of them from the full intensity of her feelings by using cancellations to decrease the hours even more. Then, a year into the analysis, she cut back to three times a week.

Dr. C., responding, in part preconsciously, to Ms. Z.'s expectation of being dominated, harmed, and influenced by his similar fears, focused on what he and the analysis could do *to* Ms. Z., not on what he could do *for* her.[9] He worried that loss of face-to-face contact would render her too vulnerable and regressed to tolerate her feelings. For the analysis to begin, Dr. C. had to endure his fear of her vulnerability, potential for regression, and incapacity to tolerate feelings, as well as his own similar fears. He also had to bear and contain his fear of failing her, which for the first year of treatment he was able to do.

Initially, Dr. C. displaced his struggle with Ms. Z. over frequency to a struggle with his institute, which he experienced as rigid and controlling. Although on good days he was able to hold on to his analytic mind and consider the seeming impasse as meaningful, on bad days he lost track of his patient's urgent need for intensive psychological help and externalized the therapeutic necessity for frequent meetings to the institute's "sadistic" requirements.

Encouraged by an instructor to take a third look[10] at the analysis and recognize that Ms. Z. wanted as much contact as possible and valued his help, Dr. C. felt more optimistic and able to look deeper into himself. He slowly discovered that because of his own fears he'd inadvertently pulled back from the patient emotionally and was participating in the standoff. Now able to see his patient's needs and fears more accurately, and less afraid of her, Dr. C. could relate to Ms. Z. in a way that helped her feel safe enough to reengage more intensively with him and with herself.

Learning to recognize difficulty finding cases as a sign of understandable, and expectable, ambivalence and to help candidates use that ambivalence to explore their own conflicts and traumas, as well as their patients', can help us in helping candidates become analysts.[11] Psychoanalytic training can give candidates the option to practice as clinical psychoanalysts beyond graduation by teaching them that the essential step in finding patients is an internal process that generates room in the analyst's mind (Ehrlich 2013) sufficient to allow the fullest possible appreciation of the patient's suffering and the hope and the will to be of help.

When a candidate's primary conscious motivation for finding a control case or maintaining immersion is progression, it's worth considering whether he or she is defensively attributing the desire to practice analysis to the institute. It's often a sign that the candidate needs assistance engaging with the essence of psychoanalytic work: experiencing and making use of the emotional storms within and between each analytic participant to help the patient become emotionally integrated and more intimately engaged with others.[12]

When candidates deny and project their own desires and fears in relation to their patients, as Dr. C. did, they can experience training requirements as arbitrary, controlling, and even sadistic demands. Paradoxically, it's these challenging requirements—for immersion, frequency, number of cases, and treating both genders—that provide candidates like Dr. C. the opportunity to learn how to contain and work with both their patients' and their own intolerable desires and fears.[13]

Unless candidates learn to anticipate, tolerate, and make use of disturbing feelings in thinking about doing analysis or consulting with a potential control case, they'll continue, even as graduate analysts, to turn away from opportunities to begin intensive treatments or to more deeply engage patients already in treatment. Candidates experience daily, and supervisors witness, how difficult it is to recognize, bear, and make use of the intensely disturbing feelings (e.g., terror, longing, desire, hatred, helplessness, despair, love, excitement) at play in the beginning and indeed throughout any meaningful intensive treatment.

Fears about finding cases or about immersing oneself in the work with a specific patient become interferences only when candidates deny those fears or externalize them. As long as candidates attribute the desire to do analysis to the institute and its graduation requirements or refrain from offering analysis to patients, citing imagined external obstacles like an unwillingness or inability to attend frequently, they miss the opportunity to explore how these fears, including the fear of desiring to do analysis, get in the way of finding cases and practicing analysis.

How do we help candidates recognize and work with their fears? To summarize:

- Encourage candidates to consider that external difficulties in finding cases and maintaining immersion are signals of conflict or trauma, which have psychological meanings and can be understood.
- Help candidates identify their conscious reservations about recommending analysis and consider that conscious reservations about analysis (e.g. suitability) also contain their fears.
- Assist candidates in learning how to link their reservations/fears to their patients' difficulties.[14]
- Encourage candidates to use that link to address patients' reservations about engaging more intensively and getting the treatment they need.

Manifestations of candidates' fears

Since candidates' fears are often unconscious, how do we help to identify them? Below, I'll offer thoughts about how these fears manifest themselves in different aspects of case finding.

Fears in relation to referrals

Candidates often wait for referrals for psychoanalysis. It might be helpful to consider with candidates that, given present-day realities, expecting referrals for analysis is unrealistic and a possible sign of fear and uncertainty about working as an analyst.[15] Whatever the source of this uncertainty,[16] helping candidates frame delays in finding cases as reflecting, in part, an internal hesitancy will put them in a better position to search for and identify the emotional obstacles that hinder their generating analytic referrals or helping an existing patient participate in treatment more intensively.

Pessimistic statements about analysis, such as "patients aren't interested in analysis" or "patients can't afford analysis," often reflect candidates' fear of working analytically and seeking referrals. Similarly, delaying finding a couch or a proper office can point to unrecognized fears. Other signs of ambivalence can include not returning referral calls promptly, seeming uninterested or ambivalent when responding to such a call, or trying to negotiate the conditions of treatment such as fees or schedule with the referral source.

Because most patients don't come asking for analysis and very few referrals for treatment are specifically for analysis, how *do* candidates find control cases? I've repeatedly observed that after candidates explore their fears about analysis, especially fears of engaging more deeply, they recognize that they don't need to search for control cases. Instead they realize that they already have them in their practices and have been seeing them once, twice, or even three times a week. Sklar and Parsons (2011), reflecting on a seminar for newly graduated analysts offered at the British Psychoanalytical Society, suggest that internal self-authorization is a crucial aspect of analytic identity and of the analyst's capacity to offer analysis: "We regularly observed that when the seminar helped new analysts recognize how the training has begun to make possible the internalization of this available space, analytic patients emerged after all. The prospective patient who comes for consultation to someone operating on this wavelength may sense that he or she is in contact with a particular kind of awareness and be willing to follow that, even without knowing, at that stage, quite what it is" (p. 147).[17]

Fears in the initial consultation

Several analysts have suggested that initial encounters are disturbing in ways that we don't consciously perceive but that both participants, unconsciously or preconsciously, register and react to (Ogden 1992; Rothstein 1995; Ehrlich 2004, 2010, 2013; Levine 2010). Findings from qualitative research by the Working Party on Initiating Analysis (clinical workshops studying initial interviews) provide further support for this view: (1) regardless of how tranquil it might appear, the initial encounter between the patient's and the analyst's intense fears and wishes precipitates an emotional storm (Reith 2010, 2012; Reith et al. 2012); (2) for analysis to begin, the analyst must bear the initial transference-countertransference and transform it into a beginning appreciation of the patient's suffering and its meaning (Reith 2012; Vermote 2012); (3) which patient is analyzable is determined not by objective criteria but by whom the analyst thinks it possible to work with (Møller 2014; Wegner 2014). Observing that analysts in the workshops often disagreed as to which patient should be offered analysis, Møller (2014) concludes that "it is something in the individual analyst's way of reacting to the patient that determines the outcome, and not some constant called analyzability" (p. 494).

Based on our current understanding of the dynamics of initiating psycho-analysis, several analysts have suggested that it's more fruitful to shift the focus to the *analyst's* degree of readiness (Rothstein 1995, 2006, 2010a, 2010b; Ehrlich 2004, 2013; Levine 2010; Wille 2012). I've come to think that the most helpful question for candidates to ask themselves in a consultation is not why they would offer analysis to a prospective patient but why they wouldn't. If a prospective patient is in a lot of psychic pain, has been unable to make his or her life work, and is asking for the kind of help that only analysis can provide, why should the opportunity for deep change and lasting relief be denied?

The literature and my clinical and supervisory experience suggest that learning how to begin analysis is less about conceptual and technical skills, though these are important, and more about finding a way to support oneself from within (one's good internal objects) and from without (supervision, analysis, readings) in order to generate the courage to withstand the disturb-ing feelings encountered in initiating analysis and to do the psychological work necessary to understand them. The work at the beginning is to survive the storm inherent in most consultations and to remain emotionally engaged.[18] Part of surviving the storm is recognizing and understanding the inclination to pull back from engagement. Frequently, the analyst's emotional pulling back is contained in her reservations about initiating analysis and the rationalizations and the externalizations about why analysis in general or analysis with a particular patient isn't possible or can't deepen or continue (Rothstein 1995, 2003, 2006, 2010a, 2010b; Ehrlich 2004, 2010, 2013; Levine 2010; Wille 2012).

The candidate's inclination to move away from engagement with the patient and her suffering takes many forms:

- Focusing on patient suitability (patient too naive, fragile, or disturbed to be in analysis).
- Focusing on patient availability (patient too busy, too poor, too uninterested).
- Focusing on a unilateral assessment of feasibility—whether analysis is practically possible. Personal and supervisory experience has led me to conclude that the analyst, hard as he or she might try, isn't able to imagine or construct *alone* how the patient and analyst *together* might eventually create the conditions for intensive treatment (distance, fre-quency, fees, etc.).
- Discussing feasibility before establishing an implicit or explicit under-standing with the patient that intensive treatment is vital. I've found that a patient's capacity to arrange to be in treatment changes in relation to how clearly the patient appreciates the extent and depth of his difficulties and senses that the analyst also appreciates them and is willing to with-stand the rigors of helping him.

- Underestimating the extent and degree of the patient's distress (its intensity, depth, duration, transferability, and portability) and therefore the need for intensive help.[19]
- Failing to adequately recognize one's disturbing feelings in relation to the patient and consequently not being able to use them to understand the patient's difficulties.
- Underappreciating the patient's strengths.
- Focusing on the patient's defenses and fears and overlooking or underestimating the patient's wish for and willingness to get help and establish intimacy.
- Joining the patient in externalizing obstacles to intensive treatment.
- Taking a potential patient's reservations about beginning at face value rather than understanding them as evidence of the patient's fears about beginning.

Fears of recommending analysis

In thinking about initiating analysis it's important to remember an obvious but often neglected truth: unless the analyst recommends analysis, there won't be an analysis. Candidates often experience recommending analysis as a response to external pressures: the need to see a patient on the couch at an analytic frequency; to obtain the supervisor's approval about the suitability of the case; for the patient to remain in analysis long enough for the case to "count." These external pressures, though often real, also signal the analyst's hesitancy and her not fully owning her wish to work analytically. Candidates who focus on the internal work necessary to prepare themselves to extend a genuine offer for analysis appear more successful in recommending analysis and in engaging patients than those who focus on training requirements (Rothstein 2010a).

The critical part of the recommendation is the work that takes place in the candidate's mind before he or she utters a word to the patient. When the candidate has a place in her mind for the analysis of the patient, the how, when, and what will be said is intersubjective, that is, created by the often preconscious or unconscious negotiation between patient and analyst; it isn't prepackaged. The analyst builds her recommendation based on how the patient responds to her each step of the way: to the analyst's understanding of the patient, to the suggestion that treatment is needed, to the proposal that intensive treatment is needed, etc.

It's crucial that candidates not take their reservations about recommending at face value; they must learn to consider them meaningful communications from their unconscious, provoked in part by the patient's fears and reservations. Anticipating a patient's reservations and using them as a reason not to recommend analysis is a sign of countertransference. For example, when I find myself calculating what various patients can afford, thinking about babysitting arrangements for them, or considering that they live too far away or will likely not stay in treatment long enough to benefit from it, I take such thoughts as indicating fears generated in me by contact with the patient. I examine these fears, looking for their unique meaning for that patient and me.

Institutional solutions

How can our institutes better help candidates contain and understand their anxieties about initiating analysis so they can use these anxieties in finding control cases and maintaining immersion? Some analytic educators suggest that given the widespread difficulty candidates have in finding cases, we might need to modify the requirements for graduation (Katz, Kaplan, and Stromberg 2012a). I disagree. While requiring less analysis might allow some candidates to graduate who might not otherwise, or allow others to graduate sooner, it will also provide them less opportunity to learn to understand and use their difficulties finding cases and maintaining immersion so that after graduation they might be more open to engaging in analytic work. Instead of requiring less immersion, I suggest we redouble our efforts to incorporate in our teaching and supervising our understanding of the challenges of initiating analysis and of the importance of the transference-countertransference as an avenue into the difficulties experienced by analyst and prospective patient alike.

What can we do differently, and who is best suited to do it? Although I can't address this question in depth here, I'll offer a few brief thoughts. In my experience, everyone who comes in contact with a candidate has an opportunity to help, in whatever way and however little or much: training analysts, supervisors, instructors, advisors, the progression committee, visiting faculty, fellow candidates, etc. Although every graduate analyst can potentially help, those of us who recognize our own ongoing anxieties about engaging intensively with patients, and how these anxieties manifest themselves in our reservations about offering or even practicing analysis, can provide candidates with more substantive help.[20]

To help candidates, institutes must address graduate analysts' discouragement and pessimism about beginning new analyses and maintaining immersion. In my experience, though some analysts are irreparably discouraged, and some are no longer interested in practicing analysis at all, there are many, some of us institute faculty, who want to be doing more analysis but feel stuck. To help candidates, I propose that we engage in faculty development, offering seminars, study groups, and peer supervision groups, in which, using detailed clinical material, we help one another stay in affective contact with the terrors and storms experienced as we begin each new treatment. Only with a faculty that is sensitized and helped with our own anxiety can we help candidates deal with theirs. I've witnessed graduate analysts benefit enormously from forums in which they were reminded that fears about beginning are ubiquitous, explicable, and expectable.[21] They were then able to reduce their own shame and subsequently help candidates better identify and contain their own fears.[22]

What specific courses, programs, and activities can be encouraged or implemented to assist candidates in this regard?

- The opportunity for candidates to be a patient in and to conduct five-times-weekly analysis. The chance to work as intensively as possible as an analysand and as an analyst during training allows candidates to work with their fears enough to be able to internalize the capacity to re-create these optimal analytic conditions when treating patients after graduation. "The point about working five times a week … is not to demonstrate empirically that it produces different results from three times a week. Five times a week represents a unique kind of space available for a patient in the analyst's mind. We regularly observed that when the seminar helped new analysts recognize how the training has begun to make possible the internalization of this available space, analytic patients emerged after all" (Sklar and Parsons 2011, p. 148).
- Mentoring programs designed specifically to help candidates find control cases and to enhance candidates' psychoanalytic immersion. At NYU, Rothstein (2010a) reports that a highly individualized tutorial with a focus on developing cases has been successful at helping candidates find cases: "readying candidates to engage in intensive work" she writes, "is as important as developing analytic patients" (p. 101). At the Michigan Psychoanalytic Institute, when a candidate is admitted, he or she is assigned a mentor who meets with the candidate weekly until the candidate finds a first case, which most candidates begin by the middle of their first year of candidacy.[23] The explicit goal of meeting with the mentor is to discuss patients in order to initiate analysis.
- Courses about beginning analysis with an emphasis on exploring transference-countertransference dynamics in the beginning of treatment, from referral to recommendation. These courses should include (1) a shift in emphasis from identifying a good case to discussing difficulties in initiating a case and what these tell us about the patient's difficulties and the reasons he or she needs intensive help; (2) the framing of a difficulty in finding a case and maintaining immersion as meaningful; (3) the framing of fears about initiating as ordinary and expectable in order to normalize them.
- Ongoing study groups on initiating psychoanalysis. Such groups can provide peer support for recognizing the omnipresence of ambivalence and reducing the shame of countertransferences and disturbing feelings;[24] an opportunity to work through idealizations of the analytic process and of experienced analysts, including the assumption that analysts face difficulties only in the beginning of their careers, or that analysts should work independently, or that disturbing feelings are signs of the analyst's pathology and dysfunction.
- Continuous case seminars in which senior faculty present and discuss their own beginning work, including detailed process material from initial consultations sessions. These seminars would model openness and consultation,

provide invaluable demystification, lessen idealization, bolster analysts' courage to do the work, and support positive identifications.

- Encouraging candidates to attend national discussion groups or workshops such as the Working Party on Initiating Psychoanalysis offered at each IPA Congress or the North American Working Parties' Workshops offered yearly.

Concluding remarks

In response to surveys indicating that candidates have difficulty finding control cases and maintaining immersion and that graduate analysts have similar challenges, I've suggested that psychoanalytic training doesn't prepare candidates well enough to find patients and practice analysis while in training and, for many, after graduation. I've also suggested that though the external challenges can indeed be formidable, it's by identifying and making use of the internal challenges to finding cases that a candidate can develop the analytic mind necessary—the identity, approach, and skills—not only to graduate but to be able to practice clinical psychoanalysis post-graduation.

More specifically, noting that the use of countertransference is central to any helpful analysis, I've proposed that we help candidates recognize the value of identifying and making use of transference-countertransference dynamics as they search for control cases in general and as they consider an individual patient. I've offered examples illustrating my observation that when we help candidates frame their concerns about external obstacles to finding cases, or about offering analysis to patients (Is the patient suitable, the analysis practically feasible? Will the case fulfill graduation requirements?) as possible signs of countertransferential fears and view them as windows into the patient's mind and difficulties, they'll be more likely to find patients and engage them.

I have argued earlier that analysis begins in the analyst's mind. Psychoanalytic education offers candidates the chance to develop an analyst's mind. As surveys show, training holds that possibility, but doesn't guarantee its realization. Doing and being in analysis provides the analyst-in-training the opportunity to come into contact with her own inner conflicts and past developmental disruptions and traumas. The demands of the training situation, especially finding and engaging patients in analysis, provide candidates the chance to understand more deeply their own fantasies and fears of judgment, humiliation, control, exploitation, rejection, seduction, etc. Taking responsibility for their difficult feelings during training and not externalizing them onto graduation requirements or the institute, while simultaneously allowing themselves to be grateful for the strengths and grieve the limitations of their analysts, supervisors, and teachers, is the single most important challenge candidates face. How they respond to that challenge determines in great part how successful they will be in finding and engaging patients in analysis.

We do not become analysts simply by learning a skill set, by applying a series of techniques, or by fulfilling a set of graduation requirements. Instead, candidates must use what's offered in analysis, supervision, seminars, and collegial interactions to access and cultivate capacities to think, listen, and intervene that are dramatically different from their mindset before beginning the analytic journey. By learning in training to appreciate the power of the mind in shaping mood and behavior, candidates find the capacity to function as the kind of helper who can recognize, withstand, and make use of patients' and their own intense, confusing, and disturbing emotions.

I believe that now is the best time ever to become a psychoanalyst. What makes it so? It's a time of uncertainty about the structure of our organizations and widespread questioning about the usefulness and effectiveness of analytic training and practice. While we can see these as causes for pessimism and a sense of futility about the future; from a different perspective, we can view this uncertainty and self-examination as the most fertile soil for developing independent-minded, creative analysts. Today's analysts can't just bask in the glow of the golden age of psychoanalysis, when analysts' ambivalence about practicing analysis was easily quieted by the popularity of psychoanalysis and by the many patients clamoring for it. Today we have to work and rework our own fears and hesitancy about engaging with our own and our patients' internal lives so we can find the courage, hope, and determination to use our minds analytically to perceive our patients' needs and to engage in helping them intensively.

> As you set out for Ithaka
>
> hope the voyage is a long one,
>
> full of adventure, full of discovery.
>
> Laistrygonians and Cyclops,
>
> angry Poseidon—don't be afraid of them:
>
> you'll never find things like that on your way
>
> as long as you keep your thoughts raised high,
>
> as long as a rare excitement
>
> stirs your spirit and your body.
>
> Laistrygonians and Cyclops,
>
> wild Poseidon—you won't encounter them
>
> unless you bring them along inside your soul,
>
> unless your soul sets them up in front of you.

From "Ithaka," by C.P. Cavafy, 1911

Notes

1 Rothstein observes that candidates, when confronted with the prospect of not advancing along with their cohort, somehow managed to find a case.
2 The Columbia University Center for Psychoanalytic Training and Research, the New Center for Psychoanalysis (NCP) in Los Angeles, and the Cincinnati Psychoanalytic Institute (CPI) in Cincinnati.
3 A brief search of the PEP Web database suggests that this number has quadrupled in the years since Target's review appeared.
4 Indirect countertransferences, Jaffe (2001) maintains, "are distinct from direct countertransference reactions, which are based on the patient's inner object world, because they introduce a complication into the analytic process that lies outside the patient-analyst dyad" (p. 841).
5 Identifying it if it's conscious, striving to recognize its signals if it's preconscious or unconscious.
6 Parsons (2006) writes: "The analytic process, whatever the situation with particular patients, will by its nature stir up, to some degree or other, conflict and anxiety in the analyst. The quality of an analyst's engagement with her own countertransference to this process will determine the quality of her engagement with the patient. If the analyst discovers that engaging with the conflicts and anxieties stirred up in her refreshes her own freedom and flexibility, and enlivens the dynamic flow of her psyche, then the analyst's engagement with the patient will be a therapeutic one" (pp. 1195–1196).
7 This means recognizing the powerful, ongoing influence of the unconscious mind on one's emotional life and behavior, privileging the consideration of subjective reality and meaning in understanding symptoms and behavioral manifestations, and appreciating the healing power of reclaiming and experiencing one's dissociated or defended thoughts/feelings in the context of an intimate analytic relationship.
8 Including fear of shame, sadness, remorse, guilt, and, of course, fear of pleasure, excitement, sense of satisfaction, and, last but not least, one's desire to engage in analysis.
9 Dr. C.'s private worry that Ms. Z.'s dream of the out-of-control ambulance reflected her experience of him as out of control for recommending analysis was one manifestation of his identification with his patient's sadomasochistic view of relationships. Dr. C.'s own fears around issues of control did not allow him to recognize the patient's projections.
10 In stalemated control analyses, it's worth considering getting a second opinion from a consultant outside the supervisory triad. Ehrlich et al. (in press), based on the analysis of qualitative data from the Working Party on the End of Training Evaluation, conclude that supervisory countertransference is ubiquitous, at times disruptive, and suggest remedies for supervisory blind spots.
11 Kravis (2013) speaks to this point: "We need more research, but we also need less defensiveness about the ambivalence of doing analytic work. I am arguing for a less shame-driven and defensive engagement with the narcissistic vicissitudes of being an analyst" (p. 20).
12 The fact that candidates have several patients they see daily doesn't mean they've encountered and wrestled with their ambivalence and disturbing feelings in relation to their patients.
13 Selling analysis to patients (Jacobs 2013) is as much a sign of countertransference as not initiating analysis.
14 Boesky (2000) suggests "that an essential component of the communication of the patient's affects in the interaction with the analyst is the inevitable *misunderstanding* by the analyst of the patient's feelings and his necessary later discovery of that misunderstanding, followed by a better understanding" (p. 259).

15 I take it as a given, of course, that behavior is multiply determined.
16 These sources can include wishes to be taken care of by the institute and one's elders; fear of the anticipated intensity of feelings within the therapeutic encounter; fear of one's inadequacy or possible success; and fantasies that others will provide what is needed.
17 Bernstein (2000) and Levine (2010) make similar observations.
18 "The experience of profound connectedness and affective interpenetration enables the patient to feel deeply what a psychoanalysis may have to offer. This experience will unquestionably have a powerful effect on the patient's motivation and trust in psychoanalysis. Trust based on emotional experience has particularly persuasive power" (Wille 2012, p. 890).
19 Grusky (1999) explores how the analyst's conviction regarding the usefulness of analysis affects the patient's willingness to accept a recommendation for analytic treatment.
20 Faculty members who are discouraged by intensive analytic work but remain involved in candidate training can add to candidates' anxieties. One of my many encounters with this unfortunate phenomenon occurred while I was serving as visiting faculty at another institute and spoke to a group of candidates about my practice. A candidate in the group expressed his relief hearing that one can make a good living doing analysis. He shared his experience at his admission interview when the faculty interviewer asked why he would apply for a long and expensive training when one can no longer practice analysis.
21 On several occasions, analysts reported that as they listened to others present stormy beginning clinical material and resonated with analysts' reported fears and their use to understand the patient, they felt capable of recognizing the need for intensive treatment in their own patients and imagined themselves capable of facilitating more intensive work.
22 From anecdotal reports, I've reached the conclusion that most graduate analysts who are immersed in analysis seek regular consultation and often reanalysis. I believe it crucial for the future of our profession to modify our hidebound professional notions and come to consider consultation and reanalysis not as shameful signs of an incomplete analysis or of inadequacy, but rather as essential aspects of continuing education.
23 The candidate may opt to continue with the mentor as supervisor of his or her first control case but is free to choose another supervisor.
24 This can mitigate the "shame about shame" (Buechler 2008) that candidates feel about discussing difficult feelings regarding their patients.

References

Baranger, M. & Baranger, W. (2008). The analytic situation as a dynamic field. *International Journal of Psychoanalysis*, 89: 795–826.
Berman, E. (2004). *Impossible training: A relational view of psychoanalytic education.* Hillsdale, NJ: Analytic Press.
Bernstein, S.B. (2000). Developing a psychoanalytic practice. *Psychoanalytic Inquiry*, 20: 574–593.
Bion, W.R. (1962). *Learning from experience.* New York: Basic Books.
Boesky, D. (1990). The psychoanalytic process and its components. *Psychoanalytic Quarterly*, 59: 550–584.
Boesky, D. (2000). Affect, language and communication. *International Journal of Psychoanalysis*, 81: 257–262.

Bollas, C. (1979). The transformational object. *International Journal of Psychoanalysis,* 60: 97–107.

Brodbeck, H. (2008). Anxiety in psychoanalytic training from the candidate's point-of-view. *Psychoanalytic Inquiry,* 28: 329–343.

Bruzzone, M., Casaula, E., Jimenez, J.P. & Jordan, J.F. (1985). Regression and persecution in analytic training: Reflections on experience. *International Review of Psychoanalysis,* 12: 411–415.

Buechler, S. (2008). Shaming psychoanalytic candidates. *Psychoanalytic Inquiry,* 28: 361–372.

Cabaniss, D.L. (2008). Becoming a school: Developing learning objectives for psychoanalytic education. *Psychoanalytic Inquiry,* 28: 262–277.

Cabaniss, D.L. & Roose, S.P. (1997). The control case: A unique analytic situation. *Journal of the American Psychoanalytic Association,* 45: 189–199.

Cabaniss, D.L., Schein, J.W., Rosen, P. & Roose, S.P. (2003). Candidate progression in analytic institutes. *International Journal of Psychoanalysis,* 84: 77–94.

Casement, P. (2005). The Emperor's clothes. *International Journal of Psychoanalysis,* 86: 1143–1160.

Cavafy, C.P. (1911). Ithaka. In *Collected Poems,* ed. Savidis, G., transl. Keeley, E. Rev. ed. Princeton: Princeton University Press, 1992, pp. 36–37.

Cherry, S., Cabaniss, D.L., Forand, N., Haywood D. & Roose, S.P. (2004). Psychoanalytic practice in the early postgraduate years. *Journal of the American Psychoanalytic Association,* 52: 851–871.

Ehrlich, J. (2003). Being a candidate: Its impact on analytic process. *Journal of the American Psychoanalytic Association,* 51: 177–200.

Ehrlich, L.T. (2004). The analyst's reluctance to begin a new analysis. *Journal of the American Psychoanalytic Association,* 52: 1075–1093.

Ehrlich, L.T. (2010). The analyst's ambivalence about continuing and deepening an analysis. *Journal of the American Psychoanalytic Association,* 58: 515–532.

Ehrlich, L.T. (2013). Analysis begins in the analyst's mind: Conceptual and technical considerations on recommending analysis. *Journal of the American Psychoanalytic Association,* 61: 1077–1107.

Ehrlich, L.T., Kulish, N.M., Hanly, M.A.F., Robinson, M. & Rothstein, A. (2017). Supervisory countertransferences and impingements in evaluating readiness for graduation: Always present, routinely under-recognized. *International Journal of Psychoanalysis,* 98: 491–516.

Gabbard, G.O. (1995). Countertransference: The emerging common ground. *International Journal of Psychoanalysis,* 76: 475–485.

Grusky, Z. (1999). Conviction and conversion. *Psychoanalytic Quarterly,* 68: 401–430.

Heimann, P. (1950). On countertransference. *International Journal of Psychoanalysis,* 31: 81–84.

Israelstam, K. (2011). The interactive category schema of candidate competence: An Australian experience. *International Journal of Psychoanalysis,* 92: 1289–1313.

Jacobs, T.J. (1973). Posture, gesture, and movement in the analyst: Cues to interpretation and countertransference. *Journal of the American Psychoanalytic Association,* 21: 77–92.

Jacobs, T.J. (1991). *The use of the self: Countertransference and communication in the analytic situation.* Madison, CT: International Universities Press.

Jacobs, T.J. (2013). Discussion of "The analyst's hatred of analysis." *Psychoanalytic Quarterly,* 82: 115–119.

Jaffe, L. (2001). Countertransference, supervised analysis, and psychoanalytic training requirements. *Journal of the American Psychoanalytic Association*, 49: 831–853.

Junkers, G., Tuckett, D. & Zachrisson, A. (2008). To be or not to be a psychoanalyst: How do we know a candidate is ready to qualify? Difficulties and controversies in evaluating psychoanalytic competence. *Psychoanalytic Inquiry*, 28: 288–308.

Kaplan, M., Pretsky, J., Wininger, L., Roose, S.P. & Cherry, S. (2009). Poster summary: A profile of analytic practice across the country: Immersion data for three institutes. *Journal of the American Psychoanalytic Association*, 57: 1169–1173.

Katz, D.A., Kaplan, M. & Stromberg, S.E. (2012a). A national survey of candidates: I. Demographics, practice patterns, and satisfaction with training. *Journal of the American Psychoanalytic Association*, 60: 71–96.

Katz, D.A., Kaplan, M. & Stromberg, S.E. (2012b). A national survey of candidates: II. Motivation, obstacles, and ideas on increasing interest in psychoanalytic training. *Journal of the American Psychoanalytic Association*, 60: 1015–1055.

Kernberg, O.F. (1986). Institutional problems of psychoanalytic education. *Journal of the American Psychoanalytic Association*, 34: 799–834.

Kernberg, O.F. (2000). A concerned critique of psychoanalytic education. *International Journal of Psychoanalysis*, 81: 97–120.

Kernberg, O.F. (2007). The coming changes in psychoanalytic education: Part II. *International Journal of Psychoanalysis*, 88: 183–202.

Kernberg, O.F. (2010). A new organization of psychoanalytic education. *Psychoanalytic Review*, 97: 997–1020.

Kernberg, O.F. (2014). The twilight of the training analysis system. *Psychoanalytic Review*, 101: 151.

Kirsner, D. (2001). The future of psychoanalytic institutes. *Psychoanalytic Psychology*, 8: 195–212.

Kirsner, D. (2010). Training analysis: The shibboleth of psychoanalytic education. *Psychoanalytic Review*, 97: 971–995.

Körner, J. (2002). The didactics of psychoanalytic education. *International Journal of Psychoanalysis*, 83: 1395–1405.

Kravis, N. (2013). The analyst's hatred of analysis. *Psychoanalytic Quarterly*, 82: 89–114.

Levine, H.B. (2010). Creating analysts, creating analytic patients. *International Journal of Psychoanalysis*, 91: 1385–1404.

Møller, M. (2014). The analyst's anxieties in the first interview: Barriers against analytic presence. *International Journal of Psychoanalysis*, 95: 485–503.

Ogden, T.H. (1992). Comments on transference and countertransference in the initial analytic meeting. *Psychoanalytic Inquiry*, 12: 225–247.

Ogden, T.H. (1994). The analytic third: Working with intersubjective clinical facts. *International Journal of Psychoanalysis*, 75: 3–19.

Parsons, M. (2006). The analyst's countertransference to the psychoanalytic process. *International Journal of Psychoanalysis*, 87: 1183–1198.

Racker, H. (1957). The meanings and uses of countertransference. *Psychoanalytic Quarterly*, 26: 303–357.

Raubolt, R. (2006). *Power games: Influence, persuasion, and indoctrination in psychotherapy training*. New York: Other Press.

Reith, B. (2010). The specific dynamics of initial interviews: Switching the level, or opening up a meaning space? *Bulletin of the European Federation of Psychoanalysis*, 64(Suppl.): 57–80.

Reith, B. (2012). What interpsychic conditions lead to full analysis? Some findings from the Working Party on Initiating Psychoanalysis 2: Part I: The analyst's internal frame. *Bulletin of the European Psychoanalytic Federation*, 66: 94–102.

Reith, B., Lagerlöf, S., Crick, P., Möller, M. & Skale, E. (2012). *Initiating psychoanalysis: Perspectives*. London: Routledge.

Rothstein, A. (1995). *Psychoanalytic technique and the creation of analytic patients*. Madison, CT: International Universities Press.

Rothstein, A. (2003). Changing psychoanalytic psychotherapy into psychoanalysis: A trusting model for helping patients begin a trial of analysis. *Journal of Clinical Psychoanalysis*, 12: 109–115.

Rothstein, A. (2006). Reflections on the concept "analyzability." *Psychoanalytic Review*, 93: 827–833.

Rothstein, A. (2010a). Developing psychoanalytic cases and the candidates who will analyze them: An educational initiative. *Journal of the American Psychoanalytic Association*, 58: 101–136.

Rothstein, A. (2010b). Psychoanalytic technique and the creation of analytic patients: An addendum. *Psychoanalytic Quarterly*, 79: 785–794.

Rothstein, A. (2017). Fostering the educational value of candidate evaluation. *International Journal of Psychoanalysis*, 98: 1641–1668.

Sandler, J. (1976). Countertransference and role-responsiveness. *International Journal of Psychoanalysis*, 3:43–47.

Schneider, J., Wilkerson, D., Solomon, B., Perlman, C., Tsioles, D.D., Shelby, D., et al. (2014). Psychoanalytic training experience and postgraduate professional development: A survey of six decades of graduate analysts. *International Journal of Psychoanalysis*, 95: 1211–1233.

Sklar, J. & Parsons, M. (2011). The life cycle of the psychoanalyst: Reflections on a seminar for newly qualified analysts. In *Landscapes of the dark: History, trauma, psychoanalysis*, ed. Sklar, J. London: Karnac Books.

Smith, H.F. (2000). Countertransference, conflictual listening, and the analytic object relationship. *Journal of the American Psychoanalytic Association*, 48: 95–128.

Target, M. (2001). *Some issues in psychoanalytic training: An overview of the literature and some resulting observations*. Paper presented at the 2nd Joseph Sandler Research Conference, University College London, March.

Tuckett, D. (2005). Does anything go? Towards a framework for a more transparent assessment of psychoanalytic competence. *International Journal of Psychoanalysis*, 86: 31–49.

Vermote, R. (2012). Preliminary sessions: The resistance of the patient is the resistance of the analyst. *Bulletin of the European Psychoanalytic Federation*, 66: 103–106.

Ward, A., Gibson, W. & Miqueu-Baz, C. (2010). Between paranoia and creativity: Candidates' experience of psychoanalytic training. *Journal of the American Psychoanalytic Association*, 58: 891–925.

Wegner, P. (2014). Process-orientated psychoanalytic work in initial interviews and the importance of the opening scene. *International Journal of Psychoanalysis*, 95: 505–523.

Wille, R. (2012). The analyst's trust in psychoanalysis and the communication of that trust in initial interviews. *Psychoanalytic Quarterly*, 81: 875–904.

Winnicott, D.W. (1949). Hate in the counter-transference. *International Journal of Psychoanalysis*, 30: 69–74.

Part Two

Developing the Capacity to Deepen an Analysis

Chapter 4

Continuing and deepening an analysis

As analysts we recognize that even our most cherished values and ideals are infused with ambivalence. Notably, however, we tend to overlook or under-estimate our ambivalence about practicing as analysts and its effects on our daily practice. In an earlier chapter, I examined the analyst's reluctance to begin a new analysis. There I focused on the analyst's ambivalence about making a recommendation for analysis and then addressing energetically the patient's resistances to the recommendation.

As I have practiced more analysis and listened to more analytic accounts from supervisees and colleagues, I've come to believe that the analyst's ambivalence is, to varying degrees, pervasive and ongoing, not only at the beginning of an analysis but *throughout* each analysis. I've seen the analyst's ambivalence take many forms. It can take the form of general reservations about why it's not possible to do analysis in the current socioeconomic climate or, more specifically, why it's not possible to analyze a specific patient. I've observed that, within a given treatment, an analyst's reservations about beginning or continuing analysis tend to complement the patient's fears and rationalizations and are frequently woven into ongoing enactments. In the current economic crisis,[1] when patients are facing real and/or imagined financial adversities that lead them to rationalize or justify their fears about beginning or continuing analysis, I believe that identifying our own fears about analyzing is crucial to our being able to practice analysis.

In this chapter, I'm going to focus on the analyst's reluctance to continue an analysis—that is, to preserve and deepen the intensity of the analytic engage-ment.[2] More specifically, I'll examine the analyst's reluctance to maintain an analytic frame of mind as it relates to frequency and fees. I'll illustrate these manifestations of the analyst's ambivalence with a detailed case example.

Many analysts have written about the psychology of the analyst at work, including the conflicts that invariably inform analytic functioning. I'll mention only a few. Abend (1986) suggests in a groundbreaking paper that analysts' capacity to analyze is a compromise formation that undergoes fluctuations each day and with each patient. He recommends that analysts not overlook these everyday fluctuations in their inner lives and attend to their own resistances.

Schafer (1979) also speaks to the changeability of the analyst. He suggests that, because of tensions inherent in analytic work, an analyst is never a finished product. According to Schafer, becoming an analyst entails an unending effort that includes tolerating confusing uncertainties about our understanding of our patients and our role in effecting therapeutic change.

Others discuss the challenges of maintaining a psychoanalytic identity. Blum (1981) suggests that in the face of internal or external pressures, even experienced analysts with strong analytic identities and ideals waiver in their conviction about psychoanalysis and in their commitment to its ideals. More recently, Wille (2008) conceptualizes analytic identity as an internalized object. Its core elements include a focus on understanding inner reality and trust in the relationship between patient and analyst and in the analytic setting as sources of meaning. He suggests that in varying degrees all analysts struggle to maintain their analytic identity.

From my own clinical and supervisory experience and from listening to the clinical presentations of colleagues, I've come to appreciate that there are many sources of the analyst's reluctance to analyze. I'll highlight a few here that I've found to be most consequential:

- The paradox that unless we believe we can be helpful, we can't engage optimistically in an analytic process. Yet, we can't know if we'll be helpful until an analysis ends—and sometimes not even then.
- Our reluctance to tolerate our confusion and shame at not understanding a patient at any given moment. More broadly, our reluctance to bear our shame about the limitations of our skills and our method.
- Our reluctance to bear feelings of loss, sadness, and grief—separateness, premature or timely termination.
- Our reluctance to bear aggression and sexuality—our own and our patients'.
- Our reluctance to tolerate our ongoing conflict and ambivalence about our own analysis. Did it help? What was useful? What was not useful? Yet assessing the usefulness and the limitations of a training analysis is subject to ongoing transferential distortions and post-termination mourning processes (Ehrlich 2004).
- Our reluctance to accept our anxiety about using, exploiting, or abusing that is an inevitable part of working with the traumatized or masochistic patient. This anxiety is exacerbated by patients' accusations that we are hurting them or not helping.
- Our reluctance to recognize the driving power of the transference in shaping our patients' thoughts and actions. Our fear of recognizing the central role we play in our patients' inner lives. At the same time, our reluctance to recognize the limitations of our influence and how, despite our best efforts, our patients are ultimately responsible for how they lead their lives.

I would like to share with you a few words about frequency and frame. In part because of different theoretical orientations, analysts hold divergent points of view as to what constitutes a good-enough analytic frequency. I take it as a given that analytic engagement and emphasis on the interpretation of resistance and of enactments are more fundamental to the development of a lively and meaningful analytic process than frequency or use of the couch. However, based on experience, I've concluded that higher frequency allows for a richer analytic engagement by affording a greater opportunity to recognize resistances and counter-resistances and to understand transference-countertransference manifestations. In most cases, I've observed that five sessions are more facilitating of a deeper process than four, and four more facilitating than three.

Other analysts report a similar experience. Gedo and Cohler (1992) found that for the "average expectable dyad" the increase in frequency led to an increase in the quality of the clinical material and an improvement of each participant's capacity to use it. In a panel discussion (Richards 1997), Milton Horowitz reported that in comparing his own experience with frequencies ranging from three to six times a week, he concluded that greater frequency facilitates greater intensity and more change, particularly in areas involving sadism and aggression. He remarked further that with greater frequency the analytic dyad is more likely to relive the past in the form of enactment, rather than just talk about it, and will have a greater opportunity to verbally express affect and arrive at insight. In keeping with the argument I'm offering here, Horowitz also observed that in every case presented, when patients cited cost and limited time as reasons for lower frequency, the patients' fears of intimacy and object loss were the most influential unconscious motivations.

In our era of theoretical and technical diversity, one can find varied and contradictory discussions about the psychoanalytic frame and its functions. I have found discussions by Bass (2007), Boesky (2009), Langs and Stone (1980), Mitchell (1993), and Parsons (2007) particularly illuminating. I define the analytic frame as the necessary and optimal conditions that further the development of an analytic engagement and the discovery and/or creation of psychological meaning. I see the frame as both external and internal. The external aspect includes the analytic space, the analyst's approach to setting and keeping appointment times, fees and interruptions, cancellation policies, etc. I view the analyst's internal frame in ways similar to Parsons (2007), who suggests that "the analytic setting exists ... internally as a structure in the mind of the analyst"; it is "a psychic arena in which reality is defined by such concepts as symbolism, fantasy, transference and unconscious meaning" (p. 1441). In my experience, this internal analytic setting within the analyst's mind is shaped by the analyst's conviction about the usefulness of analytic work, her privileging psychic reality, her commitment to understanding her own thoughts and feelings, and her commitment to her patient's best interest.

Now I'll present a case to illustrate the analyst's reluctance to continue an analysis by taking at face value the patient's intention to modify the analytic frame and reduce the frequency of her sessions.

Clinical example: Ms. A.

Ms. A., a lawyer in her mid-forties who worked in a federal agency, contacted me for a psychotherapy consultation. Statuesque and elegant, she conveyed strength and determination. Married and the mother of a two-year-old son, she reported feeling deeply ambivalent about having children. Although she had wanted to be a mother, at the same time she felt doubtful about her capacity to provide emotionally for her child. Also, while her marriage was better than many previous relationships, she struggled with negative feelings toward her husband and reported that at times they fought bitterly. Additionally, Ms. A. complained about her professional life. She spoke of being dissatisfied with working in an agency where she was poorly compensated. Yet, insecure about her abilities, she felt incapable of launching her own practice.

Ms. A. was an only child whose parents divorced when she was four. Shortly after the divorce, her father, who had been involved actively in her care for the first four years, moved overseas, at which point his contact with her became sporadic and felt dutiful. Ms. A.'s mother, a nurse, suffered from chronic, at times debilitating, anxiety and worked long hours away from home. Ms. A. was cared for by a relative who physically and sexually abused her. Ms. A. recalled several additional incidents of abuse by relatives and strangers during her childhood and early adolescence. As an adult and while in law school, she became involved with a married law professor who was her mentor. After recognizing the exploitation in the relationship, she filed a complaint against him for ethical violations.

At the end of the consultation, I shared with Ms. A. my opinion that understanding her worries about being a mother, her dissatisfaction with her husband, and her insecurities about work would be crucial to her achieving her life goals of having fulfilling relationships and a satisfying career. I also shared with her that I believed we could work well together. I suggested that intensive treatment was the treatment of choice for her because it would provide the time and the continuity necessary to help us understand what gets in the way of her aspirations. I recommended that she consider as many sessions a week as possible. Ms. A. responded to my recommendation by stating emphatically that she did not want analysis. She proposed that we start with a twice-a-week schedule. I agreed.

Privately, I thought Ms. A.'s emphatic denial of her interest in analysis was a positive sign that although scared, she was considering being in analysis. Consciously, I felt willing to begin an analysis with her and thought the only obstacle was *her* resistance. At the time, I guessed that given her level of inhibition and her fears about relationships it might take her a long time to arrange an analytic frequency. I later realized that my prediction was based as much on my own unconscious hesitation to become more engaged with her as on my assessment of her anxiety. When I look back, I recall an unpleasant sense of unease while listening to Ms. A.'s history of abusive relationships and hearing that she had been involved in a sexual relationship with a mentor against whom she later filed a complaint. With the benefit of hindsight, I recognize that though consciously I felt ready to begin to meet with Ms. A. at an analytic frequency, unconsciously I felt hesitant. Although I recommended analysis, I believe that I conveyed hesitancy and caution in my recommendation. This, in turn, might have added to her fears of beginning. This was, of course, a meaningful enactment whose significance did not become obvious until later.

As we began to meet, Ms. A. questioned her need for treatment altogether.

She now thought she might have exaggerated her dissatisfaction with her marriage and her work. Perhaps, she mused, she was indulging herself with the luxury of two sessions a week. I suggested that perhaps her concerns about starting led her to want to forget the frustrations and regrets that brought her to treatment in the first place. In response, Ms. A. disclosed that she had been struggling with whether I was qualified enough to treat her. Could she trust me to be strong enough to "handle" her? She knew herself to feel very competitive with women. What if I couldn't tolerate her aggressive and demeaning competitiveness toward me?

While working on a case with an expert witness, a male colleague and collaborator of mine, she was frightened and gratified by what she thought was his special attention and regard for her. Maybe she should have seen him instead. Maybe he was more interested in her than I was. I suggested to Ms. A. that she was helping us appreciate that she had many fears about beginning relationships, fears that led her to want to call them off. I suggested that more time together would allow us to consider her fears in greater detail. Ms. A. responded with both relief and alarm. She appeared relieved that I appreciated she was frightened. At the same time, she was suspicious of my motives. Was I trying to manipulate her into an arrangement that would serve my needs alone? How could she trust me that I didn't just need to fill another billable hour? Privately, I reconsidered my motives: did I think Ms. A. would benefit from additional time or was my offer to see her mostly self-serving? Becoming aware of my unpleasant concern that I might be using her, I was able to stay the course with interpreting her fears of beginning treatment with me. Six months into the therapy, she accepted my offer to add a third session.

Adding a session indeed gave us time to consider in greater detail her fears about beginning treatment. Ms. A. wondered if analysis was the right treatment for her. Was she going to rely on me and lose her capacity to think independently? Would I then take advantage of her and even abuse her? She recalled spending her entire ninth year feeling frightened of being poisoned by her mother and refusing to eat her mother's food. She also remembered not being able to sleep at night thinking that someone was going to break through the window and kill her. She alternated between talking about her anxiety about her safety and her fear of her destructiveness. She related an episode at home in which she'd become furious at the clutter and threw out a set of her husband's prized collection of magazines. The day after I announced an upcoming interruption, she found herself furious with the babysitter for not helping enough around the house. In her rage, she kicked a wall, hurting her foot and damaging the plaster.

While listening to her fear and fury, I found myself wondering whether she could work analytically. Was she more troubled than I'd appreciated? Did she have the necessary ego strength for analytic work? Evoking diagnostic concerns alerted me to the possibility that I was more reluctant than I had consciously known. I observed that I'd pulled away affectively and, through that observation, became aware of my fear of her hurting me.

Ms. A. began to realize that she felt ashamed to notice that she had reactions when we didn't meet. Yet, at the same time, she felt relief to know that there was meaning to her otherwise inexplicable feelings of loss, hurt, and anger associated with weekends and vacations. She made several "mistakes" coming for a session on a day when she didn't have an appointment. Initially, she didn't think of these lapses as meaningful. In time, however, she realized that indeed she had been thinking about what it would be like to add another session. She found that the time between sessions felt too long and that sometimes she started to talk about something important that felt stale by the time she came back two or three days later. She became aware that she wanted and needed more time to be able to understand her thoughts and feelings more thoroughly. Yet, she claimed that it was financially impossible to increase the number of her sessions.

Privately, I found myself thinking about the reasons she couldn't add another session: her relatively low-paying government job and the fact that she cared for her young son. But I gradually realized that I was making excuses for her in my own mind. Realizing that *I* felt reluctant, I was freed up to inquire about *her* fears. I asked her if in addition to money she might have other reasons for not wanting to come more often. Ms. A. described her trepidation that analysis would induce more of her neediness. What if, after adding a fourth session, she wanted a fifth or a sixth or a seventh? What if she learned to depend on me and then was unable to function on her own? Or what if she ran out of money and was not able to continue? I suggested that once again she was limiting herself from seeking what she needed out of fear. I offered that her long-standing strategy of dealing with her fears by holding herself back had added to her present sense of unhappiness and deprivation.

As we identified and put those concerns into words, Ms. A. began to appreciate the cost of running from her fears. She recognized that she had deprived herself of having a child earlier, of forming an intimate and sexually satisfying relationship, of setting up her own practice, and of having the treatment she optimally needed. She then began to talk about her desire to explore her concerns more deeply.

In her aspiration to be a good mother to her child, Ms. A. recognized an additional incentive to want to sort out her feelings. Slowly she put things in place to be able to attend more often. She reported being better able to function as a lawyer. She started her own practice, which allowed her to work less, make more money, work closer to home, and therefore have more time for her child. With some reservations about whether this might be "too much" for her, she requested a fourth session to be added the following winter.

Once we went to four sessions weekly, Ms. A.'s worries intensified. While earlier she'd been uneasy about being needy, she now feared she would become voracious. Instead of her earlier worry about being hurtful, now she felt scared that she would destroy me the way she felt she had destroyed an earlier therapist, who was diagnosed with cancer while she was in treatment with her. Ms. A. also expressed a long-standing fear that if she allowed herself her feelings she would lose control and become as disorganized and frantic as she had experienced her mother to be.

A few months after adding a fourth session, Ms. A. spoke of financial difficulties. She reported that her husband, whose business was related to the automotive industry, had lost an important contract and that their income had dropped significantly. She thought that the monthly amount of lost income was significant enough to require that they change their priorities.

For several sessions, Ms. A. spoke about her financial concerns and her fears that she wouldn't be able to afford to continue her analysis at its current frequency. She anticipated that she'd have to either reduce the number of sessions or to interrupt the analysis altogether. Ms. A. reasoned that because of the economic climate, her husband wouldn't be able to drum up more business and that because of her child-care responsibilities she wasn't in a position, even if she had the referrals (which she didn't), to increase her billable hours. I listened to her speaking tearfully about the financial crisis and how hard it had hit the country—especially Michigan, which was in the eye of the auto industry's financial storm. I found myself resonating with her concerns by thinking about my retirement account and the menacing economic predictions in the news.

Ms. A. also fearfully anticipated that her husband's conflicts would interfere with his ability to find more business. This, too, sounded plausible to me given her description of her husband as someone who suffered from inhibitions. Next Ms. A. considered, and promptly dismissed, the possibility of increasing her own income. She'd determined that in order to take proper care of her child, she had to limit her work schedule to 25 hours weekly. She concluded that being a mother with a toddler precluded her making a better living. Having myself faced the pleasures and challenges of being a mother while pursuing a career, I could more than empathize with her reasoning. It seemed to me at that moment that Ms. A. didn't have many alternatives to reducing the frequency of her analytic sessions.

Privately, I considered lowering my fee. Yet, from what I knew about her and our work together by that time, I didn't think it would serve her well to be beholden to me or for me to feel underpaid by her. I thought it might make sense for us to go back to meeting three times a week because that would make life easier for her. But would it? I thought about her traumatic history, my experience of her anxiety and distress, her wish for her marriage to last, her conflicts about her work, and her earnest hope not to repeat with her child the losses and traumas of her own childhood, and reconfirmed in my own mind that the quality of the rest of her life depended on her ability to come to terms with herself. She and I had worked well on a three-times-a-week basis. However, adding a fourth session had increased her anxiety and defensiveness and was a signal that we were closer to some important conflicts and traumas. Was it possible that she and I were backing away from that recognition?

I slowly came to the realization that inadvertently I'd been planning privately to see her less frequently and that I'd agreed with her in my own mind that her reasons for wanting to reduce the frequency of her sessions were based solely on external reality. I also realized that although her external circumstances were compelling, my unexamined focus on them was uncharacteristic and worth noting. I reminded myself of several of my patients who, having come to understand some of their fears about beginning, had creatively arranged to finance their analysis. Why did I think of Ms. A. as less competent than these other patients? What in her specific situation might have led me to underestimate her abilities? When I thought of joining her in actualizing her fantasy of decreasing her sessions, I wondered about my motivations. Did *I* want to see her less frequently? What might *I* be trying to avoid? I recognized a variety of unpleasant feelings, including a sense of myself as greedy and exploitative. I noted the unpleasantness of such feelings and realized that they must have meaning within our relationship. Although the meaning wasn't obvious to me at the time, I began to recognize my reluctance to proceed.

Yet, there was still the issue of the fee. I entertained the idea that my unwillingness to lower it might be part of *my* reluctance to continue to work with her intensively. I therefore decided to revisit the issue if, after exploring her resistance, it became clear that lowering the fee was the only way she could continue at the present frequency. At this point, I became aware that I didn't know in detail the facts of Ms. A.'s finances and realized that we'd been avoiding looking at the reality of her situation. I called this to her attention. When she looked at her income and expenses, she concluded that her situation was not as dismal as she'd thought. Despite that conclusion, she continued to passively predict that her analysis was in danger. I observed that although she claimed she wanted to continue in analysis, she did nothing to solve the problem and make that happen. I interpreted that perhaps for some reason she was hesitant to continue.

In the weeks that followed we discovered many different sources for her unwillingness. We discovered that Ms. A. had the expectation that the end of her analysis and losing me were as inevitable as her parents' divorce and the loss of her father. Turning passive into active, she wanted to leave me before she was left. We understood also that now that we met more frequently, she was concerned that she couldn't interest me and therefore couldn't keep me, just as she'd felt she couldn't sustain her father's interest beyond her fourth year.

Another aspect of her motivation to run out of money was her feeling that she was entitled to be seen for free in compensation for the child support her father hadn't sent and for his love that she couldn't have as a child. In addition, by exploring Ms. A.'s unconscious motivation to end we discovered the extent to which she experienced our analytic arrangement as being all on my terms: the fee, the place, the time, the frequency. By understanding her deep resentment at what she experienced as the one-sided nature of our relationship, we came to appreciate how hurt she had felt by the post-divorce contact with her father. Experiencing me as demanding—just like her father—that she make all the effort, she rebelled by not doing what was necessary to safeguard her treatment.

Gradually, Ms. A. devised creative ways to market her law practice, increased her own low fees, and billed more hours. In addition, she helped her husband think through possible business opportunities that he then pursued successfully. The issue of the fee receded to the background, and she no longer spoke about ending her analysis precipitously.

Once Ms. A. settled back into the analysis, she slowly revealed a set of concerns that were even more disturbing to her. Beginning with a dream in which a bouncy chair doubled as a vibrator, Ms. A. introduced her fear of overstimulating or hurting her son and provided more details of her own abuse, now reporting instances perpetrated by boyfriends and her mother's lovers. In addition, she recalled with difficulty and shame feeling over-stimulated and confused by her mother's nudity, by the sexual noises coming out of her mother's bedroom, and by sleeping with her mother, who she suspected soothed herself to sleep by masturbating while lying next to her.

Her sharing with me her vision of a giant pubic mound that she was forced to touch at the end of one of our sessions during this time led us to understand her experience of my questions and interpretations as overstimulating; it also led to her worry that she was overstimulating *me*. We began to appreciate her conviction that relationships are exploitative—the only ambiguity being about who is exploiting whom at any given moment. We also identified a fundamental feeling of danger in relationships that rested on her repetitive experiences of abuse by a person who was supposed to be protecting her. Ms. A. recognized that because of her need for attention and affection she'd allowed herself to be used by her mother and also by her mentor. For my part, I recognized that my concern about using her and taking advantage of her was a necessary experience with this multiply traumatized patient, an experience I needed to bear and continue to analyze.

Discussion

Using Freud's sculpturing metaphor, Loewald (1960), in his renowned paper on therapeutic action, suggested that during an analysis the analyst is actively creating and holding in his mind an image of who the patient could be without the neurotic distortions: "In analysis, we bring out the true form by taking away the neurotic distortions. However, as in sculpture, we must have, if only in rudiments, an image of that which needs to be brought into its own. The patient, by revealing himself to the analyst, provides rudiments of such an image through all the distortions—an image which the analyst has to focus in his mind, thus holding it in safe keeping for the patient to whom it is mainly lost" (p. 17). Thus, Loewald recognizes the analyst's active role in creating and maintaining the analytic process within his own mind.

Obviously, for an analysis to begin and proceed, patient and analyst must cooperate in creating the conditions to make that possible. Rothstein (2000, 2006) has helped us appreciate a crucial dimension of that process: unless the patient is first created in the analyst's mind during the consultation, there will be no analysis. Had I not allowed myself to create an image of Ms. A. as an analytic patient, I would not have invited her to attend as frequently as possible. Had I not envisioned that at some point she and I would be capable of engaging in a deep analytic process in order to understand her difficulties, I would not have been motivated to think of her objections to analysis as meaningful and related to her fears of beginning a relationship with me.

I believe it is the analyst's task to re-create and safeguard a view of the patient as someone capable of making good use of the analyst and the analytic process, not only in the beginning but time and again throughout the treatment. I also believe that it is the analyst's task to maintain an inner analytic perspective and to sustain the analytic frame.

I've heard the argument that maintaining the frame is a vestige of an old-fashioned analytic rigidity. I agree that it can be, but it doesn't have to be. I've come to think of it as a crucial aspect of the analytic situation and the development of an enlivened analytic process (Ogden 2002). No matter how compelling the external obstacles, I find it useful to consider any request for modification of the external frame, the customary way that an individual patient and I work, as evidence, at least in part, of the patient's anxiety and conflicts.

I agree with those who observe that the external frame and its meaning are mutually negotiated between patient and analyst and are dynamic within each analysis (Bass 2007; Boesky 2009; Gabbard 2007). The analyst's internal frame is also dynamic, representing at any given point a compromise between different tendencies and internal and external pressures. I suggest that it must be nurtured and preserved by the analyst's self-analysis, including the analysis of any signals of the analyst's ambivalence about privileging inner reality. I suggest that the analyst's inclination to initiate changes to the external frame should at least be considered a signal of the analyst's fears and a possible enactment of conflict or trauma.

Correspondingly, I also find it useful to consider my inclination to accommodate patients' requests for a change in the frame as a possible manifestation of my own fears of facing something difficult within myself. Böhm (2004) talks about changes in the frame (outer changes in the setting or inner changes by prematurely foreclosing certain issues) as "countertransference signals of an unresolved life theme in the analyst" (p. 9). Boesky (2009) discussed the function of the frame at a panel of the American Psychoanalytic Association (Levine 2009). With his customary incisiveness, he suggests that the value of the frame rests on a central paradox that "without having it to maintain we could not eventually *fail* to maintain it. Then we would lose the chance to make our most important discoveries" (p. 11).

After adding a fourth session, Ms. A. faced an intensification of her worries. Her financial difficulties at that time, though real, also served the very real defensive function of giving her a possible escape from the increasing intensity of her feelings and of her worries of what was to come. Her suggesting that we cut back or interrupt the analysis and my taking her suggestion at face value were together a cocreated manifestation of our fear of proceeding. After framing it that way, first recognizing her fears and then my reluctance to see Ms. A. and then hers to see herself, I was able to ask her about her fears about continuing, and our understanding of her deepened.

Because many factors affect how deeply a patient engages in treatment, examining my own willingness to engage hasn't, of course, made analysis possible for all my patients. Yet, even with patients who don't attend more than one or two times a week, I've found that examining my fears to see them more frequently frees me up to engage with them with more immediacy and energy. Further, I've observed that when I extend an open invitation to them to increase sessions, many become more anxious and at the same time more engaged affectively and more hopeful. The treatment deepens whether they accept the invitation or not.

Time and again I've marveled at how creative and resourceful many of my patients or other analysts' patients have been in constructing the conditions necessary for engaging in intensive treatment. Any attempt on my part to think for them, or even with them, about how to arrange to make it happen, or any gloomy forecasts about their inability to do so, has become a signal to me that I need to examine *my* willingness to engage with them.

If we're to do justice to the complexity of our work as analysts, we have no resting place regarding understanding our motivations. As soon as we've identified our reluctance to analyze, we need to question our analytic zeal. We must ask how our agenda to do more analysis and to have analytic practices affects our engagement with our patients. Lazar (2000) speaks of the analyst's zeal and warns that if the goal of the analyst is to intensify the treatment for her own reasons, she won't be respectful or optimally responsive to patients who aren't capable of initially engaging in a deep and intensive analysis. She recommends that "the analyst's primary focus should be to provide an availability to work on the patient's conflicts and developmental needs with a respect for the timing of their emergence and expression within a treatment frame that invites but does not prematurely elicit and confront" (p. 556). I think it critical that we strive to recognize and understand how the analyst's needs affect her participation at any point in an analysis (Boesky 1990). The analyst's zeal can be as much an impediment to understanding the patient as the analyst's reluctance. I find it helpful to be mindful of both tendencies.

Lazar voices an additional concern by questioning the view that analysis is the treatment of choice for most patients who seek an analyst and that patients' objections are "resistances" to be "analyzed." She maintains that some difficult and disturbing patients do not have the "ego strength" or "cohesiveness of the self" or "capacity and tolerance for continuity in relationship" to participate in an intense therapeutic engagement (p. 568). Who can benefit from analysis and under what conditions is a particularly complex issue that leads inevitably to questions about how one defines "benefit" and how one defines "analysis." I believe we don't yet have the data to be able to assert confidently which patients are capable of participating in analysis. While some patients might not be capable of this participation, at least with me, I find it useful to begin by asking about *my* willingness and capacity to engage with a particular patient. My concerns about Ms. A.'s ego strength and capacity to participate in an intensive treatment were in part a reflection of my fear of engaging with her. While it's important to be respectful of the patient's pace, rhythm, and wishes, it's also essential that we don't use these as rationalizations for our fears.

Some analysts have warned that the practice of "creating" analytic patients is disrespectful of patients because it undermines their autonomy or creates sadomasochistic struggles by forcing them into analysis (Allison 2000; Bassen 1989; Lazar 2000). Like any other analytic interaction, recommending analysis can have a sadomasochistic cast. However, the outcome depends, in part, on the analyst's primary intention. If the analyst intends to control and use the patient, destructive battles are likely to follow. If she intends to create the conditions for a richer analytic engagement and process, the ensuing enactments should provide an opportunity for deeper understanding. I'd further propose that in many cases *not* envisioning the patient as capable of engaging in analysis is compromising the patient's autonomy. Analysts can enact their hostility or sadism by coercing patients into analysis as much as they can by withholding from them the analytic frequency they need.

Given Ms. A.'s history and dynamics, sadomasochistic enactments are not simply inevitable; they're, in fact, an integral aspect of the psychoanalytic process. While Ms. A. has been reliving her traumas and internal struggles in the analysis, her life outside my office has improved. She's been reporting a mostly joyful engagement with her son and decreasing battles with her husband. Although her work doesn't have center stage in her life at this time, she maintains a stable law practice and continues to develop her skills as a lawyer.

Concluding remarks

The capacity to privilege the role of the unconscious in motivating thought and behavior and the belief in the therapeutic value of reliving and understanding traumas, conflicts, and identifications within the analytic relationship are essential components of a strong psychoanalytic identity. In addition to our private uncertainties, analysts face harsh external realities: a societal devaluing of analysis, a trend for evidence-based everything, and economic realities that are scary to analysts and patients alike. How then is an analyst to maintain an analytic identity?[3] I suggest that the most fruitful way is to begin by looking within ourselves. Whether informed by our ongoing internal dialogue with the important figures in our past, including our analyst, or by what's evoked by a particular patient or particular circumstances in our lives, we all have to contain distressing states of mind to be able to engage in analysis. I concur with those who suggest that the outcome of an analysis rests in great part on the analyst's capacity to analyze her own conflicts (Poland 1986; Bernstein 1990; Ogden 1991; Orgel 2000). A ubiquitous conflict that the analyst must analyze, as Ehrlich (2004), Wille (2008), and Gabbard and Ogden (2009) have discussed, is the analyst's ambivalence about practicing as an analyst. I'd add that, paradoxically, recognizing this ambivalence can strengthen one's analytic identity and increase one's capacity to continue and deepen an analysis.

Knowing that ambivalence is a feature of analysis, how do we maintain optimism about the usefulness of psychoanalytic work? During my daily work as an analyst I find it helpful to anticipate my ambivalence at any time during a treatment and in relation to all my patients. I work hard to be patient and to be kind to myself in the face of manifestations of my ambivalence about practicing as an analyst and to let myself know about my reservations about the usefulness of a particular analysis, worries about my capacity to understand a particular patient, or even, at times, questions about the analytic endeavor as a whole. At the same time, I strive not to take my reservations at face value but rather to think of them as thoughts with meaning regarding myself and my patients.

While working to maintain my analytic identity, I've found additional sources of assistance and inspiration. In a plenary address titled "Privacy and Disclosure in Psychoanalysis," Kantrowitz (2009) spoke of the importance of ongoing professional consultation with colleagues: "To know and share with a colleague our own internal conscious conflicts increases our chances of discovering *unconscious* conflicts and their ramifications. Telling someone else what we think and feel in our work makes it clearer and more understandable to us; it can normalize what we intellectually understand to be universal yet may experience as personally unacceptable" (p. 790). She addressed our unrealistic organizational ideal that we shouldn't need consultation once we get the "green light" to practice independently. I concur with her experience that presenting to colleagues is essential for every analysis. One could argue that it's an ethical imperative.

Writing up my cases for presentation or publication has allowed me the chance to think through my work carefully and has been invaluable. I continuously find inspiration in the writing of colleagues who are immersed in analytic work and who report with pleasure and conviction.

To close, I believe that at present many analysts have swung from an earlier tendency to idealize analysis to its polar opposite, a tendency to devalue it. Instead of our past view of psychoanalysis as a cure-all, we tend to view it as of no help at all—too expensive, too impractical, too uncertain an outcome. I consider both positions defensive. Either can be used to hide our reluctance to engage meaningfully with our inner lives and those of our patients.

Notes

1 This, too, refers to an earlier economic environment and is outdated.
2 Although a detailed discussion of the term *to deepen* is beyond the scope of this paper, it might be of help to describe how I use the term. I think of an analysis as deepening when my patient moves toward an increased recognition of her fears and wishes within our relationship, an increased capacity to think freely and psychologically, an increased capacity to recognize and tolerate a wider range and greater intensity of feelings, and an increased capacity to recognize and tolerate different views of herself and of me, among others. I have found that such an increase in my patient's capacity corresponds to a parallel increase in my ability to recognize transference-countertransference manifestations, think freely, feel deeply and intensely, and tolerate previously intolerable views of the patient and of myself.
3 Wille (2008) offers a rich discussion on the development of psychoanalytic identity and the causes for its instability, as well as suggestions about how to maintain a sturdy analytic identity beyond graduation.

References

Abend, S.M. (1986). Countertransference, empathy, and the analytic ideal: The impact of life stresses on analytic capability. *Psychoanalytic Quarterly*, 55: 563–575.

Allison, G.H. (2000). The shortage of psychoanalytic patients: An inquiry into its causes and consequences. *Psychoanalytic Inquiry*, 20: 527–540.

Bass, A. (2007). When the frame doesn't fit the picture. *Psychoanalytic Dialogues*, 17: 1–27.

Bassen, C. (1989). Transference-countertransference enactment in the recommendation to convert psychotherapy to psychoanalysis. *International Journal of Psychoanalysis*, 16: 79–92.

Bernstein, S.B. (1990). Motivation for psychoanalysis and the transition from psychotherapy. *Psychoanalytic Inquiry*, 10: 21–42.

Blum, H.P. (1981). The forbidden quest and the analytic ideal: The superego and insight. *Psychoanalytic Quarterly*, 50: 535–556.

Boesky, D. (1990). The psychoanalytic process and its components. *Psychoanalytic Quarterly*, 59: 550–584.

Boesky, D. (2009). *Bending the frame*. Unpublished presentation to panel "Bending the Frame and Judgment Calls in Everyday Practice," American Psychoanalytic Association, New York, January.

Böhm, T. (2004). Inner and outer frame breaks: Countertransference, enactments and whose life history? *Scandinavian Psychoanalytic Review*, 27: 2–11.

Ehrlich, L.T. (2004). The analyst's reluctance to begin a new analysis. *Journal of the American Psychoanalytic Association*, 52: 1075–1093.

Gabbard, G. (2007). Flexibility of the frame revisited: Commentary on Tony Bass' "When the frame doesn't fit the picture." *Psychoanalytic Dialogues*, 17: 923–929.

Gabbard, G.O. & Ogden, T.H. (2009). On becoming a psychoanalyst. *International Journal of Psychoanalysis*, 90: 311–327.

Gedo, P.M. & Cohler, B.J. (1992). Session frequency, regressive intensity, and the psychoanalytic process. *Psychoanalytic Psychology*, 9: 245–249.

Kantrowitz, J. (2009). Privacy and disclosure in psychoanalysis. *Journal of the American Psychoanalytic Association*, 57: 787–806.

Langs, R. & Stone, L. (1980). *The Therapeutic Experience and Its Setting*. New York: Aronson.

Lazar, S.G. (2000). Should analytic patients be "created"? Reflections on Arnold Rothstein's "Psychoanalytic technique and the creation of analytic patients." *Psychoanalytic Inquiry*, 20: 556–573.

Levine, A.R. (2009). Panel report: Bending the frame and judgment calls in everyday practice. *Journal of the American Psychoanalytic Association*, 57: 1209–1215.

Loewald, H.W. (1960). On the therapeutic action of psychoanalysis. *International Journal of Psychoanalysis*, 41: 16–33.

Mitchell, S.A. (1993). *Hope and Dread in Psychoanalysis*. New York: Basic Books.

Ogden, T.H. (1991). Analysing the matrix of transference. *International Journal of Psychoanalysis*, 72: 593–605.

Ogden, T.H. (2002). A new reading of the origins of object-relations theory. *International Journal of Psychoanalysis*, 83: 767–782.

Orgel, S. (2000). Letting go: Some thoughts about termination. *Journal of the American Psychoanalytic Association*, 48: 719–738.

Parsons, M. (2007). Raiding the inarticulate: The internal analytic setting and listening beyond countertransference. *International Journal of Psycho-analysis*, 88: 1441–1456.

Poland, W.S. (1986). The analyst's words. *Psychoanalytic Quarterly*, 55: 244–272.

Richards, A.K. (1997). Panel report: The relevance of frequency of sessions to the creation of an analytic experience. *Journal of the American Psychoanalytic Association*, 45: 1241–1251.

Rothstein, A. (2000). A response to the contributors. *Psychoanalytic Inquiry*, 20: 611–627.

Rothstein, A. (2006). Reflections on the concept "analyzability." *Psychoanalytic Review*, 93: 827–833.

Schafer, R. (1979). On becoming a psychoanalyst of one persuasion or another. *Contemporary Psychoanalysis*, 15: 345–360.

Wille, R.S. (2008). Psychoanalytic identity: Psychoanalysis as an internal object. *Psychoanalytic Quarterly*, 77: 1193–1229.

Chapter 5

Teleanalysis

Slippery slope or rich opportunity?

Anecdotal reports, surveys, and a growing number of publications devoted to the subject indicate that more and more often analysts are treating patients through teleanalysis—that is, analysis conducted over the telephone or via online videoconferencing platforms such as Skype or Zoom (Richards 2001). In addition, more candidates are being taught, treated, or supervised via online videoconferencing or the telephone than ever before (Manosevitz 2006; Fishkin et al. 2011; Scharff 2013a, 2015; Merchant 2016). While many analysts still question the practice of teleanalysis,[1] the rapidly expanding presence of technology in our everyday lives, and our growing reliance on it, suggest that the question for analysts should be how best to practice teleanalysis, not whether to. Anyone invested in the future of psychoanalysis, if not having done so already, must grapple with the practice of telephone or online analysis and its conceptual and technical underpinnings (Litowitz 2012).

When considering whether to practice teleanalysis, a newcomer faces many questions. Is psychoanalysis possible on the phone or through online videoconferencing? How does it compare to in-person analysis? What do we know about its usefulness, and what are the sources of our knowledge? What might be its limitations? Advantages? Who is it most useful for? When? Does online analysis provide an enlarged opportunity for analysts to practice analysis, or does it represent analysts' accommodation to patients and their own resistances to in-room treatment? As Tao (2015) asks, "How does technology affect the psychoanalytic situation in particular? Does a secure connection on the Internet offer a 'good enough' setting for psychoanalysis, with enough oxygen in the atmosphere for the survival of the analytic couple and the analytic process? Or does it indulge an omnipotent fantasy of the analyst ...?" (p. 105).

The increasing body of literature addressing different aspects of teleanalysis is characterized by wide differences of opinion and controversy about its usefulness. At one end of a continuum are analysts who practice teleanalysis and have found it functionally equivalent to and at least as effective as in-office analysis (Spiro and Devenis 2000; Leffert 2003; Hanly 2007; Carlino 2011; Migone 2013). Less ardent proponents of teleanalysis maintain that teleanalysis is a valuable second choice to in-office analysis, a way of helping patients who otherwise couldn't be helped to receive the intensive treatment they need (Lindon 1988; Zalusky 1998; Mirkin 2011; Scharff 2012). These analysts report that teleanalysis, when practiced with analytic thoughtfulness and skill, can produce good analytic results, comparable to those of successful in-room analyses. At the other end of the continuum, critics argue that teleanalysis, at its best, is less effective because its frame doesn't support a deep psychoanalytic process or its analysis (Bayles 2012; Essig 2015; Russell 2015; Turkle, Essig, and Russell 2017). Critics point to the limiting effects of technology on free association and on communication between analyst and analysand and therefore on the analytic process (Brainsky 2003). Some even suggest that teleanalysis undermines analytic practice and is a slippery slope leading to the extinction of any form of analysis (Essig and Russell 2017), or is such a diluted treatment that it doesn't merit the designation of psychoanalysis (Argentieri and Mehler 2003).

While the number of books and papers on teleanalysis increases, there's still a lack of objective research on the topic. In addition, only a relatively small number of publications provide clinical material to support these varying opinions. I'll argue here, using detailed clinical material, that teleanalysis is not inherently "analysis-light" or resistance to analysis but can serve as another opportunity to help patients who need intensive work but can't be present in the analyst's office.

Selective literature review

I'll begin with a selective review of the critics and skeptics of teleanalysis. Argentieri and Mehler (2003), arguing against telephone analysis, conclude that speaking with patients over the phone doesn't constitute analysis. Using as a springboard for discussion Zalusky's comprehensive report of analytic work with a patient who participated in an analysis conducted partly over the phone (1998), they suggest that in telephone analysis analysts accommodate, rather than help analyze, the anxieties inherent in separations and termination. They suggest further that practitioners of telephone analysis might be enacting omnipotent rescue fantasies and fostering omnipotent fantasies in their patients by denying the limitations of phone conversations. Argentieri and Mehler base their conclusions on their own telephone work with patients who were prevented from attending in-person because of illness, work obligations, or living in an area lacking access to analytic treatment.[2] Summarizing that work, they conclude that although "good work" took place in many of their cases, "nevertheless, there was a clear, explicit and mutual awareness of the fact that we were *not doing* or *continuing* to do analysis. We were *doing something else* like psychotherapy, post-analytic occasional follow-up, support therapy or simple human supporting contact. Undeniably, the telephone might occasionally be a useful therapeutic tool as well; but it simply is not compatible with a psychoanalytic process" (p. 18).

Argentieri's and Mehler's frequently referenced paper usefully calls our attention to the possibility that telephone analysis can be used as a resistance to analytic engagement. However, their conclusion that teleanalysis isn't analysis isn't based on analytic data. Although they use Zalusky's work as a starting point for their views on teleanalysis, they don't base their comments on the actual work of Zalusky, who offers detailed analytic process of a telephone analysis,[3] nor do they furnish their own analytic data to support their claims. By their own account, they never attempted to practice psychoanalysis when they met with patients on the phone. Their claim that telephone analysis is not analysis, therefore, rests primarily on their *beliefs*, even, perhaps, their biases, regarding telephone analysis.

Essig (2015) invited analysts to recognize biases for and against teleanalysis. Referring to relationships mediated by technology as "screen relations," he encourages clinicians to pay attention to both gains and losses involved in Internet treatment. Essig calls clinicians' intense, visceral, a priori rejection of therapeutic experiences mediated by technology "simulation avoidance" (p. 687). He suggests that clinicians under the influence of simulation avoidance focus on the losses and can't consider gains. Conversely, when clinicians suffer from what Essig calls "simulation entrapment" (p. 689), they're unable to register any differences in relating through technology and act as if the results of their actions within technologically mediated treatments are identical to those produced in the office setting.

Essig, in a later collaboration with Russell, is more critical of teleanalytic work and expresses concern about its deleterious effects on practitioners and the field more generally.

Skype treatment really is paving the road for something like "Freud: The App." It's harsh to say, but those routinely treating at a distance via screen relations are unwittingly serving the needs of technology entrepreneurs who want to replace therapists with apps and programs. Such a practice does the work of what Turkle termed the robotic moment to turn us into creatures looking to machines rather than people for love and care (Essig and Russell 2017, p. 135).

Essig and Russell also predict that teleanalysis will disrupt the mental health market the way Amazon and Uber have disrupted the bookstore and taxi markets.

Turkle similarly suggests that teleanalysis moves away from the demands and difficulties inherent in psychoanalysis, such as the anxieties of "embodied empathy, of being together in a messy way" (Turkle, Essig, and Russell 2017, p. 244). She observes that analysts often see teleanalysis as progress, a treatment that embraces the realities of contemporary culture and keeps psychoanalysis relevant, profitable, and more portable. Turkle argues that these positive views are rationalizations: analysts use them to justify practicing a treatment that avoids the difficult therapeutic conversations that promote vulnerability and full presence, elements essential to emotional healing.

Many reports of successful teleanalyses (e.g., Robertiello 1972; Lindon 1988; Zalusky 1998; Leffert 2003; Bassen 2007; Eckardt 2011; Mirkin 2011; Scharff 2010, 2012, 2013a, 2013b; Hanly 2007; Essig 2015; Lemma 2015; Abbasi 2016; Merchant 2016; Wooldridge 2017) contradict Turkle's, and Argentieri and Mehler's claims that teleanalysis is untenable. In my opinion, their claim that distance analysis is a priori defensive doesn't account for the fact that patients seek teleanalysis for a wide range of reasons, not purely defensive, and that defensive reasons, if in fact present, can be analyzed. As I intend to demonstrate in the case examples that follow, even if some patients might seek teleanalysis for primarily defensive reasons, such as a need for fierce distancing; teleanalysis provides the only setting flexible enough to contain them and allow for their eventual analysis. Also, although patients might be compelled to seek teleanalysis for external factors such as issues of confidentiality, promoting one's career or following a spouse by relocating, scarcity of analysts or lack of the right therapeutic match in one's geographic location, each of which might contain some defensive elements. However, the overall opportunities for emotional growth and health are greater in teleanalysis than in choosing to forgo analysis altogether or continuing to meet in an in-person analysis and relinquishing other relationships or opportunities for growth.

Russell (2015) has written the most comprehensive critique of teleanalysis to date. In *Screen Relations: The Limits of Computer-Mediated Psychoanalysis and Psychotherapy*, she set out to explore the therapeutic effectiveness of teleanalysis after observing that her computer-mediated treatments weren't functionally equivalent to treatments where she and the patient met in the same room. Adding to her own observations, Russell interviewed many colleagues and patients who have had experience with teleanalysis and who contributed clinical vignettes and anecdotes to her book.

Borrowing Essig's term (2015), Russell concludes that screen relations[4] are not conducive to "an optimally effective therapeutic process" for three main reasons: first, the absence of physical co-presence; second, the incapacity to "kiss or kick"; and third, the supposed fact that the balance of communication between patient and therapist is tilted in favor of the explicitly verbal mode. Russell suggests that while computer-mediated treatments are "better than nothing" (p. 181), analysts must not present them to patients as being equivalent to in-office treatment.

Russell found that analysts practicing teleanalysis didn't attend to the frame as diligently as they did in in-office treatments.

It did not occur to most of the analysts I interviewed to discuss with their patients the issue of the safety of the environment and establish a working framework before embarking on computer-mediated treatment. This is despite the fact that all the analysts I have spoken to recognize the importance of this and are scrupulous in providing such a setting in their traditional, shared environment practices. The mere act of establishing contact was their prime aim, whether the patient was in a sitting room, car seat, or a bed, and overshadowed the necessity to create some mutual form of a reliable and predictable setting (Russell 2015, p. 11).

In addition, analysts tended to ignore, rather than consider for possible meaning, difficulties inherent in Internet connection involving "poor sound, grainy visuals and frequent interruptions" (p. 3). Russell also reported that analysts observed in themselves and their patients a diminished capacity to concentrate, pay attention, engage with their own reverie, be silent, or feel intimate with each other:

> We had curious lapses. It was easy to forget treatment sessions and the times of our peer group meetings. We were likely to bring a cup of tea or glass of water to a session, something we did not do in co-present sessions. We did more talking with our patients about the comparative times and weather. We did more talking in general, as silences were not so easy. We felt less in touch, less intuitively connected.
>
> (Russell 2015, p. 3)

Noting the lack of psychoanalytic research in this area, Russell turned to neuropsychological and memory research (Moser and Moser 2014; Buzsáki and Moser 2013; Clayton et al. 2007) to help explain clinicians' memory lapses and difficulty maintaining a therapeutic frame. She suggested that the two-dimensional nature of computer-mediated treatments affects memory, contributing to clinicians' difficulty in keeping the patient in mind as they would in an in-office treatment. Russell further asserts that the reason analysts don't attend to the therapeutic frame as diligently as they would in person is that patients are in a different location. Presence, she remarks, "requires the sense of bodies together. We know that it is dependent on recognizing the other as an intentional self, located in a shared physical space with the potential to interact with the other" (p. 179).

Referencing developmental research on communication (Boston Change Process Study Group 2008) and highlighting the importance of implicit communication in creating and maintaining intimacy, Russell also suggested that the nature of computer-mediated communication, with its narrow attentional focus, intrinsic two-dimensional nature, and limits of movement and action taking place within a common space, compromises communication and intimacy. Applying right brain research to teleanalysis (Schore 2005, 2011), she hypothesizes that use of the computer compromises right brain function in both clinician and patient by impeding the transmission of "finely nuanced, nonconscious information such as gestures, smells, and pheromones" (p. 97).

In addition to affecting memory, communication, and intimacy, Russell suggests, the screen in teleanalysis prevents the patient from experiencing the full potential for destructiveness in the analytic relationship, such as the potential for "kissing or kicking" the analyst. Using Winnicott's idea of object usage (1969), Russell argues that in teleanalysis use of the screen and awareness of simulation limit patients' imagination and thereby their chance of acting out their omnipotence and test analysts' capacity to maintain their separateness: "In 'screen relations,' the patient can never truly test the analyst's capacity to survive. The extent to which the patient can 'imagine' the destruction of the analyst (by zealous love or hate) is bounded by the barrier of the screen ... Therefore, the use of the object is foreclosed by the limitations of the medium" (p. 35).

Russell offers the account of Patrick, an Australian analyst, as an example of an analysis where meeting on Skype foreclosed the patient's use of the analyst. After relocating and beginning to meet online, Patrick reports, the patient would blow up and express contempt and rage toward him and had difficulty calming down and reflecting on his experience. Patrick referred the patient to another analyst for in-office treatment, and he is quoted by Russell as concluding "it felt like there was something about being on Skype that made it just not possible" (p. 38).

Russell presents a wealth of clinical examples to support her thesis. In my opinion, however, her examples for the most part present problematic applications of teleanalysis, such as not being able to create an analytic frame that can contain the anxieties of patient and analyst sufficiently that they can be examined analytically. A second problem is that she bases her discussions on brief examples that lack detail and specificity. As a result, when she discusses these clinical examples using a psychoanalytic lens, the lack of process, context, and historical background doesn't allow the psychoanalytic reader a complex analytic consideration of the data to determine the veracity of her assertions and conclusions.

A third problem arises when she attempts to understand analysts' difficulties by importing findings from other fields without accounting for psychoanalytic findings. For instance, she uses a neuropsychological/cognitive focus and ignores the role of unconscious motivation. Thus, Russell explains analysts' and patients' symptomatic behaviors as reactions to the actual setting, rather than considering them as reactions associated to the *meaning* of the teleanalytic setting. For example, when analysts report that they tend to speak to patients on Skype more than usual, she explains their behavior as reactions to meeting on Skype, rather than behavior with deeper personal meaning—a manifestation of anxiety about the meaning of meeting on Skype[5] that needs to be thought about and understood in the context of the analyst's history and countertransferences, rather than as simply reactive to the medium. Similarly, Russell attributes forgetting "technologically mediated" sessions to the two-dimensional experience of screen relations and doesn't consider forgetting to be a highly motivated symptom that reflects an attempt to manage and disguise consciously unacceptable difficult feelings. Consequently, although her collection of problematic behaviors and lapses usefully alerts analysts to possible enactments and countertransferential challenges associated with teleanalysis, I consider her attempts to illuminate these observations psychoanalytically disappointing and her conclusions unconvincing.

Fourth, in her effort to explain the difficulties she and other analysts have faced while practicing teleanalysis, Russell creates a straw man. She juxtaposes teleanalysis with what many analysts would recognize as a utopian version of in-room treatments. In this idealized version, analysts are assumed to be consistently and effectively attending to all therapeutic variables that render analysis optimally effective: the physical body and its role in the analytic process are attended to and understood[6]; free association and reverie are facilitated; challenges to the internal or external therapeutic frame by patient or analyst are considered diligently as evidence of the patient's or analyst's reluctance to understand or to engage in analytic intimacy; and patients' explicit or implicit modes of communication are recognized and used productively.

Some of Russell's criticisms about teleanalysis point to areas of difficulty in any analysis—for instance, the tendency to drift away from what's difficult emotionally and take refuge in external distractions. Are analysts prone to look or wish to look at their Smartphones only when meeting with patients on the Internet? Are analysts inclined only when they meet online not to question when the patient participates in ways not conducive to analysis?

Russell's account of Patrick typifies her clinical examples. By not providing more analytic data, she can easily frame his dilemmas as a teleanalysis problem rather than a countertransference problem of the sort analysts might struggle with in any analysis. She leaves many questions unanswered: How did Patrick feel about the patient's move away from him and about their new videoconferencing frame? What was the transferential source of the patient's rage and contempt? How did the patient's rage and contempt connect to relocating away from his analyst and meeting teleanalytically? Without a closer look at the analytic process, it's impossible to ascertain whether this impasse is an example of possible limitations in the teleanalytic frame generally or an example of the analyst's incapacity to survive the patient's rage—an enactment of unrecognized and unaddressed feelings about the change in frame and its meaning for patient and analyst.

A fifth flaw in Russell's argument pertains to her assertion that teleanalysis limits the full expression of the patient's destructive and loving feelings and the analyst's capacity to survive them. Clinical experience refutes this assertion. The analyst's capacity to survive is not foreclosed by the screen but exists in the analyst's mind, her capacity not to withdraw or retaliate emotionally in the face of the patient's hatred, defiance, disappointments, and challenges.

As evidenced precisely in Russell's example of Patrick, patients *can* "kick" or even "kill" the analyst when they meet online. The telephone and Skype screen do not limit the enactment of unconscious fantasy or the patient's expression of unformulated experience, any more than using the couch and not seeing the analyst does. Unconscious fantasies of seducing or destroying the analyst are integral to every analysis, products of the patient's (and analyst's) mind regardless of the analytic setting. Whether in person, on the telephone, or through videoconferencing, analysts are "kicked and kissed" daily

by their patients' evocative words, tones of voice, silences, detailed porno-
graphic or gruesome accounts, and much more.[7] If simulation precluded
imagination and the manifestation of unconscious fantasy, then analysis, itself
a simulation, wouldn't be useful in any setting, not just teleanalytically.

A sixth shortcoming involves Russell's equation of physical distance with
emotional distance and lack of connection. This concrete interpretation of
physical distance doesn't support what we know about emotional communication and connection.[8]

As I've argued elsewhere (Ehrlich 2004, 2010, 2013), the analyst's resistance to
analysis is vastly underestimated with in-office treatment. Russell's clinical examples confirm that this is true also for teleanalysis. Although the specific form
resistance takes in any analysis is uniquely shaped by each analytic pair, I suggest
that Russell's many anecdotes alert us to some of the common forms that resistance takes in online treatment. Difficulties in concentration, memory, attention,
and sense of connection to the patient, reported by many of Russell's respondents,
can be understood as manifestations of analysts' emotional distancing.

Russell's book helps analysts rethink therapeutic action in analysis in any
setting by highlighting the need to bring analytic attention to the body and its
meanings, the importance of the analyst's emotional presence, the necessity of
attending to the frame, the need to take into account the explicit and verbal
as well as the implicit and nonverbal aspects of the patient's communications,
and the vital role of containment and the analyst's capacity to survive. I
believe it also underscores the need for the analyst's self-discipline and
uncompromising commitment to self-assessment and consultation.

Case examples of teleanalysis

M. When open-ended in-person analysis is not possible

Several years ago I was presented with a clinical dilemma. A man in his early
30s, deep in despair and suffering from self-hatred and suicidal thoughts,
came to see me for a consultation after breaking up with his fiancée. He told
me he had been in intensive treatment twice before—for two-and-a-half years
each time—and that professional moves had led these treatments to end. He
left each of these experiences feeling better about himself and thinking the
treatment had been helpful. He recalled thinking, after each termination, that
he had understood his difficulties with bouts of despair and sexual inhibition
and that his self-regard had improved lastingly. Subsequently, though,
romantic disappointments led him to realize that his gains were temporary,
and he felt he had no choice but to return for further treatment.

During our second consultation meeting, he told me he had definite plans to
move to another state in about two years when he finished a project. He suggested that we meet weekly while he was in Michigan and that I provide a
referral for an analyst in his new location when he moved. I wrestled with several

considerations in my effort to determine how best to proceed. I contemplated his current painful state of mind and his account of his long-standing distress, which called for the intensive, long-term help that only psychoanalysis can provide. At the same time, I considered his history of previous treatments and noted his propensity to walk away before his treatment needs were met.

To further appreciate his fears and hopes in relationships, I took stock of how my encounters with M. affected me. I observed that during our first meeting when he appeared overwhelmed and desperate for relief, I'd registered clearly his plea for urgent help and, simultaneously, a disconcerting feeling that I couldn't reach him. I felt surprised when he came to our second session visibly less distressed. Yet my sense that he couldn't be reached persisted throughout the second session. In reflecting on the discrepancy between my perception of his relief and my feeling that he couldn't be affected, I realized that M. felt some release in the process of unburdening himself by laying out his symptoms and feelings but not necessarily from any sense of emotional contact with me or hope that I could help him.

In the third meeting, after M. revealed more about his experiences and expectations of relationships, I further appreciated some of the meanings contained in my experience of him. He delineated his many efforts to find relief of his mood and physical symptoms by enlisting physical therapists, chiropractors, and yoga teachers, efforts that produced only temporary, limited results. M. clearly implied that he had low expectations for anything different happening in the future; though he was not explicit, he conveyed the message that he viewed health care providers as capable of offering only temporary, impersonal relief and as interchangeable.

I recognized that M. saw me as one more anonymous, expendable helper whom he was seeing in order to vent or to straighten himself up, rather than someone he could rely on to help him in a substantive, deeply personal way. I became aware that M., though forthcoming with symptoms and facts, was cautious with his thoughts and feelings at a deeper level. I sensed that he profoundly doubted anyone's capacity to understand him or contain his feelings and questioned people's motives for offering to help. Instead, he expected others to buckle under the weight of his feelings or the power of his intellect and withdraw or retaliate for his view of them as inadequate or inferior. I thought that if he and I could find a way to understand these protective walls, perhaps our work together would allow him to feel more trustful of himself and others and therefore more likely to find and sustain intimacy.

Despite his vulnerabilities, M. had considerable strengths. Although in pain and unable to sustain intimate love relationships, he was a capable man who distinguished himself in most endeavors he engaged in. He was articulate, ambitious, determined, and extremely perceptive. His high standards, when not used self-punitively, led him to excel and to be a valuable partner in all he did. I thought M. had the raw material to be a great psychoanalytic partner and, if he could engage long enough, benefit from analysis.

It was clear M.'s difficulties hadn't been addressed sufficiently by earlier treatments. His subsequent efforts to find solutions, such as becoming entirely self-sufficient, moving frequently, focusing on career success, and having a big network of friends, had helped some. Underneath it all, however, he still struggled with emotional difficulties that prevented him from loving intimately and feeling worthy of love.

Given the nature and extent of his difficulties, M. needed immediate, frequent, reliable, and open-ended help. Yet, given that he was planning to leave, how could I help him get the treatment he needed? M. had an early history of losses and having had less help than he needed, including parents who couldn't help him regulate his feelings, his mother's post-partum depression after the birth of his brother when he was a toddler, the death of his father when he was in elementary school, and a beloved aunt who lived with the family and left when M. still needed her. As an adult, he tried to protect himself from loss by remaining emotionally unattached. Repeating his history, he repetitively left locations and therapists and fell in love with women he left or were emotionally unavailable.

What appeared to be an impossible external predicament mirrored one of M.'s central internal dilemmas: desperately needing help and simultaneously dreading it. During the consultation, I experienced at first hand M.'s ambivalent approach to relationships. I felt at the receiving end of his great need for both relief and emotional distance. By announcing from the outset his intention to leave and find another analyst, M. attempted to proactively limit the duration and potential of our relationship. It was left to me to manage my feelings of disappointment, concern, apprehension, insecurity, frustration, and fear in order not to lose touch with his suffering, his need for intensive help, and my desire to provide it.

At that moment, so early in my relationship with him and not seeing a clear path forward, I contemplated all options. I considered going along with his stated wishes to be seen weekly and then facilitate a referral in his new location. However, this didn't seem like a good option because he was in profound distress and needed more than weekly treatment immediately. Also, given his tendency to turn passive into active and leave before he was left, I thought chances were high he wouldn't settle down in the next treatment either. I also presumed that if I agreed to his proposal to work together temporarily, I'd be joining him in repeating his history of losses without the conditions necessary to help us understand it. Convinced that unless he was helped to understand this repetition sooner rather than later he'd continue to enact it, I decided against going along with his proposed plan. Instead, I offered to be his analyst.

In my recommendation to him, I acknowledged his suffering and outlined what I perceived to be his difficulties, recognizing that he'd made many good efforts to address them. I also told him that he and I knew that there was work left to be done in addressing some very painful long-standing feelings that recede when times are good but persist, raw and unintegrated, inside of him. In times of stress, I said, these powerful feelings erupt and blindside him, knocking him off his feet.

M. agreed with my assessment and expressed chagrin that all his previous years of treatment hadn't cured him. I told him that based on his account I thought they had helped some. However, the problem seemed to be that the treatments ended because he moved, not because he was truly ready to stop. I let him know that I thought it was important to do it differently. I suggested we meet daily in an open-ended way and take as long as needed to make sense of the profound pain he had struggled with for so long.

M. responded by saying he was still planning to leave and so didn't see how we could meet in an open-ended way. Still, he agreed that, given his current distress, more than weekly sessions were needed. He proposed coming four times a week, the frequency of his previous analyses. I agreed to begin on these terms and said I hoped that he and I would continue to discuss frequency, as well as how to arrange to work in an open-ended way. Although I had a feeling that he considered these issues settled and was humoring me by agreeing to discuss them further, M. began analysis. Shortly after we began, after examining some of his fears of working teleanalytically, we agreed that we would work via videoconferencing once he moved.

Two years into the analysis and a couple of months before he planned to move, M. announced that, in anticipation of relocation expenses, he wanted to reduce his sessions from four to three times a week. At this point, having worked together productively and having evidence of the benefits of our work, I felt even more confident in my assessment that M. needed as intensive a treatment as possible. After exploring the timing of his request and discovering his expectation that his move would be the beginning of the end of my investment in him, I told him I thought cutting back wasn't the solution. Summoning my courage, I said that in fact I thought it would be best if we met five times weekly. The emotional storm that followed fleshed out more explicitly and vividly some of M.'s fears in relationships: being exploited and sexually misused, losing control and feeling uncontrollable voraciousness and rage, having a partner with very thin skin whom he could destroy with his honesty or successes, and losing his sense of himself and his ability to please and hold on to his partner. Realizing that similar concerns had gotten in the way of his relationships with his ex-fiancée and previous girlfriends, M. agreed to add a fifth session to better understand those concerns.

M.'s many resources, intellectual and financial, had allowed him to defend against fears of entrapment through frequent moves. In the beginning of our relationship, M. reminded me of Margaret Wise Brown's very young runaway bunny (1942), who left his mother prematurely. Teleanalysis allowed me to be the mother/analyst who could follow him long enough and persistently enough to help him recognize and begin to address the fears that motivated him to run self-defeatingly from himself and from intimate relationships. Over the years of his long analysis we met teleanalytically for the most part; three times a year, he would come to Ann Arbor for several in-office sessions.

Teleanalysis allowed us to accommodate M.'s fears of entrapment and dependency and examine them long enough and intensively enough to slowly understand their many sources. Beginning teleanalysis with M. was not a defense against analysis but the only condition under which analysis could continue to take place. The determining factor for helping M. was not meeting exclusively in person. Rather, it was creating the conditions where we would have enough time and opportunity to identify the ongoing oscillations in his and my capacities to think, feel, and together make sense of M.'s unprocessed raw, intolerable states of mind and the symptomatic manifestations of his unconscious fantasies. Working together long enough and intensively enough provided him greater access to his mind and to ways of managing his feelings with increased tolerance. He became less self-attacking and dissociative and less phobic of emotional contact with others, beginning with me.

M. and I were able and willing to work well teleanalytically and achieved good therapeutic and analytic results. Would he have achieved greater gains if I'd seen him in my office for the entire analysis? Although, of course, the question can't be answered, I'm doubtful. One of the many difficult realities that psychoanalytic practitioners must contend with is that analytic results can't be compared. It's as impossible to know what he and I would have accomplished in my office together as it is to know what we would have accomplished at another period in his life.

Nevertheless, during the many years of our working together, as he felt "held" teleanalytically and during in-office sessions, we identified many fearful and shameful states of mind that contributed to his dread of connection and dependency and his efforts at omnipotent self-sufficiency. He gained better access to himself, felt more integrated, and eventually was able to allow others, including me, to know him and move closer to him. As he repeatedly encountered his difficulty sharing his achievements with me, M. became familiar with his unconscious guilt about his successes. Recognizing that he equated his successes with destructive triumph over less successful loved rivals, including his dead father, freed him from the need to deny them and to enjoy them more.

The juxtaposition of in-office and teleanalytic sessions gave us unique opportunities to understand his tendency to form long-distance relationships that would eventually fizzle, as well as his avoidance of intimacy. A pattern of starting affairs just before he was scheduled to visit for in-person sessions, and ending them right after he left, led us to his shame and guilt over his passionate sexual feelings toward me. M. tried to create a buffer between us because the contact with me felt like a siren song: luring, overwhelmingly exciting, and very dangerous. We learned that his experience of the in-office sessions felt more real but intolerable, and his experience of the telesessions felt more tolerable but less real. Recognizing the extent to which he held back his *real* feelings in telesessions, especially negative feelings, allowed him to feel more real in the telesessions but also overwhelmed. We understood better that physical distance served as an emotional retreat. By unconsciously designating the telesessions as distant sessions, he tried to restore his sense of control and safety. Understanding the multiple functions of his need for distance and control in relationships allowed him to better engage with me and eventually find a physically, emotionally available partner.

My concern with M. was how to create external and internal frames that would allow him to get the help he needed. Having determined that he needed analysis, my consideration wasn't whether in-person is better than tele-analysis, but how to provide the frequency, continuity, and safety he needed to address his inability to feel safe enough within himself and with another.

P. When career opportunity calls

P., a middle-aged university professor, had been in analysis with me for five years when he was invited to join the faculty of a renowned university overseas. The invitation included funds and resources unavailable in his current position. P. felt torn. He wanted to accept the invitation not only because it was an honor but because the university overseas had a department known for innovative work in his area of expertise and for supporting creative original research. At the same time, he still suffered from sexual and writing inhibitions, social anxiety, and occasional panic attacks. Having gained some relief from our work but still suffering, P. didn't want to end analysis.

P. had a helpful first analysis when in his 20s. However, because he had an unproductive experience with phone sessions during that analysis, he felt that working teleanalytically might compromise our work. In exploring his earlier telephone experience, we found that when P. left town for a sabbatical semester, he and his analyst reduced their sessions from four to one a week. P. hated the phone sessions and described feeling panicked in anticipation of each session and distant from his analyst when they spoke. P. initiated the reduction in sessions because he'd privately thought that speaking on the phone would be difficult. He interpreted his analyst's unquestioning agreement as confirmation that he, too, didn't like meeting by phone. After recognizing that his negative reaction to speaking by phone was partly a response to having spoken less often and having felt rejected by his analyst, P. was more optimistic about using phone sessions to speak to me productively. He briefly considered videoconferencing but decided he preferred speaking by phone because in his mind it replicated most closely his experience of using the couch, which he found helpful. At that point, ten months before he would have needed to move, he decided to accept the job and, after moving, continue to meet teleanalytically five times weekly.

The months preceding the move proved to be very productive for our work. Initially, after making his decision, he spoke with dread about the logistics of the move and anticipated many difficulties when he arrived, including problems adjusting to his new environment, being disappointed by his future colleagues, and not being able to work creatively enough. Noting that he was focused on the destination and not the departure, I suggested that he might be having difficulty thinking about what it would be like leaving his home in Ann Arbor and our way of working together in-room. Initially he dismissed my suggestion and maintained that, since we would be continuing phone sessions at the same frequency, he didn't anticipate any changes. However, after repeated allusions to professional collaborations in Michigan falling apart following his move, he reluctantly recognized that, despite our plan to continue, at some level he expected our relationship to end. Once identified, P.'s fear of losing me transformed into a haunting certainty. He experienced waves of panic states and an inability to sleep, work, and even think. At times he appeared robotic and distant or hypervigilant. Recognizing that he was lost in states of mind he couldn't verbalize, let alone explain, I reached into my own mind to find any thoughts, sensations, or feelings that might help us understand him. At moments I felt lost myself and wondered privately whether he could manage the move psychically and doubted the wisdom of arranging to meet by phone.

As we looked for meaning within these disturbing feelings, slowly we began to make out different facets of P.'s emotional experiences. Although we'd previously identified the traumatic impact of a surgery and hospitalization when he was a toddler, at this juncture we understood their emotional effect with unprecedented immediacy and resonance. As the months passed and the date of the move approached, we came to experience between us the separation-individuation struggles that P. described having had with his parents, especially his mother. At moments, he experienced his decision to leave as if *I* were leaving him. He imagined I was eager not to have him around and to be free from what he thought I experienced as his demanding presence. "Why didn't you stop me from committing to go? If you cared, why would you agree to continue remotely and not see me in person?" he asked. At other moments, he reversed himself and felt suspicious of my interest in his feelings about leaving. He feared I was encouraging him to share his feelings to create a need in him and manipulate him to want to stay. He further imagined that I wanted to hold him back in order to feel wanted and needed. When he thought of me as unable to release him because of my own needs, he worried that when he left I'd retaliate and disengage from him, and he'd have to manage without my attention, care, or help.

P.'s growing ability to share his negative views of me, including fears of my fragility and likelihood of retaliation if he disclosed these "horrible" views of me, contributed to a growing sense of trust between us. At the same time, our joint efforts to tolerate his states of mind, find words to speak about them, and understand what they represented gave me hope that we could carry these gains into our telesessions. Yet, with the move in sight, questions remained: Could he feel his sense of abandonment and loss without devaluing me, as he characteristically stopped himself from experiencing loss in the past? Would he be able to bear feelings of deprivation without falling into a paranoid state and experiencing me as a frightening stranger?

P. had always felt that his sense of freedom and independence and the security of relationships were mutually exclusive. Now, as the time to leave approached, he felt pleased he could envision something different and would be pursuing his interests while continuing to have my help and support. Although regretful for having made similar arrangements in his first analysis, he felt grateful we could do so now.

During our first calls after the move, P. commented with relief that having talked about the way he disengaged and withdrew paid off and he retained his sense of my presence and investment in him. P.'s characteristic mode of defending was, of course, available to him, and he'd deployed it regularly since the beginning of the analysis. However, it became more prominent after his decision to move. His move gave us a chance to identify his emotional withdrawal more clearly, understand the suffering that catalyzed it, and be better able to help him with it. He became more capable with me and in other relationships of monitoring himself for emotional distance and becoming more present. Regular in-room visits helped us identify elements he defended against in telephone sessions, such as longings to be physically close and the presence of a suspicious, persecutory way of looking at himself that close physical presence could activate.

Of the many difficulties we worked on, one stands out because it highlights an advantage of working teleanalytically. A news story involving a priest accused of molesting children brought up his own molestation by a beloved priest, which he had mentioned in an in-office session. In the past, during in-room sessions, he'd been seized with panic when he thought of the event and had been unable to share details. Now, as he spoke of details of the news story, he slowly recalled the specifics of his abuse with fear, shame, and eventually fury. He volunteered that speaking on the phone felt safer. He recognized that at some level he worried that I, too, would be a predator and overstimulate him or traumatize him.[9]

S. When issues of confidentiality preclude in-person analysis

S., a professional woman from another city, contacted me for a consultation after a period of depressive symptoms that interfered with her capacity to work. S. had heard about me from her husband, a mental health professional who had attended a workshop where I presented on the analyst's reluctance to deepen analysis. Her hopelessness had begun a few months earlier, after her daughter was diagnosed with a major mental illness. S. had been in analysis previously, but her analyst had since died. For reasons of confidentiality—her husband was well known in the mental health community—she didn't want to be seen locally. After a brief consultation, we decided that her symptoms had been persistent and debilitating enough to require intensive help. Blaming herself for her daughter's illness but determined not to burden her with her own distress, S. was strongly motivated to reenter analysis. We agreed to meet for a five-times-a-week analysis over the phone.

S.'s first analysis had helped her identify that her mother's suicide when she was four years old, her parents' sadomasochistic relating while her mother was alive, the birth of her two younger siblings, and the elaboration of these realities and experiences in her own mind had contributed to her painful emotional states and a pervasive sense of insecurity about her worth and lovability. Because of the help that she received, S. had lived with less discontent after ending her analysis 15 years earlier and until her daughter's diagnosis.

During the termination phase of our work six years later, as we reflected on what we had accomplished, S. suggested that she and I hadn't discovered much that was new to her in terms of historical events in her early life. Yet she observed that our collaboration had afforded her a deeper, fuller emotional appreciation of how her mother's suicide disrupted her sense of herself as safe, stable, and good and profoundly affected her development and relationships thereafter. Despite the physical distance, by attending to what emerged in her mind and our interactions within each session, we were able to move emotionally close to the origins and meanings of her deep feelings of guilt and self-recriminations, her fear of her hostility and her love, her pervasive but unconscious sense of omnipotence and grandiosity, and her shame for her vulnerability, longings, and suffering.

In time, we understood that her daughter's illness had reawakened the loss of her mother, activating a depth of anguish S. didn't know existed within her and leading her to call me. At that time, I had some psychotherapy experience working teleanalytically but had never begun an analysis remotely. Yet, given her concerns about confidentiality, referring her for in-office psychoanalysis was not an option. Responding to her desolation and my own undefined but distinct sense that working together could help her, I offered her analysis. Although, of course, it's not possible to know what she and I could have accomplished if we'd met in person, her resulting relief from depression, increased capacity to self-regulate and self-analyze, and expanded ability to be present to herself and relate to others led us to conclude that this had been an effort worth undertaking.

Discussion

I came of age analytically when in-person analysis and supervision were the norm. I remember driving an hour each way once a week to meet with one of my supervisors, and forty-five minutes each way a different day to see a second supervisor. I imagined but never seriously considered speaking on the phone for supervision. It was just not done. At present, analyzing, supervising, and consulting teleanalytically with occasional in-person meetings are regular facets of my practice.

I approached teleanalysis with some apprehension,[10] rooted in part in the presumption that what teleanalysis offered was inevitably second best. In retrospect, I think this belief rested partly on my underappreciating the importance of the analyst's emotional engagement and overestimating the importance of physical presence.[11] I was confusing distance analysis with distant analysis. I think my apprehension was also related to insecurity stemming from my lack of training and experience doing teleanalysis. I'll address these issues briefly later.

What I've learned from working teleanalytically has surprised me and led me to revise earlier preconceptions. My work with M., P., and S. has contributed to my understanding that, in certain circumstances, teleanalysis is not just the only opportunity for analysis—and not offering it is a resistance to engaging intensively with a patient—but can offer results indistinguishable from those of in-office analysis.

Over the years, I've presented process material from teleanalytic sessions to study groups of senior analysts and to senior consultants. Time and again I was surprised to find that the "telematerial" was indistinguishable from in-room process to my colleagues[12] unless I specifically told them, or it was explicitly contained in the process—when, for example, the patient and I were addressing the teleanalytic frame. I'm not suggesting that there are no differences. There are. However, if one uses an analytic lens to consider reactions to the frame, the differences provide not liabilities but rich sources of meaning that can add to the understanding of the patient's psychology. For example, as seen with M., physical distance and physical presence were used both defensively and adaptively. He defensively and unconsciously designated the in-room sessions as the "close" and scary sessions and the teleanalytic sessions as the safer retreats. Identifying and speaking to the defensive uses of these designations—that is, not taking them at face value—allowed for their analytic consideration. The analyst's and patient's attention to the *meanings* of the setting constitute an analysis, not the setting itself.

My experience with P. provides further confirmation. In anticipating a move and major separation while knowing we would still be working together, P. felt contained enough and at the same time activated enough that he experienced unprocessed early separation trauma with unprecedented intensity. Only then did we have the chance to appreciate in an experience-near way the full force of his trauma. Although his decision to move contained elements of resistance to deepening the analysis, it also contained his attempt to rework his earlier trauma. Our consistent, close attention to his thoughts and feelings about the move and about working teleanalytically, before and after he moved, allowed us to analyze the passive-into-active enactment of his early separations and resulted in a deepening of the analysis.[13]

In teleanalysis I stay as close to an analytic frame as possible. I recommend that patients attend five times weekly, use a couch, and speak as freely as they can. When videoconferencing, I greet and say good-bye to patients face to face. After greeting me, patients lie on their couch with the computer placed in the position I would assume if I were in the room with them and in a way that I can see their whole body and they can turn around and see me if they wish. Patients begin and end sessions by initiating and ending calls, similar to their entering and leaving my office. I expect payment at the same time and charge for missed sessions in the same way as with the in-office setting. I ask that patients tell me in advance if they plan to meet with me in a location other than what is usual for us. Similarly, when on a few occasions I've needed to meet with a patient from my home office, I informed her and attended to her conscious and unconscious reactions to my announcement of this change of location. I don't accept meeting arrangements that are distracting to me and interfere with my ability to analyze, such as the patient's driving or being at a noisy place where we can't hear each other clearly.

Since my analytic training didn't include instruction or supervision in teleanalysis, and certainly not a training teleanalysis, I found it very useful to consult with and read the work of analysts who practice teleanalysis. Reading the literature has sensitized me to ways I've normalized technological difficulties and avoided acknowledging them. Essig's and Russell's writings alerted me to analysts' tendency to deny the differences, difficulties, and losses that inhere in meeting online and try to ignore, compensate for, or accommodate them. In retrospect, these attempts to protect myself and my patients from difficult feelings created an atmosphere of distance and falseness. Addressing with patients the painful realities of teleanalytic interruptions and malfunctions, or their frustrated yearnings to smell me or lie on my couch, resulted in a stronger sense of emotional connection. As I've felt more confident in the usefulness of teleanalysis and my capacity to practice it, I've become better able to acknowledge and speak to patients' perceptions of differences and limitations in telesessions and their meanings.

In addition to strong motivation and commitment from analyst and patient, I can identify a few other elements that were consequential in teleanalytic work with M., P., and S.: rigorously establishing and holding an internal and external analytic frame; periodic in-office visits; recognizing my patients' and my thoughts and feelings about the teleanalytic and in-office settings and seeking to understand their meanings as well as their use as resistance;[14] and the energetic analytic exploration of resistance and transference-countertransference enactments and fantasies. I've found that frequency, continuity, and safety, and a focus on explicating transferential and countertransferential experiences and enactments determine the usefulness of a treatment, whether it takes place in the office or teleanalytically.

Most analysts would agree that establishing and maintaining an analytic frame requires ongoing emotional effort and resolve. In my work and in supervising others, I've found that analysts, including myself, can countertransferentially slide into underappreciating the role that the analytic frame of mind and setting plays in supporting a lively, effective analytic engagement and process (Ehrlich 2010). As important as paying analytic attention to the frame is for in-office analysis, I've found it to be even more so in teleanalysis. As we saw in Russell's examples, the inherent flexibility of the teleanalytic setting provides fertile ground for unexamined enactments that undermine analytic work.

Is the heightened anxiety reported by analysts about maintaining the connection with their patients catalyzed by physical distance in teleanalysis, or is it just more obvious? My experience leads me to conclude that the physical distance inherent in teleanalysis poignantly evokes patients' and analysts' painful early experiences of emotional distance, separations, and losses and therefore strong resistances.[15] In working teleanalytically, establishing an explicitly stated, dependable frame, and regarding variations in the frame as meaningful, helped contain my patients' and my own anxieties about distance, loss, and separation enough for us to understand their meanings. I believe it also conveyed the seriousness of my commitment to them and my confidence in the value of our analytic collaboration, which in turn helped them prioritize it.

How do analysts' identity and conviction affect our capacity to do teleanalysis? As with in-office analysis, I've found that analysts' confidence in the teleanalysis is a function of many variables, including our confidence in analysis in general, prior experiences with teleanalysis, facility with technology, and a capacity to address difficult frame issues. Given that our confidence depends in large measure on having benefited from personal analysis, does the fact that most analysts haven't benefited from teleanalysis as patients preclude us having the same level of conviction about its therapeutic value as we have regarding in-office analysis? Although our confidence in our capacity to be helpful can transfer to teleanalysis, I've found that having had a helpful teleanalytic experience as a patient or supervisee adds considerably to our conviction about its usefulness and feasibility. Even though I practiced teleanalysis before having my own analytic experience with teleanalysis, since then I have a more visceral conviction regarding its value and helpfulness.

Concluding remarks

Asking whether teleanalysis is useful is not the most pertinent question. More germane is the question: Are analyst and patient able and willing to do the emotional work necessary to create a good-enough analytic frame and work analytically while meeting teleanalytically? I've argued here that teleanalysis, if practiced with an analytic frame of mind and setting, doesn't constitute a move away from analysis, as some maintain. Instead, it can offer additional rich opportunities for patients to receive analytic help and for analysts to practice analysis. Teleanalysis will not destroy analysis if analysts practice *analysis* within the teleanalytic setting.[16]

In contrast to critics of teleanalysis, I've found that the physical distance and occasional technological difficulties don't limit or preclude useful analysis as long as analysts pay disciplined, thoughtful attention to establishing and maintaining an external and internal analytic setting conducive to analysis; identify, contain, and analyze our and our patients' responses to the setting, including anxieties about meeting at a distance and experiencing technological disruption; arrange to meet with patients periodically in person; and want to practice teleanalysis.

Comparing analytic process from in-office analysis and teleanalysis, I've found that analysts' emotional engagement and working affectively close to patients is more consequential than physical distance. Recognizing how analyst and patient use physical distance to create emotional distance provides valuable analytic information. When considered analytically, the feelings and thoughts distance evokes are not insurmountable obstacles. On the contrary, they help deepen an analysis. In addition, the juxtaposition of the experiences of the in-person and the "tele" settings provide increased, unique opportunities for analysis because they activate different transference-countertransference wishes, fears, and states of mind.

In earlier work (Ehrlich 2004, 2010) I identified different manifestations of the analyst's reluctance to engage in analysis, including taking at face value patients' scheduling conflicts and their apparent lack of interest in analysis. Adding to the list, I believe that focusing on physical distance or potential technical difficulties when teleanalysis is the only way a patient can have or continue to have an analytic experience can be another manifestation of the analyst's reluctance to engage in analysis. In my direct and supervisory experience with teleanalysis, I've found that not offering teleanalysis, or practicing it sloppily by not adhering to a consistent and reliable internal and external analytic frame, often reflects manifestations of additional, more contemporary versions of the analyst's reluctance.

I don't believe that any patient/analyst pair can or should engage in teleanalysis. When proposed by patient or analyst primarily as a matter of convenience, I would suggest it constitutes a move away from inconvenient emotional truths that need to be identified and understood. Also, some patients and analysts, for various internal or external reasons, can't work well within the teleanalytic setting.[17] For example, those of us who don't believe the teleanalytic setting is effective won't engage in it with the same determination and conviction they would in the in-office setting and consequently won't get good results.

Analysts who practice teleanalysis would benefit from clinical accounts addressing a number of questions: Under what conditions is teleanalysis most effective? When should distance analysis be offered? What should the training for it be? What are some technical considerations specific to distance analysis? When is accepting the patient's request to meet remotely a rationalized resistance on the analyst's part, and when is it a necessary adaptation that allows patients to receive the intensive help they need and otherwise would not receive?

Notes

1 To make the reading of this chapter less laborious, I will be referring to both telephone sessions and online videoconferencing as *teleanalysis*.
2 "We, like most analysts, have come across situations that have prevented the regular analytic process from developing (or continuing) within 4–5 analytic sessions implying the couch and a regular frame, such as: a woman patient, aged over 65, travelling to Rome from an island and only able to have occasional vis-à-vis sessions; lengthy letters during a long absence due to work abroad; pilots or stewards

who can only have extemporaneous sessions according to flight schedules; actors filming or on stage far from the analytical venue for long periods at a time; accidents requiring patients' long hospitalization" (Argentieri and Mehler 2003, p. 18).

3 Zalusky (1998) demonstrated in her account that she paid careful attention to the setting, interpreted in the transference, and identified and analyzed her countertransferences and both hers and the patient's resistances to deepening the analysis.

4 Essig (2015) defines screen relation as "a technologically mediated simulation of a traditional physically co-present relationship experience" (p. 685).

5 Scharff (2012) also observes the analyst's anxiety in teleanalysis: "Therapeutic regression occurs in analysis by telephone and on the Internet as it does in traditional analysis. However, it must be admitted that this is more anxiety-provoking for the analyst who may experience increased anxiety about doing harm and being censured" (p. 84).

6 On the contrary, the literature suggests that historically analysts have neglected to examine how the patient's and analyst's bodies affect analytic process. In recent years, from different theoretical traditions and with different emphases, Balsam (2011, 2013, 2015), Balsam and Harris (2012), Lemma (2014a, 2014b, 2014c; Lemma and Caparrotta 2014), and Sletvold (2011, 2012, 2014, 2016) have highlighted the clinical usefulness of focusing on the patient's and/or the analyst's body and have called for analysts to attend to and make use of bodily experiences and representations.

7 Loewald (1975) speaks to language's capacity to serve as action: "Language is not merely a means of reporting action, it is itself action; narrative has a dramatic potential of its own … One might express this by saying that we take the patient less and less as speaking merely *about* himself, about his experiences and memories, and more and more as symbolizing action in speech, as speaking from the depth of his memories, which regain life and poignancy by the impetus and urgency of re-experience in the present of the analytic situation" (pp. 293–294).

8 The Boston Change Process Study Group (2002) speak to this: "If two animals are put in the same space, a complicated process of regulating the physical distance, of moving towards and away from one another, will occur … With humans, this process is largely mentalized, meaning that the exploration, regulation and establishing of proper contours, boundaries and temporal structures to the interaction will occur mainly in the intersubjective rather than in the physical space. But it occurs nonetheless. It is a process of trying to get closer, or further away, or to avoid something happening, or to get something to happen, or to increase or decrease the state of arousal, or to shift the affective state, in relation to the other. These might be called 'mentalized kinesics'. It is on the basis of such back and forth movement that we arrive at the feeling of being 'in sync' with another or are left with the feeling that the other is a million miles away … This negotiation occurs in the implicit domain of interaction, even though in the analytic situation it would be mediated through verbal exchange" (p. 1053).

9 Scharff (2012) also reports on how the teleanalytic frame affected the emergence and working through of sexual trauma.

10 Lindon (1998) finds that "the analyst initially seems more ill at ease than the patient" (p. 526). He further reports that the anxiety related to telephone analysis dissipates with more experience and over time. I agree with the many authors who suggest that the analyst's comfort with the medium determines in part the ease with which she can listen and intervene. Beginning on the Internet for an analyst is anxiety-producing in the same way as being behind the couch for the first time, whether she knows it consciously or not.

11 Lemma and Caparrotta (2014) agree that although Skype and telephone analysis affect each member of the analytic couple and bring "an additional dimension to the therapeutic relationship that requires analysis, the analyst doing teleanalysis is no different from an analyst who works with his patient in the actual consulting room" (p. 14).
12 Lindon (1988) reports that he, his patient, and his study group couldn't distinguish between in-person and telephone sessions in terms of the quality of the therapeutic rapport or the dyad's ability to do analytic work. Similarly, Neumann (2013) suggests that process from telesessions and in-office sessions couldn't be distinguished by reviewers.
13 I agree with Migone (2013), who thinks that what's most important in deciding whether to begin an analysis in any setting, including online, are the patient's treatment needs, his or her ego function, and the transferential and counter-transferential meaning of the setting for patient and analyst. He offers the useful reminder that to achieve a "truly psychoanalytic way of thinking," an analyst must strive to hold in mind the meaning of the choice of setting, not only at the beginning but throughout the analysis, so that it can remain available for ongoing understanding (p. 293).
14 For example, when a patient has consciously or unconsciously decided that the telesessions are the "safe" sessions while the in-office sessions can be dangerous, or that the in-office sessions are real while the telesessions are the pretend sessions.
15 Lindon (1998) reports feeling deprived by the patient's physical absence. I, too, have found that separation and physical distance evoke poignant memories and experiences like those evoked by the analyst's vacations or other analytic separations or disruptions.
16 I concur with Migone (2013), who contends that neither in-room nor virtual presence is analytically inferior or superior to the other. He suggests that they constitute two different kinds of experience and that each experience, when explored analytically, yields valuable information with meanings specific to each individual patient.
17 For indications and counterindications, see discussions provided by Zalusky (2005), Eckardt (2011), and Scharff (2012).

References

Abbasi, A. (2016). Beyond the miles, memories, and usual modes of functioning: How we change as we help our patients change. Clinical plenary address, American Psychoanalytic Association, Chicago, June 18.
Argentieri, S. & Mehler, J.A. (2003). Telephone 'analysis': 'Hello, who's speaking?' *Insight*, 12: 17–19.
Balsam, R. (2011). *Women's bodies in psychoanalysis*. New York: Routledge.
Balsam, R. (2013). (Re)membering the female body in psychoanalysis: Childbirth. *Journal of the American Psychoanalytic Association*, 61: 447–470.
Balsam, R. (2015). Eyes, ears, lips, fingertips, secrets: Dora, psychoanalysis, and the body. *Psychoanalytic Review*, 102: 33–58.
Balsam, R. & Harris, A. (2012). Maternal embodiment: A conversation between Rosemary Balsam and Adrienne Harris. *Studies in Gender & Sexuality*, 13: 33–52.
Bassen, C.R. (2007). Telephone analysis. *Journal of the American Psychoanalytic Association*, 55: 1033–1041.

Bayles, M. (2012). Is physical proximity essential to the psychoanalytic process? An exploration through the lens of Skype. *Psychoanalytic Dialogues*, 22: 569–585.

Boston Change Process Study Group (2002). Explicating the implicit: The local level and the microprocess of change in the analytic situation. *International Journal of Psychoanalysis*, 83: 1051–1062.

Boston Change Process Study Group (2008). Forms of relational meaning: Issues in the relations between the implicit and reflective-verbal domains. *Psychoanalytic Dialogues*, 18: 125–148.

Brainsky, S. (2003). Adapting to, or idealizing, technology? *Insight*, 12: 22–24.

Brown, M.W. (1942). *The Runaway Bunny*. New York: Harper & Row.

Buzsáki, G. & Moser, E.I. (2013). Memory, navigation and theta rhythm in the hippocampal–entorhinal system. *Nature Neuroscience*, 16: 130–138.

Carlino, R. (2011). *Distance Psychoanalysis*. London: Karnac Books.

Clayton, N.S., Salwiczek, L.H., & Dickinson, A. (2007). Episodic memory. *Current Biology*, 17: 189–191.

Eckardt, M.H. (2011). The use of the telephone to extend our therapeutic availability. *Journal of the American Academy of Psychoanalysis & Dynamic Psychiatry*, 39: 151–153.

Ehrlich, L.T. (2004). The analyst's reluctance to begin a new analysis. *Journal of the American Psychoanalytic Association*, 52: 1075–1093.

Ehrlich, L.T. (2010). The analyst's ambivalence about continuing and deepening an analysis. *Journal of the American Psychoanalytic Association*, 58: 515–532.

Ehrlich, L.T. (2013). Analysis begins in the analyst's mind: Conceptual and technical considerations on recommending analysis. *Journal of the American Psychoanalytic Association*, 61: 1077–1107.

Essig, T. (2015). The gains and losses of screen relations: A clinical approach to simulation entrapment and simulation avoidance in a case of excessive Internet pornography use. *Contemporary Psychoanalysis*, 51: 680–703.

Essig, T. & Russell, G.I. (2017). A note from the guest editors. *Psychoanalytic Perspectives*, 14: 131–137.

Fishkin, R., Fishkin, L., Leli, U., Katz, B., & Snyder, E. (2011). Psychodynamic treatment, training, and supervision using Internet-based technologies. *Journal of the American Academy of Psychoanalysis & Dynamic Psychiatry*, 39: 155–168.

Hanly, C. (2007). Case material from a telephone analysis. In *Psychoanalysis Online 2: Impact of Technology on Development, Training, and Therapy*, ed. J.S. Scharff. London: Karnac Books, 2015, pp. 133–137.

Leffert, M. (2003). Analysis and psychotherapy by telephone: Twenty years of clinical experience. *Journal of the American Psychoanalytic Association*, 51: 101–130.

Lemma, A. (2014a). The body of the analyst and the analytic setting: Reflection on the embodied setting and the symbiotic transference. *International Journal of Psychoanalysis*, 95: 225–244.

Lemma, A. (2014b). *Minding the Body: The Body in Psychoanalysis and Beyond*. New York: Routledge.

Lemma, A. (2014c). Off the couch, into the toilet: Exploring the psychic uses of the analyst's toilet. *Journal of the American Psychoanalytic Association*, 62: 35–56.

Lemma, A. (2015). Psychoanalysis in times of technoculture: Some reflections on the fate of the body in virtual space. *International Journal of Psychoanalysis*, 96: 569–582.

Lemma, A. & Caparrotta, L., eds. (2014). *Psychoanalysis in the Technoculture Era.* New York: Routledge.

Lindon, J.A. (1988). Psychoanalysis by telephone. *Bulletin of the Menninger Clinic*, 52: 521–528.

Litowitz, B.E. (2012). Psychoanalysis and the Internet: Postscript. *Psychoanalytic Inquiry*, 32: 506–512.

Loewald, H.W. (1975). Psychoanalysis as an art and the fantasy character of the psychoanalytic situation. *Journal of the American Psychoanalytic Association*, 23: 277–299.

Manosevitz, M. (2006). Supervision by telephone. *Psychoanalytic Psychology*, 23: 579–582.

Merchant, J. (2016). The use of Skype in analysis and training: A research and literature review. *Journal of Analytical Psychology*, 61: 309–328.

Migone, P. (2013). Psychoanalysis on the Internet: A discussion of its theoretical implications for both online and offline therapeutic technique. *Psychoanalytic Psychology*, 30: 281–299.

Mirkin, M. (2011). Telephone analysis: Compromised treatment or an interesting opportunity? *Psychoanalytic Quarterly*, 80: 643–670.

Moser, E.I. & Moser, M.B. (2014). Mapping your every move. *Cerebrum: The Dana Forum on Brain Science*, 4: 1–10.

Neumann, D. (2013). The frame for psychoanalysis in cyberspace. In *Psychoanalysis Online: Mental Health, Teletherapy, and Training*, ed. Scharff, J.S. London: Karnac Books, pp. 171–182.

Richards, A.K. (2001). Talking cure in the 21st century: Telephone psychoanalysis. *Psychoanalytic Psychology*, 18: 388–391.

Robertiello, R.C. (1972). Telephone sessions. *Psychoanalytic Review*, 59: 633–634.

Russell, G.I. (2015). *Screen Relations: The Limits of Computer-Mediated Psychoanalysis and Psychotherapy.* London: Karnac Books.

Scharff, J.S. (2010). Telephone analysis. *International Journal of Psychoanalysis*, 91: 989–992.

Scharff, J.S. (2012). Clinical issues in analyses over the telephone and the Internet. *International Journal of Psychoanalysis*, 93: 81–95.

Scharff, J.S. (2013a). *Psychoanalysis Online: Mental Health, Teletherapy, and Training.* London: Karnac Books.

Scharff, J.S. (2013b). Technology-assisted psychoanalysis. *Journal of the American Psychoanalytic Association*, 61: 491–509.

Scharff, J.S., ed. (2015). *Psychoanalysis Online 2: Impact of Technology on Development, Training, and Therapy.* London: Karnac Books.

Schore, A.N. (2005). A neuropsychoanalytic viewpoint: Commentary on paper by Steven H. Knoblauch. *Psychoanalytic Dialogues*, 15: 829–854.

Schore, A.N. (2011). The right brain implicit self lies at the core of psychoanalysis. *Psychoanalytic Dialogues*, 21: 75–100.

Sletvold, J. (2011). "The reading of emotional expression": Wilhelm Reich and the history of embodied analysis. *Psychoanalytic Dialogues*, 21: 453–467.

Sletvold, J. (2012). Training analysts to work with unconscious embodied expressions: Theoretical underpinnings and practical guidelines. *Psychoanalytic Dialogues*, 22: 410–429.

Sletvold, J. (2014). *The Embodied Analyst: From Freud and Reich to Relationality.* London: Routledge.

Sletvold, J. (2016). The analyst's body: A relational perspective from the body. *Psychoanalytic Perspectives*, 13: 186–200.

Spiro, R.H. & Devenis, L.E. (2000). Enhancement in the therapeutic process. In *Use of the Telephone in Psychotherapy*, ed. Aronson, J.K. Northvale, NJ: Aronson, pp. 45–79.

Tao, L. (2015). Teleanalysis: Problems, limitation and opportunities. In *Psychoanalysis Online 2: Impact of Technology on Development, Training, and Therapy*, ed. Scharff, J.S. London: Karnac Books, pp. 105–120.

Turkle, S. (2015). *Reclaiming Conversation: The Power of Talk in a Digital Age*. New York: Penguin.

Turkle, S., Essig, T., & Russell, G.I. (2017). Afterword: Reclaiming psychoanalysis: Sherry Turkle in conversation with the Editors. *Psychoanalytic Perspectives*, 14: 237–248.

Winnicott, D.W. (1969). The use of an object. *International Journal of Psychoanalysis*, 50: 711–716.

Wooldridge, T. (2017). Now I see you, now I don't: Screen services, short stature, and the fear of being seen. *Psychoanalytic Perspectives*, 14: 193–205.

Zalusky, S. (1998). Telephone analysis: Out of sight, but not out of mind. *Journal of the American Psychoanalytic Association*, 46: 1221–1242.

Zalusky, S. (2005). Telephone, psychotherapy and the 21st century. In *Dimensions of Psychotherapy, Dimensions of Experience: Time, Space, Number and State of Mind*, ed. Stadter, M. & Scharff, D.E. London: Routledge, pp. 105–114.

Part Three

Sustaining the Capacity to Listen and Intervene Analytically

Chapter 6

Maintaining an analytic mind and the confidence and desire to practice analysis

As I discussed in an earlier chapter, surveys on psychoanalytic practice reveal that many analysts practice little or no analysis after they graduate. Once they terminate with their control cases, they begin few or no new analytic cases (Cherry et al. 2004; Kaplan et al. 2009; Schneider et al. 2014). This is so, despite having undergone a lengthy, demanding training program. These findings suggest that as difficult as it is to learn to function as an analyst, it's even harder to sustain this capacity past graduation.

Given this stark reality, I think it's critical for our profession to find answers to the following questions: What allows some analysts to sustain the confidence, interest, and determination to offer and practice analysis given the internal and external challenges of practicing analytically in today's fast-paced, evidence-based world? What permits us to sustain belief in the healing power of analysis after graduation when we're no longer bolstered by the confidence of our own analysts and supervisors and have had inevitable disappointing experiences in our own analyses and in practicing analysis?

In this chapter, I aim to articulate my experience of what interferes with and what sustains me in functioning as an analyst and also what I've witnessed to be sustaining to colleagues to whom I provide consultation and colleagues with whom I collaborate closely in study groups and other professional activities. Striving for clarity, I divide my observations into distinct categories although, of course, in practice there is overlap.

(I) The nature of the analyst's beliefs about practicing psychoanalysis and their interfering and facilitating impact

    (A) Beliefs about the quality of the analyst's effort
    (B) Beliefs about the nature of the analyst's commitment to analysis
    (C) Beliefs about the extent of the analyst's capacity to practice without help
    (D) Beliefs about the quality of the analyst's confidence
    (E) Beliefs about the results of analysis

(II)   The nature of the analyst's engagement and its interfering and facilitating impact

    (A)   Analytic frequency
    (B)   Transference-countertransference
    (C)   Tensions and paradoxes

I The nature of the analyst's beliefs about practicing psychoanalysis and their interfering and facilitating impact

I'll discuss how analysts' beliefs about what's required to practice analysis interfere with or facilitate their capacity to offer and practice psychoanalysis.

A Beliefs about the quality of the analyst's effort

Interfering: the belief that practicing analysis can be effortless

I'll begin with an example. An early career analyst consulted with me about his practice. He was interested in doing more analysis but had been unable to begin a new case since graduation. He told me that he was receiving referrals for treatment, identifying patients for analysis, and even recommending analysis to them. He sought supervision to explore what might be getting in the way of facilitating beginnings. Together we looked at the process of his last consultation for possible answers. It turned out that his most recent prospective patient had agreed to his recommendation for analysis and had scheduled four meetings per week. However, when he returned for what was to be his first analytic session, he announced that, because of financial concerns, he could only come twice. When the analyst suggested they further discuss the patient's thoughts about beginning analysis, the patient offered compelling facts to argue that the reality of his financial circumstances necessitated a lower frequency and that there was nothing more to discuss. Thwarted, the analyst agreed to the patient's proposal and they had been meeting at that frequency ever since.

Among the several factors we discussed that contributed to this couple's retreat from analysis was the analyst's taking the patient's concerns about cost at face value, thus missing the opportunity to explore the possible emotional reasons for that withdrawal—for example, his fears about the high *emotional* cost of analysis. Contributing to the analyst's inhibition was his misinterpreting the patient's retreat as an indication that the analyst wasn't capable enough. The analyst shared with me that he expected that, once he made recommendations and patients agreed, analysis should proceed as smoothly, as he imagined beginnings unfolded for successful analysts with lively analytic practices. When beginnings didn't go as smoothly as his idealized expectation, he felt clumsy, amateurish, and discouraged. Denigrating himself, he did not consider patients' reactions as a meaningful communication and part of engaging in a deeper exploration.

As seen in the above example, the nature of analysts' expectations about practicing analysis and their own functioning can weaken or support their analytic identity and practice. I've observed in myself and in colleagues that, during training and early in one's career, most analysts rely on some idealization to maintain their confidence in the usefulness of analysis and be inspired to become better skilled in its practice. Early on in their careers and still unsure about their capacity to help, beginning analysts idealize the analytic role and analysis as a defense against the narcissistic vulnerability inherent in analytic practicing. Although experienced analysts tend to idealize less and are more likely to recognize that tendency, during challenging times in the analytic relationship, they also resort to idealization. When persistent, unidentified, and unexamined, analysts' idealization of analysts and analysis gets in the way of their continued analytic development and practice.

In providing tips for aspiring Op-Ed NY Times' writers, Bret Stephens offers: "If you find writing easy, you're doing it wrong."[1] Like writing, practicing psychoanalysis is hard. Yet, I have observed that many graduate analysts, including myself at times, imagine that it can or should be easy. In my own work and in consulting with analysts who want to practice more analysis, I have experienced and witnessed analysts' discouragement and, for some, even a sense of futility when our belief that initiating or practicing analysis should be easy clashes with realities in the consulting room.

When we expect practicing analysis to be easy, we are likely to see analytic difficulties as reflecting *our* shortcomings, as opposed to an inherent challenge for *all* analysts. Consequently, we experience ordinary analytic challenges—such as negative transferences, patients' temporary emotional regressions, and acting out around the frame—as extraordinary and a negative reflection on our ability or talent. Similarly, we interpret our negative feelings about analysis or about a specific patient as evidence of their inadequacy or unsuitability. When we expect analysis to be easy, we are unable to view our patients' and our own analytic difficulties as meaningful and use them to further the analysis. I've observed that when analysts feel discouraged, we move away from analysis by practicing it less, or feeling defeated, or proceed in practicing but go through the motions.

Facilitating: expecting to exert ongoing emotional effort while practicing analytically is a prerequisite to understanding patients' suffering

Lamott, a successful writer, understands well the effort required to gain access to emotional truth. She writes:

> It is a fantasy to think that successful writers do not have these bored, defeated hours, these hours of deep insecurity when one feels as small and jumpy as a water bug. They do. But they also often feel a great sense of amazement that they get to write, and they know that this is what they want to do for the rest of their lives.
>
> (Lamott 1995, p. 48)

Writing, Lamott (1995) tells us, requires reckoning with oneself, one's amorphous and familiar emotional demons—insecurities, self-loathing, sadness, shame—and giving them a new form. Lamott's description of the experience of the process of writing resonates with me, not only as a writer but also as an analyst and supervisor. As Lamott observes about writers, I've found that even when analysts have the conscious intentions and the requisite technical skills, practicing psychoanalysis entails inevitable times of inner struggle. In psychoanalysis as in writing, it's through this struggle that something authentic and meaningful materializes, and the analyst—like the writer—experiences the wonder of having discovered something true about the patient and herself.

From my experience and in observing other analysts, I've found that recognizing and working on our ability to tolerate and make use of our deepest feelings—our affect tolerance—is key to sustaining oneself as an analyst. Our deepest feelings are "the raw clay that you pull out of the river," (p. 11) as Lamott calls it, that we can shape creatively. Analysts' capacity to access and use their feelings to cognitively and viscerally understand their patients constitutes a hard-earned, continuously fluctuating capacity (I will elaborate on this later in the chapter). Practicing analysis well enough necessitates not backing away from identifying and reflecting on difficult feelings, our patients' and our own.

Despite our experiences as graduate analysts, I don't think we communicate enough to candidates or with each other that training doesn't guarantee a clinician will become capable of initiating and practicing analysis after graduation. We fail to emphasize that resistance to one's inner life and engaging intimately with another is not only patients' domain. Nor do we divulge often enough that graduate analysts—even the most committed and passionate—struggle with their fears of feeling vulnerable and of connecting intimately with their patients. We rarely convey the ongoing effort, courage, and determination analysts must exert to help patients with their deepest suffering and conflicts.

B Beliefs about the nature of the analyst's commitment to analysis

Interfering: the belief that analysis can be practiced without ambivalence

I've observed that analysts' expectation of practicing without ambivalence and therefore overlooking or not fully appreciating their reluctance represents another important and related factor that undermines analysts' capacity to practice analytically. As I've written elsewhere (Ehrlich 2004, 2010, 2013, 2019) analysts' reluctance is expected, unavoidable, and often preconscious or unconscious.

The problem isn't analysts' reluctance per se. Reluctance is intrinsic to doing analytic work. Difficulties arise when analysts don't anticipate having fears and subsequently fail to recognize their manifestations. When we don't recognize signals of our reluctance, we don't have the chance to use them analytically. Instead, we become likely to accept patients' and our own reservations about analysis at face value.

I've observed that regardless of how reasonable analysts' reservations appear in relation to beginning or deepening an analysis, they inevitably also signal countertransferential reluctance. As seen in the earlier example and other examples throughout this book, money, time, other obligations, and analyzability are among the many external impediments that analysts evoke for not recommending or practicing analysis.

Facilitating: anticipating, tolerating, and analyzing the analyst's ambivalence

For me, one of the greatest aids in being able to build an analytic practice was that the Institute's green light was not enough to feel that I could continue to practice analysis post graduation. I needed to find inner authority and conviction to initiate analysis and continue to practice analytically. Considering my worries about not being able to practice once I graduated as a signal, in part, of preconscious fears of offering/engaging in analysis was an important first step toward my finding the confidence to recommend analysis post-graduation. Paradoxically, my first step toward self-authorization was identifying my doubts about my helpfulness, my fears about intense engagement, and my unconscious worry that patients would agree to be in analysis with me.

As a beginning analyst, I found it extremely useful to consider that as eager as I was to practice analysis, I was also scared of it. I learned that if I paid attention to signs of my reluctance in relation to a patient, I could understand something meaningful about what scared me about working with that patient. More aware of my fears, I was less likely to enact them by staying away from patients. Knowing *my* fears, I could identify and work better with my patients' fears and desires and help them increase their treatment involvement and deepen their engagement.

Despite what many analysts used to believe, and some still believe, managing ambivalence is not reserved for beginners and does not signal inadequacy or emotional weakness. On the contrary, managing reluctance about analysis constitutes an essential component of effective psychoanalytic functioning. I've observed that regardless of level of experience, skill, or talent, if an analyst is engaged enough and not too defended, she must contend with insecurity, pessimism, and frustration. Recognizing that this ever-present challenge is a way of life for analysts has added to my confidence and sense of determination to keep meeting that challenge.

C Beliefs about the extent of the analyst's capacity to practice without help

> The psychoanalytic method entails anxieties of insecurity, of perceptual conflicts, of aporia, invasion, of the threat of being confused and of not being able to tolerate one's incompetence in the face of the real psychic structure of the analysand. These are anxieties about the loss of one's therapeutic omnipotence.
>
> (Danckwardt 2011, p. 21)

Interfering: the idea that analysis can be practiced self-sufficiently

We internalize an expectation during training that a well-analyzed, adequately trained analyst should be able to practice self-sufficiently. This belief gets in the way of seeking ongoing routine help and extra consultation when needed. Analysts' notions that wanting consultation is a sign of inadequacy or incomplete analysis doesn't reflect what we know about the complexity of the human mind and the analyst's ongoing countertransferences (I will elaborate on this notion in the next chapter on consultation).

I've had the experience more than once with well-meaning consultants that they were incredulous when I called asking for help. They appeared surprised and asked me to tell them why exactly I was calling and, after I shared with them what was troubling me, made comments like "you already knew this" or "I didn't tell you anything you didn't know," conveying that they did not view consultation as an ordinary part of professional practice but as a sign of insecurity or inability.

Facilitating: identifying and accepting the analyst's fundamental need for ongoing help

SUSTAINING ONESELF THOUGH CONSULTATION, PEER SUPPORT, AND CONTINUING EDUCATION

Contrary to what I wanted to believe earlier in my career, but in keeping with what we know about the human mind, the capacity to practice analysis is dynamic. Despite having developed a baseline of receptivity, I vary in my capacity to listen, make use of what I hear, and participate analytically. I've seen that this is true as well for analysts whose work I've listened to in some detail. As mentioned previously, one of many tensions I've found helpful to hold in mind is that regardless of seniority, experience, or skill, each of us must find and refind ourselves as analysts, moment to moment in every session from the beginning to the end of every analysis. This awareness allows me, most of the time, not to get discouraged and pull back or become complacent and accept stalemates at face value. It also allows me to seek help when I need it.

Extensive literature and our own daily experiences reveal that counter-transference is our constant companion, sometimes facilitating, sometimes obstructing. I've suggested throughout this book that our appreciation of the ongoing effects of unconscious conflict and the omnipresence of counter-transference leads to the inevitable conclusion that analysts need ongoing help to function effectively. I'll discuss consultation and my experience with peer supervision more extensively in the following chapter.

In addition to much internal work in three analyses, committed self-analysis, ongoing peer supervision, and extensive reading, I sustain myself by reading the writing of other analysts, who I imagine in their consulting rooms, earnestly working to find ways to help others with their daily suffering. I've found reading about analysts' more personal accounts of their thoughts about analysis and their own work extremely valuable. Their resolve, determination, doubts, and hope-fulness give me courage and inspiration. In addition, writing, presenting, teaching, and administrating help me maintain a place in my mind to think analytically and be receptive to my fears about and the pleasures of analytic work.

SEEKING REANALYSIS

Most contemporary analysts would agree that seeking to understand one's mind is a never-ending endeavor. As analysts it's vital that we find ways to continue to look honestly, determinedly, and with a sense of hope within our thoughts and feelings as a source of meaning and wisdom. While few analysts have written about it (Silber 1996; Meyer and Debbink 2003; Meyer 2007), my experience talking to colleagues suggests that most analysts who do a lot of analysis have had a lot of analysis.

I, too, sought reanalysis when I reached the limits of what I could make use of from self-analytic scrutiny, consultation, peer study group, and continuing education alone. My earliest experiences in analysis increased my confidence, providing me with experiential understanding of the determining power of unconscious fantasy and firsthand witnessing of the usefulness of the trans-ference as a therapeutic tool. I ended my first analysis shortly after having my first baby. My first analyst understood that my family finances—early in my husband's and my career—didn't permit me to support an analysis and also be the primary caregiver of an infant and helped me end that treatment even though we both knew I had more work to do.

When my youngest child was a preschooler, I sought my second analysis as a first step toward pursuing psychoanalytic training and because I suffered from bouts of insecurity about my capacity to be helpful to my psychotherapy patients. During that analysis, I learned about the nature of my preferred defenses and the distorting power of my transferential feelings. I observed the steadying function of the frame and discovered my conflicts about success, as well as a sense of my own resilience and strength. My gains served me well in being able to initiate and practice analysis. Yet, in retrospect, I recognize that I terminated my analysis relying on my identification with my analyst's sense of conviction about the usefulness of analysis and lacking a deeper, more genuine sense of conviction of my own.

When a series of personal losses activated profound feelings of sadness and grief that were both familiar and unknown, I realized I needed more analytic help. Through more analysis, I began to recognize I didn't have enough emotional understanding or empathy for my vulnerabilities, early losses, and the limitations of my earlier analyses. As I recognized the historical origins of my lack of empathy for myself, I became better able to appreciate more of what I had to endure and its effects on me and my relationships. My new gains allowed me to feel more compassion for the vulnerability inherent in every analytic endeavor from both sides of the couch.

D Beliefs about the quality of the analyst's confidence

Interfering: the impression that analysts who practice analysis are inherently and consistently confident

Based on my experience and disclosures from colleagues, I've concluded that many analysts imagine that analysts who practice a lot of analysis are consistently confident about its usefulness and their abilities. Such idealization impedes acceptance of our own fluctuations in confidence as ordinary manifestations of the analyst's unconscious at work and our ability to examine them as meaningful. When we take our lack of confidence in analysis, in general or in relation to a specific patient, at face value, we can't use it as a signal with meaning.

Facilitating: a) accepting fluctuations in confidence as normative and signals with meaning; b) trusting that analysis is helpful and that I can be of help

As I became more immersed in analytic practice, I recognized fluctuations in my confidence, interest, capacity, and desire to practice the profession that I loved. Early in my career, I found these hesitations and fluctuations worrisome, at times even alarming. I tried but was unable to dismiss them. Thinking I was alone in feeling this way, I privately worried that they indicated insufficiency in me and in my capacity as an analyst. As I have learned more about myself, have had more experience with analysis, and have become better acquainted with other analysts' functioning, I've come to understand that these hesitations and fluctuations are expectable, even desirable. When I function at my best, I can welcome fluctuations in confidence as signals of some aspect of myself that calls for my self-analytic attention.

I now think of analytic practice not just as the number of patients I see and the hours that I work applying analytic ideas and skills but as a way of exercising a patient-centered, empathic, disciplined, and self-reflective never-ending use of the self to connect with the truth in oneself and with the subjectivity and truth in another. Who I am as an analyst at any given moment of practice depends on how much conscious effort I exercise but also comes from a deeper place that isn't under my conscious control. There are days when I can be more emotionally present than others. Sometimes just observing my emotional distance allows me to reconnect. Other times associating to it is what brings me back. And, there are occasions when I just must endure this temporary inaccessibility and trust that eventually more emotional clarity will show up.

Although I'm attentive to variations in my confidence, I'm also aware of having a baseline of trust that analysis can be helpful and that I can help. Belief in analysis is multiply determined (Rothstein 1995; Grusky 1999; Smith 2000; Wille 2008, 2012; Gabbard and Ogden 2009; Ogden 2016.) While it comes primarily from firsthand experiences of the healing power of analysis, it's based on other sources including experiences in good-enough early relationships, evidence of our own or colleagues' good analytic work with patients, witnessing changes in loved ones who are or have been in analysis, good analytic writing, seminars, consultations, etc. It can also come from witnessing the power, even destructive, of the analytic relationship and from appreciating that analysis is a powerful tool. One's analytic identity, whether it is primarily in the service of defense or genuine emotional openness, is in great part based on the quality of one's own emotional work. Ongoing emotional work.

My trust contributes to my capacity for affect tolerance, patience, and persistence. While I believe deeply in analysis, I try to remain anchored in real experiences *and* acknowledge limitations and failures, in my work and others'. Being able to perceive and mourn the disappointments in my analyses and supervisions and analysis in general has been essential to my being able to sustain myself as an analyst and maintain analytic immersion.

E Beliefs about the results of analysis

> There is no perfect analysis; every analysis remains incomplete in some ways. Some limits may be due to the nature of the patient's difficulties, the accessibility and valence of particular issues at particular times in the patient's life, the patient's willingness and motivation to work on particular issues, and various forces from outside which may impinge on the work. Some of these limits also may be due to the analyst's skill, level of experience, unresolved issues, particular character and style, opinions and beliefs, motivation, and the particular time in the analyst's life.
>
> (Kantrowitz 1989, p. 915)

Interfering: idealized expectations about the results of analysis

I've observed that some analysts feel discouraged and turn away from practicing analysis when their analytic results don't match their idealized expectations of analytic outcomes. Accrued analytic experience has taught us that even when practiced at its best, psychoanalysis can't undo the wounds of trauma, can't make analysands anew, and can never make them fully known to themselves. Yet, I have encountered time and again, in myself and others, evidence that these unrealistic ideals persist and interfere with what can be realistically accomplished in analysis.

I've encountered many disappointed and discouraged analysts who believe they've failed when their patients haven't achieved these idealized therapeutic results. They don't treat their feelings of discouragement and failure as psychoanalytically meaningful, reflecting some important aspect of the patient's or their own psychology that needs to be fully felt, explored, and understood. Furthermore, by focusing on what patients have not achieved, some of these analysts overlook their patients' actual achievements in the form of increased resilience, self-recognition, self-integration, capacity to reflect, etc.

Here is one example. Dr. A., an experienced analyst, consulted with me about his work with a patient who he'd seen for several years and who complained about her progress and wanted to end analysis. In describing his work with this patient, Dr. A. emphasized the recent recurrence of the patient's hopelessness and self-loathing and delineated the patient's somatic complaints. Without explicitly stating it, Dr. A. communicated to me that he agreed with the patient's assessment of the analysis as a failure and her view of him as unable to help. As I listened further to Dr. A.'s account of the history of the analysis, I thought the patient's and analyst's shared hopelessness wasn't justified by the reality of the results of their efforts so far. Dr. A.'s account suggested that the patient had made much progress in her capacity to reflect on her difficulties, was better able to regulate herself, and had progressed toward some life goals that were important to her.

As we continued to work together, Dr. A. and I were able to frame his and his patient's assessment of the progress of the analysis as psychologically meaningful rather than objective fact. Thinking of his own hopelessness as a feeling rather than a fact, Dr. A. became better able to reflect on its personal and interpersonal meaning. He also became better able to contain the patient's hopelessness, listen to it without trying to defensively counter it or privately agree with it and, eventually, was able to invite the patient to be curious about its meaning. Instead of being the end, this moment in the analysis served as an entryway to a deeper exploration of the patient's, and analyst's, conflicts with intimacy, guilt, success, and fears of individuation and autonomy.

Facilitating: managing disappointment in analysis

From many observations of patients who have been harmed by their analysts, I've concluded that another important reason analysts don't sustain the desire or confidence to practice analysis is their conscious, preconscious, or unconscious disappointment in or hurt from their own analysts. Over the years and from various perspectives (as analysand, friend, colleague, analyst of second or third analyses, supervisor, consultant) I've witnessed the analytic relationship's potential for repetition, re-traumatization, dependency, and hostage taking through accounts of analyses where the analyst functioned omnipotently, manically, or exploitatively, rather than tending to the patient's and his own suffering and offering the chance for the patient to grieve and heal.

I've observed that the analytic identities of analysts or candidates who were treated by disturbed, impaired, or unethical analysts have been profoundly and at times catastrophically affected. Of course, each analyst who has been hurt by analysis doesn't respond the same way. I've seen some analysts turn away from or against analysis. For some, the analytic relationship repeated earlier damaging relationships and they no longer trust analysts' capacity to help. Another group of analysts who have been hurt by their analysis continue to practice analytically but don't seek further help for themselves. I've observed that in most cases this solution doesn't turn out well. This has led me to conclude that analysts, if we want to function competently and be helpful to our patients, can't overlook attending to our analytic wounds. If we don't get help for ourselves, we'll either be incapable of helping or will repeat our traumas with our own patients sooner or later. Finally, I have encountered analysts who, although wounded by an analysis, continued to look for aid, found it and, in turn, were better able to assist their patients.

Even under the best of analytic circumstances, when the analyst is skilled, experienced, and ethical and there is a great match between analyst and patient on important analytic variables, the nature of human beings and relationships is such that patients must contend with limitations in their analyst and their analysis. Under good-enough circumstances, patients who are analysts can be helped to process these disappointments in their analysis in a way that doesn't undermine their confidence in analysis or their desire to practice it.

Even if not subjected to boundary violations firsthand, most analysts have witnessed or heard of occasions when impaired analysts have misused patients or when long analysis led to no change, adding to patients' hopelessness and cynicism. For analysts who have had disappointing analyses themselves, such observations further activate their fears that analyzing can be hurtful and it affects their confidence and desire to practice analysis.

Many writers have observed that accounts of disappointing or failed treatments have been conspicuously absent from the analytic literature. In earlier decades, the North American emphasis on theory-driven formulations and paucity of clinical process deprived us from recognizing a more realistic view of analysis, especially its limitations. Increasingly, though, psychoanalytic literature explores more fully the challenges, disappointments, and failures of practicing analysis. (Chessick 1996; Mendelsohn 2002; Orgel 2002; Goldberg 2011; Bronstein 2015; Cooper 2015; Greenberg 2015; LaFarge 2015; Wilson 2015; Chused 2016). Although these accounts might cause discouragement, I've found that accounts of the challenges of analysis validate my experience and counter my unrealistic and perfectionistic ideals.

At the same time, I've observed that analysts, including myself, can use knowledge of analysts' transgressions defensively. During a session, when I find myself thinking of the analysis as destructive, futile, misguided, and exploitative, I've found it analytically helpful to consider these views, in part, as fantasies generated in me by my encounter with the patient—whether my concerns about exploitation and sadomasochistic engagement represent, in part, a retreat from something new and vital in the analysis.

Recently, after I returned from medical leave, a patient who spoke often about sadomasochistic struggles with everyone around him, insisted that because he wanted the freedom to attend midday monthly lectures at a local library, he needed to change one of his analytic appointments to an evening time. He argued that if I was well enough to return to work, then I should be well enough to add an evening appointment to my regular workday. After all, he said, he had been accommodating my schedule by waiting to see me while I was on leave over the past weeks. Initially, I registered only his entitlement and felt put off. My thoughts next went to a colleague who had confided in me that he and his analyst had monumental fights over his analytic schedule, which eventually led to an analytic impasse. Realizing that I feared, and wished, a similar ending, I redoubled my efforts to understand his demands more deeply. I slowly recognized that hiding behind my patient's wish to fight and control me lay his fear about my health and of losing me. I suggested that we put aside the schedule for a moment and discuss what it had been like for him for me to be gone, and not knowing how sick I was or when exactly I would return. In response, he eventually could identify more directly a new-found concern and care for me, in addition to his anger and frustration about not meeting with me.

Our ability to offer and practice analysis, and the future of psychoanalysis, depend in significant part on our recognizing and integrating the reality of the limitations and misuses of psychoanalysis and getting more help if we need it. One can view failures as an indictment of analysis. They would be if these were the only examples of analysis one could locate. But they're not. I find it helpful to keep in mind that it is not the method that damages but the people. The fact that some analysts take advantage of their patients does not mean all analysts are exploitative. I take it to mean that analysts need to be vigilant for signals of their own countertransference and consult regularly about their work. Given the emotional demands and complexity of analytic relationships and the human mind, I find it predictable that there are unhelpful or hurtful analyses. I find it more surprising that there are many analyses that are life transforming.

II The nature of the analyst's engagement and its interfering and facilitating impact

A Analytic frequency

Interfering: not taking advantage of the healing potential of frequent analytic meetings

Daily sessions represent an element that historically has been identified with, even defined, psychoanalysis. In recent years, though, this previously unques-tioned prerequisite has been called into question, not just by the public but by the psychoanalytic community and literature. Surveys and anecdotal reports suggest that analysts practice with lesser frequency; fewer analysts work at a high analytic frequency. At present, there are differences of opinion among analysts as to which analytic frequency best facilitates good psychotherapeutic outcomes (Lazar 2000; Wallerstein 2000; Almond 2002; Stern 2009; Conrotto 2011; Hunyady and Sauvayre 2015). Frequency has become a divisive issue.

I've encountered many analysts who think high frequency is unnecessary. Some argue that the requirement for daily sessions is impractical, a financial burden on the patient, and an antiquated relic of the past. I've heard others maintain that frequent sessions function for the financial benefit of the analyst and similar results can be accomplished with fewer sessions per week. I've seen that when analysts doubt or don't believe in the usefulness of daily meeting, they don't recommend high weekly frequency or recommend it in a way that conveys to the patient that the invitation is not genuine.

I think it's important to examine the merit of any aspect of analysis, including frequency, and to call attention to apparent misapplications. However, focusing on the misuses of frequency contribute to overlooking its healing potential. Although there are analysts who write about the usefulness of analytic frequency (Gedo and Cohler 1992; Richards 1997; Freedman et al. 1999; Schwartz 2003; Ehrlich 2010; Conrotte 2011; Ferraro 2011; Frank 2011) and articulate the generative and curative aspects of practicing with such frequency, I think that the function and therapeutic value of analytic frequency is currently underappreciated, underrecognized, and underutilized.

Facilitating: making use of the containing and healing potential of analytic frequency and of a consistent analytic frame

> An emergent pattern of meaning from outcome research is that for most people in psychoanalysis, high-intensity treatment leads to a better outcome compared to low-intensity treatment.
>
> (Frosch 2011, p. 18)

When I work at my best as an analyst, I invite, tolerate, and work with intense feelings—my patient's and my own—in a consistent-enough, reliable-enough, close-enough manner. I've found that meeting at least four, preferably five, times weekly (in what follows, I will refer to four- and five-times weekly analysis as "analytic frequency") contributes substantially to my ability to provide the consistency, reliability, and closeness, which I've found to be essential in establishing and maintaining the mutual trust and shared intimacy required to generate good analytic work.

In my experience, patients' awareness of the analyst's capacity to be reliable and to consistently show up emotionally ready to work every day, increases the chances that patients will feel safe enough to share what's most shameful and to think spontaneously about what's most conflictual. I've observed that analysts' genuine interest and willingness to help, as manifested in their consistent and reliable adherence to intensive work and clear analytic boundaries, contribute powerfully to patients' ability to invest and commit to analytic work and its eventual good outcome.

I've seen repeatedly that each frequency increase (two sessions to three, three to four, four to five) brings with it a corresponding deepening of the treatment. Most patients feel increasingly emotionally held and thus become better able to access and work with more distressing, defended, or dissociated feelings. I've witnessed many examples when just talking about the possibility of increasing frequency leads the patient to speak about something traumatic in his personal history that he hasn't yet revealed, voice feelings about the analyst that he hasn't previously shared, or reveal a secret from his current life that he has felt too ashamed to discuss.

As an example, a middle-aged woman, who attended twice weekly psychotherapy for a few months, began tentatively bringing up the topic of increasing her sessions to an analytic frequency. Although she thought increasing would be useful to allow her more time to explore her many difficult feelings about her husband, she also identified that she felt very apprehensive. After recognizing that her initial worries about cost and time were manageable, she considered other possible sources of concern. She detected worries about me and the possibility that I would change and, with increased contact, become more intrusive and overstimulating. This led her to cautiously disclose that she was taunted and overstimulated by her older brother, who was her tormentor throughout her pubescent years. Initially coerced by him and then too ashamed to tell, she'd kept this secret and protected herself by maintaining her emotional and physical distance from others.

Increasing sessions has meanings for both patient and analyst but an increase alone doesn't lead to more understanding and better emotional integration and self-acceptance. Frequent sessions must be made use of and not adopted pro forma. Showing up five times weekly can be futile, if analyst and patient don't engage, emotionally and intellectually, whatever experience is brought in by the patient or created between them.

I've witnessed that the analyst's motivation for recommending frequent analytic sessions determines whether frequency proves useful or not—more specifically, whether the analyst is primarily motivated to create more understanding and intimacy or is pursuing narcissistic aims. I've heard analysts brag about the number of analytic patients they have in their practice or about the large number of analytic patients they see in a single workday. In such instances, one questions whether the analyst's focus on frequency stems from a wish to help patients or reflects an effort to treat her own insecurities at patients' expense, both financial and emotional. Mizen (2013) writes:

> Frequency may easily become a matter of prestige or conformance for both therapist and/or patient involving subtle appeals to snobbery and unanalyzed narcissism. It may even become a kind of fetish. … it is not then [has] to do with what is relevant, singular, useful or interesting but becomes instead a matter of what is correct or incorrect, good or bad.
>
> (p. 72)

The more solid the analyst's sense of competence and of having been helped by her personal analysis, the more likely the generative reasons for recommending and engaging in daily analysis will prevail over her narcissistic or neurotic motivations.

Let me illustrate with an example. A patient, a university professor, agreed with the analyst's assessment that analysis was needed to address his long-standing insecurity and inability to achieve academically, in keeping with his talent and ambitions. Yet, he also stated that his schedule was such that it precluded the possibility of attending at a high frequency. When the analyst asked about his schedule, the patient, in a subtly but distinctly annoyed tone, explained that between work and family obligations he didn't have time to make daily analytic appointments.

Married to an academic and having children of her own, the analyst privately empathized with the patient's demanding academic schedule and family obligations. Initially, she took at face value that the difficulty was entirely external. In consultation, she reconsidered. Regaining her capacity to reflect on his response analytically, she registered the patient's inpatient tone and her own response of feeling dismissed and discouraged. Then, considering both the patient's reactions and her own unpleasant feeling of being seen as demanding, the analyst recognized that the patient, frightened about beginning for reasons that were not conscious to him at the time, was experiencing her offer of analysis as an attempt to control him.

The following session the analyst told the patient that she understood that attending more frequently wasn't possible for now and suggested that they continue to meet and see if at some later time it would become more likely. The patient agreed. Some weeks later, the patient discussed his dentist's recommendation to have more frequent visits to address the patient's many dental problems. The patient explained his dilemma: on one hand he agreed with the dentist about the need to schedule more visits; on the other, he worried that dental work could be painful because the dentist could inadvertently hit a nerve. The analyst recognized that the patient was also speaking about his fears of his wish to be in analysis and addressed his fear that analysis might be a dangerous, painful process. By identifying and speaking to the patient's many fears about what might unfold if he followed his wish to enter analysis, the analyst helped the patient feel less fearful so that he could engage more intensively.

B Transference-countertransference

Interfering: overlooking the transference-countertransference

I entered the psychoanalytic world just before a tidal wave of recognition of the analyst's inevitable emotional participation in each analytic encounter. The analyst's anxieties were still, at least at my Institute, mostly seen as an interference and therefore undesirable. Being able to be tolerate and making use of feeling scared, ashamed, doubtful, or aroused in the course of an analysis was still not recognized as part of the job description for analysts. We still operated with the impossible ideal of the fully analyzed analysts who have achieved a complete understanding of and are therefore in charge of their unconscious.

I remember vividly in the mid-80s, when early in my career one of my supervisors offered his advice for analytic success: for analysis to be successful, he declared categorically, only one person in the room must be anxious and that person should be the patient. At the time when I was contending with beginner's insecurity about the usefulness of my chosen profession and my own capacity to be of help, his pronouncement fitted seamlessly with and bolstered my own defensive idealizations of analysis and analysts. Early in my career, thinking of the analysts' anxieties as problematic and therefore unwelcome, I felt critical of parts of my emotional experience and missed many opportunities to use them to find the most inaccessible and protected aspects of my patients' suffering.

Facilitating: not losing track of the centrality of the transference-countertransference.

> Being a psychoanalyst is always passionately interesting, always challenging, but never easy. One has to be daring in order to choose it as a profession in the first place and the daring needs to be continued all along as we have tried to illustrate to you: daring to listen to our countertransference feelings, especially the negative ones, daring to take on difficult patients and enter momentarily into their mad worlds in order to gain a deeper understanding of them.
>
> (Aubry et al. 2004, p. 162)

Accepting that my difficult feelings were not necessarily a liability but could be an asset evolved over time, primarily from learning how to tolerate them and understanding their meaning in my own analyses. Contrary to my supervisor's pronouncement, psychoanalysis, when done helpfully, is never emotionally easy. I've discovered that when I feel that it is, it is often an indication that I have become complacent.

As I accrued more hours of analytic experience on and behind the couch and as the view of countertransference as facilitating became more widely reported in the literature (Boesky 1990; Jacobs 1991; Chused and Raphling 1992; Renik 1993; Schwaber 1992 Smith 2000; Ferro 2003), I began to embrace its usefulness. I slowly recognized that the more receptive I could be to my most vulnerable and disturbing feelings, the better able I was to help my patients with theirs, both in the beginning and throughout their analyses.

When I work at my best, I can keep firmly in mind that everything that disturbs the patient will eventually manifest itself in the analytic relationship and needs to be felt and understood by analyst and patient. When I can practice well enough, the question of who I am for the patient and what he is reliving with me in each analytic moment remains central in my mind throughout each session.

In most analyses, I've found that following the manifestations of the transference-countertransference proves to be a royal road that leads to my patients' unconscious feelings and motivations. In every analytic session, I aim to find the richest psychological meaning and deepest connection with a patient by experiencing and understanding her vulnerabilities, distortions, unrequited desires, shameful longings, and wishes in relation to me in as much detail as possible. I seek to flesh out my patients' feelings in their full subjectivity and specificity and avoid relying on preconceptions or theory. I'm interested in moving as close as possible to what they feel and to what I experience in each session in order to be able to understand what shames them, scares them, saddens them, and what feels intolerable in their minds and between us.

Their feelings and thoughts about me and our relationship, and what they evoke in me, is how patients and I get to experience firsthand what they have been through and what they have made of it in their minds in order to survive the challenges of their childhood and the conflicting pressures within their minds. I aim to track the transference-countertransference, but I'm also mindful not to chase it. I share my thoughts with patients only when I discern that they are closer to the surface of my patients' awareness and only when I detect that they're receptive to considering my perceptions.

At times, when I am unable to listen to a patient's transferential allusion, I lose my connection to the immediacy and poignancy of that patient's suffering and her ongoing efforts to communicate this suffering to me. When I become aware of having lost the thread to how a patient sees me transferentially, I use that realization as a signal that I'm defending against coming closer to how the patient experiences me, what she wants from me, and what her transference evokes in me.

In my clinical practice and in supervising others, I've found that working with the negative transference-countertransference while sustaining empathy for the patient and for one's sense of goodness as an analyst constitutes a fundamental clinical challenge. Over the years, my understanding of the negative transference has evolved significantly. During my training and early years, I understood patients' inhibited or directly expressed negative feelings as expressions of their innate aggression and tried to help them understand and accept its many variations. With more experience and reflection, I recognized that this formulation doesn't account for the complexity of my patients' feelings and their multiple origins. I find that considering that aggression and hostility can have many sources and can serve many functions—such as protection from sadness and vulnerability—guides me to a fuller and richer appreciation of their difficulties. This in turn leads patients to be less punitive with themselves and better able to manage and integrate their hostility. I've concluded that the more secure I feel in my goodness and my capacity to be of help, the less reactive I become in the face of patients' overt or veiled aggressive manifestations and better able to consider their multiple origins and functions.

C Tensions and paradoxes

Many analysts have noted that tensions and contradictions are inherent in practicing as an analyst (Pizer 1992, 1998; Levine 1996; Skolnikoff 1996; Parsons 2000, Ehrlich 2010). I briefly discuss how managing the tensions and paradoxes of practicing can get in the way or assist the analyst in maintaining her motivation and capacity to practice. I identify a few tensions and paradoxes that I've found consequential.

Interfering: overlooking the complexity of the analyst's emotional tasks

Given the complexity of human motivation, tension between competing desires is inherent in practicing as a psychoanalyst. At the same time, because of the privacy afforded by the analytic setting and the human mind's propensity to protect itself from disturbance, analysts seek to avoid existing tensions and contradictions by ignoring the complexity integral to daily practicing. I've given examples throughout this book of analysts, including myself, rationalizing, denying, and projecting our reluctance to analyze and our grievances about analysis and our need for supervisory help. I've observed that when analysts ignore tensions and paradoxes, we inevitably shortchange our capacity to practice analytically by understanding their meaning. I've observed that this neglect leads us to tepid superficial versions of analysis and, if our avoidance is persistent and profound, to chronic hurtful enactments.

Facilitating: recognizing and containing the tensions and paradoxes of analysis

On the contrary, although distressing at times, appreciating the tensions, dilemmas, and paradoxes inherent in practicing analytically has sustained me. This appreciation allows me to more readily recognize signs of my complacency or defensiveness and analyze their specific meanings at a given moment in an analysis.

Below are a few tensions and paradoxes, which I've found critical in sustaining myself as an analyst:

- Not underestimating the effort required to do the work and at the same time recognizing that some of the motivation to do analysis comes from deep within and can't be willed
- Striving to be authentic and creative while maintaining reliable and stable therapeutic boundaries and frame
- Aiming for increased self-compassion for one's countertransferential "mistakes" without compromising the pursuit of their meaning
- Accepting the analyst's fundamental need for ongoing help while developing one's own voice

- Engaging in rigorous self-analysis while remaining open to the need for reanalysis
- Trusting in the usefulness of the work and, simultaneously, remaining aware of what analysis can't do
- Acknowledging what was helpful *and* what was disappointing in one's analysis
- Remaining aware of both the wish to practice analysis and fears of initiating and deepening analysis
- Not denying the reality of the misuses of psychoanalysis while considering the possibility that this reality is used defensively

Concluding remarks

It's critical for our field for analysts who are immersed in analysis to try to articulate their experience of how they maintain their motivation and ability to analyze. In this chapter, I shared my observations and thoughts about what might impede and what might sustain graduate analysts' desire and capacity to practice analysis. I suggested that idealization of the analyst's functioning and of analysis and disappointment in analysis can interfere with analysts' capacity to function effectively or even to engage in the practice of analysis. I offered my experience that the nature of the analyst's beliefs and the nature of her engagement could be an interfering or facilitating factor in her practice of psychoanalysis. I identified several beliefs that have supported my capacity to immerse myself in analytic practice and function well enough as an analyst, which included anticipating analysis to be effortful, expecting my ambivalence and insecurities, trusting analysis and my capacity to be helpful while being aware of its misuses and limitations, and accepting my need for consultation. I also articulated how working within an analytic frequency, privileging transference-countertransference, and being mindful of the tensions and paradoxes of analysis have been critical in helping me uphold a solid analytic identity and practice.

Note

1 Opinion section of the NYT, August 25, 2017.

References

Almond, R. (2002). Commentary on "The holding function of theory for the analyst: Conviction derived from unitary or integrated models". *San Francisco Center of Psychoanalysis*, 1: 3.

Aubry, C., Reith, B., Bonard, O., Déjussel, G., & Quinodoz, D. (2004). Dare we be analysts? *European Psychoanalytical Federation Bulletin*, 58: 158–162.

Boesky, D. (1990). The psychoanalytic process and its components. *Psychoanalytic Quarterly*, 59: 550–584.

Bronstein, C. (2015). The analyst's disappointment: An everyday struggle. *Journal of the American Psychoanalytic Association*, 63(6): 1173–1192.

Cherry, S., Cabaniss, D.L., Forand, N., Haywood, D., & Roose, S.P. (2004). Psychoanalytic practice in the early postgraduate years. *Journal of the American Psychoanalytic Association*, 52: 851–871.

Chessick, R.D. (1996). Impasse and failure in psychoanalytic treatment. *Journal of the American Academy of Psychoanalysis and Dynamic Psychiatry*, 24(2): 193–216.

Chused, J.V. (2016). An analyst's uncertainty and fear. *Journal of the American Psychoanalytic Association*, 64: 1153–1171.

Chused, J.F. & Raphling, D.L. (1992). The analyst's mistakes. *Journal of the American Psychoanalytic Association*, 40: 89–116.

Conrotto, F. (2011). On the frequency of psychoanalytic sessions. *The Italian Psychoanalytic Annual*, 5: 123–134.

Cooper, S.H. (2015). Reflections on the analyst's "good enough" capacity to bear disappointment, with special attention to repetition. *Journal of the American Psychoanalytic Association*, 63(6): 1193–1213.

Danckwardt, J.F. (2011). The fear of method in psychoanalysis. *Bulletin*, 65: 113–124.

Ehrlich, L.T. (2004). The analyst's reluctance to begin a new analysis. *Journal of the American Psychoanalytic Association*, 52: 1075–1093.

Ehrlich, L.T. (2010). The analyst's ambivalence about continuing and deepening an analysis. *Journal of the American Psychoanalytic Association*, 58: 515–532.

Ehrlich, L.T. (2013). Analysis begins in the analyst's mind: Conceptual and technical considerations on recommending analysis. *Journal of the American Psychoanalytic Association*, 61: 1077–1107.

Ehrlich, L.T. (2019). Teleanalysis: Slippery slope or rich opportunity? *Journal of the American Psychoanalytic Association*, 67: 249–279.

Ferraro, F. (2011). Some remarks on an ongoing debate. *The Italian Psychoanalytic Annual*, 5: 135–156.

Ferro, A. (2003). The analyst as individual, his self-analysis and gradients of functioning, *Bulletin of the European Federation*, 57: 134–141.

Frank, G. (2011). The theoretical and practical aspects of frequency of sessions: The root of the controversy. *Psychoanalytic Review*, 98(1): 1–10.

Freedman, N., Hoffenberg, J.D., Vorus, N., & Frosch, A. (1999). The effectiveness of psychoanalytic psychotherapy. *Journal of the American Psychoanalytic Association*, 47(3): 741–772.

Frosch, A. (2011). The effect of frequency and duration on psychoanalytic outcome: A moment in time. *Psychoanalytic Review*, 98(1): 11–38.

Gabbard, G.O. & Ogden, T.H. (2009). On becoming a psychoanalyst. *International Journal of Psycho-Analysis*, 90(2): 311–327.

Gedo, P.M. & Cohler, B.J. (1992). Session frequency, regressive intensity, and the psychoanalytic process. *Psychoanalytic Psychology*, 9(2): 245–249.

Goldberg, A. (2012). *The Analysis of Failure: An Investigation of Failed Cases in Psychoanalysis and Psychotherapy.* New York: Routledge.

Greenberg, J. (2015). Disappointment: Something in the nature of analysis, *Journal of the American Psychoanalytic Association*, 63(6): 1215–1223.

Grusky, Z. (1999). Conviction and conversion. *Psychoanalytic Quarterly*, 68: 401–430.

Hunyady, O. & Sauvayre, P. (2015). On the enforcement of frequency. *Contemporary Psychoanalysis*, 51(4): 597–623.

Jacobs, T.J. (1991). *The Use of the Self. Countertransference and Communication in the Analytic Situation*. Madison, CT: Int. Univ. Press.

Kantrowitz, J.L., Katz, A.L., Greenman, D.A., Morris, H., Paolitto, F., Sashin, J., *et al.* (1989). The patient-analyst match and the outcome of psychoanalysis: A pilot study. *Journal of the American Psychoanalytic Association*, 37: 893–919.

Kaplan, M., Pretsky, J., Wininger, L., Roose, S.P., & Cherry, S. (2009). Poster summary: A profile of analytic practice across the country: Immersion data for three institutes. *Journal of the American Psychoanalytic Association*, 57: 1169–1173.

LaFarge, L. (2015). The fog of disappointment, the cliffs of disillusionment, the abyss of despair, *Journal of the American Psychoanalytic Association*, 63(6): 1225–1239.

Lamont, A. (1995). *Bird by Bird*. New York: Penguin Random House.

Lazar, S.G. (2000). Should analytic patients be "created"? Reflections on Arnold Rothstein's psychoanalytic technique and the creation of analytic patients. *Psychoanalytic Inquiry*, 20: 556–573.

Levine, H.B. (1996). Action, transference, and resistance: Some reflections on a paradox at the heart of analytic technique. *Psychoanalytic Inquiry*, 16(4): 474–490.

Mendelsohn, E. (2002). The analyst's bad-enough participation. *Psychoanalytic Dialogues*, 12(3): 331–358.

Meyer, J.K. (2007). Training analysis and reanalysis in the development of the psychoanalyst. *Journal of the American Psychoanalytic Association*, 55(4): 1103–1128.

Meyer, J.K. & Debbink, N.L. (2003). Reanalysis in the Career of the Analyst. *Journal of Clinical Psychoanalysis*, 12(1): 55–71.

Mizen, R. (2013). On session frequency and analytic method. *British Journal of Psychotherapy*, 29(1): 57–74.

Ogden, T.H. (2016). Some thoughts on practicing psychoanalysis. *Fort Da*, 22(1): 21–36.

Orgel, S. (2002). Some hazards to neutrality in the psychoanalysis of candidates. *Psychoanalytic Quarterly*, 71(3): 419–443.

Parsons, M. (2000). *The Dove that Returns, The Dove that Vanishes: Paradox and Creativity in Psychoanalysis*. London: Routledge.

Pizer, S.A. (1992). The negotiation of paradox in the analytic process. *Psychoanalytic Dialogues*, 2(2): 215–240.

Pizer, S.A. (1998). *Building Bridges: The Negotiation of Paradox in Psychoanalysis*. Hillsdale, NJ: The Analytic Press.

Renik, O. (1993). Analytic interaction: Conceptualizing technique in light of the analyst's irreducible subjectivity. *Psychoanalytic Quarterly*, 62: 553–571.

Richards, A.K. (1997). The relevance of frequency of sessions to the creation of an analytic experience. *Journal of the American Psychoanalytic Association*, 45: 1241–1251.

Rothstein, A. (1995). *Psychoanalytic Technique and the Creation of Analytic Patients*. Madison, CT: International University Press.

Schneider, J., Wilkerson, D., Solomon, B., Perlman, C., Tsioles, D.D., Shelby, D., *et al.* (2014). Psychoanalytic training experience and postgraduate professional development: A survey of six decades of graduate analysts. *International Journal of Psychoanalysis*, 95: 1211–1233.

Schwaber, E.A. (1992). Countertransference: The analyst's retreat from the patient's vantage Point. *International Journal of Psychoanalysis*, 73: 349–361.

Schwartz, C. (2003). A brief discussion on frequency of sessions and its impact upon psychoanalytic treatment. *Psychoanalytic Review*, 90(2): 179–191.

Silber, A. (1996). Analysis, reanalysis, and self-analysis. *Journal of the American Psychoanalytic Association*, 44: 491–509.

Skolnikoff, A.Z. (1996). Paradox and ambiguity in the reactions of the analyst at work. *Psychoanalytic Inquiry*, 16(3): 340–361.

Smith, H.F. (2000). Countertransference, conflictual listening, and the analytic object relationship. *Journal of the American Psychoanalytic Association*, 48(1): 95–128.

Stern, S. (2009). Session frequency and the definition of psychoanalysis. *Psychoanalytic Dialogues*, 19(6): 639–655.

Wallerstein, R.S. (2000). Where have all the psychoanalytic patients gone? They're still here. *Psychoanalytic Inquiry*, 20(4): 503–526.

Wille, R. (2008). Psychoanalytic identity: Psychoanalysis as an internal object. *Psychoanalytic Quarterly*, 77(4): 1193–1229.

Wille, R. (2012). The analyst's trust in psychoanalysis and the communication of that trust in initial interviews. *Psychoanalytic Quarterly*, 81(4): 875–904.

Wilson, M. (2015). Introduction: Working with the analyst's disappointments, grief, and sense of limitation in the analytic process. *Journal of the American Psychoanalytic Association*, 63(6): 1169–1172.

Chapter 7

It takes three to know one

On receiving and providing consultation

Like most candidates, by the end of my training I had many hours of opportunity for consultation per week to discuss each of my patients—five sessions of my own analysis and three supervisions per week—but I graduated with the expectation, from that moment on, that I should practice self-sufficiently.[1] Though perhaps current candidates have a different belief, I ended my training expecting that if I was confident enough, talented enough, and well trained enough, I shouldn't require further help. Having received my Institute's permission to practice analysis with a new analytic case without supervision the year before I graduated, I was under internal and external pressure[2] to end my supervisions as soon as possible. Shortly after graduation, even though I still found one of my supervisions extremely useful, I ended all supervision. In retrospect, I realize this was premature.

Since then, the more analytic hours I've been part of, as analyst, supervisor, and consultant, the more I've come to appreciate *graduate* analysts' need for regular consultation to sustain close-enough empathic involvement with patients and to think, process, and intervene well analytically. I've observed, both in myself and in working with other experienced and committed analysts, that we need regular help to face the onslaught of conflictual and traumatic feelings that are inherent in intensive analytic work.

Here's a compelling example. In my study group of 14 senior colleagues from North America, which meets over three-day weekends twice a year, each member of the group takes a turn presenting, for an entire weekend, detailed process notes from consecutive weekly sessions from three different points of an analysis. Each presentation begins on Friday afternoon and ends mid-morning on Sunday, typically involving 12 to 13 hours of analytic process from one analysis. During my time as a member of this group, I've listened to 25 presentations. Inevitably by Saturday afternoon, if not earlier, each presenter's countertransferences and how these manifested themselves in limiting the analysis have become evident to the group and, most of the time, to the presenter. Despite years of experience, skill, and confidence, each of us has been subject to manifestations of our unconscious and have benefited from the wisdom of the group in better understanding how these manifestations limited our functioning, as well as their meaning in terms of the patient's, and our own, psychology.

My focus on consultation is part of my larger interest in the analyst's mind and identifying the conditions that help analysts sustain our capacity to function analytically over time. This chapter is intended as a contribution to the small body of literature on the usefulness of consultation for graduate clinicians. My thoughts stem from my current and past experiences with consultation. At present, I receive individual consultation from two out-of-town colleagues twice a month. I also participate in two clinical study groups: a local monthly group and the national group, which I mentioned earlier. In addition, I serve as a weekly and biweekly consultant to several graduate local and out-of-town colleagues. Over the last ten years, I've had the opportunity to assist as a consultant to more than 40 graduate analysts, through individual and group consultations and case conferences. Although substantial, my experience is still just one person's. I'm offering my thoughts with the hope that knowing what has been sustaining to me will help readers think about what might be of further help to *them*.

I am writing to attest to the helpfulness of receiving and providing ongoing consultation[3] and to challenge remaining stigma attached to graduate analysts needing ongoing help. I intend to articulate my experience as both consultee and consultant of what consultation can offer; to discuss under what conditions I've found consultation useful and when it was not; and to highlight some resistances to consultation

The stigma of acknowledging the need for consultation

Compared to the extensive literature exploring supervision of candidates since the 1920s, we have remarkably few contributions on seeking consultation as a graduate analyst, all of them recent. This limited interest in discussing consultation can be understood in the context of our field's long-standing belief that analysts should be able to practice without help once we graduate.[4] Before countertransference was better understood and depathologized, analysts proceeded, at least in public, as if we could/should have a fully analyzed unconscious, which never interfered with our work. Analysts could not acknowledge our need for consultation, and therefore did not discuss consultation as a separate topic, until we began to accept and make use of the inevitability and omnipresence of analysts' countertransferential engagement. The increasing acceptance of this more honest view of the analyst's mind—as unintentionally and meaningfully responding to its own and the patient's conflicts and traumas—led to an increasing recognition in the literature that graduate analysts need help refinding our analytic bearings (Sandler 1976; McLaughlin 1981; Gill 1982; Jacobs 1983; Poland 1984; Boesky 1990) and to more interest in discussing the usefulness of consultation.[5]

Though it appears there is less stigma in acknowledging the need for consultation, the still relatively small number of papers addressing consultation for graduate analysts and observations of my own lead me to believe that we haven't fully accepted the extent of that need. In my experience, many analysts still struggle to fully embrace and integrate into our ego ideal the inevitability of our emotional involvement and participation in each analysis and their implications. I'll say more about this later.

What does consultation offer?

How does consulting enhance analysts' functioning? I provide a brief selective literature review and then offer my own thoughts.

Muller (1999) proposes that a consultant, whom he calls "a structuring Third" (p. 116), is essential in situations when the analytic dyad has regressed into prolonged power struggles, during which the autonomy and separateness of each member is obliterated in their minds and we have lost their capacity to see their responses as countertransferential rather than realistic responses to patients. Muller suggests that the role of the consultant in such impasses is "to reinstall the 'framework of the Third'—that is, an oedipal, triadic framework that contextualizes the dyad, amplifies its symbolic dimension, and introduces a space beyond transference-countertransference dynamics" (p. 116).

Gabbard (2000), who has worked with many clinicians who have committed sexual boundaries violations with patients, recommends "regular consultation" as standard practice. He has found that although consultation does not prevent boundary violations, it helps analysts identify "blind spots or transference/countertransference enactments" (p. 211) and regain their capacity to reflect upon them, rather than act. Gabbard advises that analysts should consult when they feel ashamed of their analytic conduct with a patient and want to keep it a secret, when, they have fantasies about rescuing a specific patient, or when they feel particularly attracted to a patient.

Pizer (2000) writes that all analysts, regardless of experience, if they're truly engaged in an analysis, are vulnerable to "error, boundary crossings, or potential boundary violations" (p. 198). Therefore, she proposes that we require "regular consultations as stringent as our continuing education requirements" (p. 199). She advocates that our field mandates consultation in part to alleviate the embarrassment associated with seeking consultation on one's own.

Like Gabbard, Pizer has developed a list of self-monitoring signals she uses to identify her need for consultative help. These include: the analyst's inability to use her own affects to understand the patient and feeling perplexed for an extended period; the analyst's wish to keep a secret or, alternatively, to boast or complain about the analysand; rescue fantasies, and "prolonged excitement, boredom, anxiety, dread, withdrawal, anger, and, last but not least, feeling cozy" (p. 204).

Kantrowitz (2002) speaks of the necessity for an "external observer" and suggests that consultation can offer consultees a different perspective, "an aerial view" where consultees' capacity to see is not obscured by their blind spots and other countertransferences.

Kantrowitz (2009) suggests that consultation amplifies not only what the analyst sees but what she can hear and bear. She writes that while analysts differ in our capacity for self-awareness, there are always limits to what we can see about ourselves and how much we can bear alone. She further observes that "communicating details of analytic process increases both insight and the capacity to contain intense affect" (pp. 799–800). Kantrowitz proposes that consultation can be beneficial not only in cases where there is a loss of distance but also when the analyst maintains too much emotional distance from the patient.

Ogden (2005) sees the role of the consultant as assisting the analyst to resume "genuine unconscious psychological work" when that ability "has been disrupted by the disturbing nature of the thoughts and feelings being generated in the analysis" (p. 1266). Referring to consultation as "supervision" and to the consultee as "supervisee," Ogden poignantly writes:

> The supervisee entrusts to the supervisor something highly personal—his conscious, preconscious and unconscious experience of the intimacy and the loneliness, the sexual aliveness and the deadness, the tenderness and the fearfulness of the analytic relationship. In return, the supervisor shows the supervisee what it is for him to be (and to continue to become) an analyst through the way he thinks and dreams, the way he formulates and expresses his ideas and feelings, the way he responds to the supervisee's conscious and unconscious communications, the way he recognizes the supervisee as a unique individual for whom the supervisory relationship is being freshly invented.
>
> (Ogden 2005, p. 1269)

In a later paper, Ogden (2016) suggests that one important function of the consultant is to help the analyst "survive" the destructive feelings that are mobilized in an analysis. If that is not possible and when there is a prolonged stalemate, the function of the consultant becomes to help the analyst end a destructive analysis, instead of continuing a hurtful relationship. Ogden has found that consultants can be most useful when they focus on and reflect freely upon the consultees' experiences of the analytic relationship rather than working with their understanding of the patient.

All analysts who write about consultation assert that consulting about one's cases is useful, even imperative, in case of difficulty. Few endorse ongoing consultations as standard practice. Even among the few analysts who advocate for regular consultations, only one, Kantrowitz, suggests that analysts routinely discuss each patient in their practice (Kantrowitz 2009) Kantrowitz writes:

> I have found it beneficial to present all my analytic patients throughout their treatment—not just those with whom I note a difficulty—and to

begin to do so as early in the work as possible. We must value our patients' privacy, but to keep our work totally private may seriously limit our ability to be helpful; sometimes it may do outright harm.

(Kantrowitz 2009, p. 800)

While practicing analysis myself, and receiving and providing consultations, I have observed that analysts continuously struggle with the counter-transferential wishes and fears inherent in interacting with all our patients, whether we are aware of it or not. As Mizen (2013 reminds us:

Psychoanalytic ideas have provided a potent means of understanding phenomena such as psychological projection, splitting, regression, 'acting-out' … but … it may be that this understanding has provided only a rather uncertain and unreliable inoculation against their effects. In consequence, we may be too easily drawn into overestimating our capacity to negotiate primitive affect, and be seduced into assuming immunity, when in reality we have merely been alerted to the dangers.

(Mizen 2009, pp. 63–64)

Blind spots and chronic enactments, as well as analysts' denial that they exist, have been part of every analysis I have witnessed regardless of the analyst's skill or experience. This observation has led me, like Kantrowitz, to conclude that analysts need to present their work frequently in order to remain alert to and make use of these omnipresent, ongoing interferences to optimal analytic engagement. Presenting at regular intervals (weekly or biweekly) and pursuing periodic input for each analytic and supervisory relationship needs to be seen as part of our ordinary way of practicing.

The functions of consultation

I will now share with you some aspects of consulting that I find helpful in improving my analytic functioning and sustaining myself as both analyst and consultant. I will list these and then elaborate on each one and provide brief examples. Although for the sake of clarity I am presenting them as distinct categories, in fact there is overlap.

Consultation helps me:

- Make better use of my thoughts and feelings to gain greater access to the patient's suffering
- Identify my defenses against my awareness of the prevailing transference-countertransference
- Be open to alternative meanings (i.e. not become enamored of my own ideas or interpretations)

- Sustain my optimism regarding the usefulness of analysis and a good-enough analytic frame
- Remain alert to my narcissistic vulnerability and the regressive pulls inherent in every analytic dyad
- Improve my own supervisory capacities

I Making better use of my own thoughts and feelings to gain access to the patient's associations

Discussing a patient freely with a consultant whom I trust enlarges my capacity to draw on thoughts and feelings that I had registered but did not use during sessions. I can make connections between my seemingly unrelated perceptions, thoughts, and feelings during a session and the patient's state of mind and its meanings.

In addition, the experience of speaking to a trusted colleague generates additional associations, which I can also use to further understand my patient and his experience of our relationship, if I identify and reflect on them. With an enlarged emotional capacity and better understanding of myself and the patient, I can be more effective in helping the patient bear and know what is most difficult for him.

Let me offer a brief example: Mr. A., a 45-year-old professional in the third year of a five times-a-week analysis, came for help because he found himself unable to hold back from constantly criticizing his children's behavior. A divorced parent, he feared that if he continued down this path his adolescent children would no longer want to live with him. He described a similar problem at work where he was told that his critical style of delivering feedback interfered with his collaborators' morale and performance.

Born into a household where survival required vigilance, Mr. A. was a keen observer of others and spent his analytic hours complaining about the many faults of those around him. He mostly diverted or ignored my attempts to help him reflect on his emotional experience and the meaning of his complaints. For my part, I observed that I was cautious and stilted when I spoke with Mr. A. and particularly hesitant when I addressed any evidence of his feelings about me or his experience of being in analysis. While I understood this transference-countertransference dynamic to have history and meaning, I couldn't find a way to speak to him about the distance between us that didn't lead him to retreat further into himself.

I had discussed Mr. A. previously with one of my individual consultants, with whom I take turns presenting analytic process, who had supported my sense that Mr. A. needed me to proceed slowly. During a third presentation, my consultant observed that as I presented, I appeared less patient with Mr. A.'s evasive style. She raised the possibility that my impatience might be an indication that Mr. A. and I were ready for something different between us. In response to her comments, I found myself picturing Mr. A. and me walking cautiously toward each other from opposites sides of a minefield. Catalyzed by this consultation, I slowly became more consciously able to experience the fear that had been underlying my caution and Mr. A.'s avoidance. By feeling my dread rather than just reacting to it, I became better able to appreciate that Mr. A.'s harshness with others protected him from recognizing and feeling his own horrors. Over time, Mr. A. and I discovered together that his criticisms of others hid scathing attacks toward himself and the awful expectation that others would also pounce on him to intimidate or ridicule him. Slowly, Mr. A. felt safe enough within himself and with me to share that his experience of analysis felt to him as similarly dangerous. He feared that, if he spoke freely, one of us would blow up in pieces, replicating his explosive relationship with his abusive father. I found myself freer to speak to Mr. A. and noticed that he, too, became more spontaneous and able to speak more directly with me.

2 Identify my defenses against my awareness of the prevailing transference-countertransference

Receiving consultation helps me remain alert to my tendency to defend against my awareness of the transference-countertransference—how the most distressing or most unarticulated aspects of my own and my patients' experiences manifest themselves within the analytic relationship. As I become aware of how or what I've been defending against, I experience firsthand, and thus rediscover experientially, how my pre/unconscious fears get in the way of pursuing my conscious goal of analyzing. More aware of my defenses, I thus become better able to invite the patient to share the depth, extent, and intensity of her experience inside the consulting room.

I'll provide a brief example: Ms. B., a highly capable, yet self-defeating young professional woman, with a history of childhood abuse, sought treatment after being put on work probation for poor performance and absenteeism. Although Ms. B. claimed she wanted to be in a committed relationship, when we began the analysis she was involved with a boyfriend who didn't believe in marriage and whom she suspected engaged in sexual activities with other women during his frequent business travels.

In the fifth year of a four times-a-week analysis and having progressed in her capacity to reflect on her difficulties, Ms. B. had become involved with a more emotionally available man and then accepted a job offer that advanced her career. Initially, she felt pleased with her new job. However, after a brief honeymoon, she once again created difficulty for herself by fighting unnecessarily with her new boss and two of her coworkers about her schedule and the nature of her duties. Despite our efforts to understand her motivations, she continued to fight and the situation at work worsened.

In my individual consultation with a senior colleague whom I pay to present my work to, I described this new round of Ms. B.'s self-destructiveness. While presenting, I became aware and shared with my consultant that I was feeling discouraged about Ms. B.'s capacity to benefit further from analysis. My consultant suggested that the patient had made good use of our efforts and that there was no indication that she couldn't continue to do so. He suggested that what might be difficult for me at this analytic juncture wasn't that she couldn't be helped but that she would need my help for much longer. As I considered his suggestion, I recognized that I was defending against Ms. B.'s pleas for more of my help. Reflecting on my defensiveness led me to understand that her battles at work replicated, in part, her internal battle about deepening her analysis—getting to know herself more deeply and becoming more intimate with me. Although from time to time we'd identified and talked about the realistic factors and ambivalence, which prevented her from increasing her sessions to five times-a-week, this matter had dropped off our conscious radars. I now recognized that by battling at work, Ms. B. was preconsciously trying to bring this matter back to our attention. By thinking that I couldn't help her, I disguised my wish to turn away from experiencing the full measure of longing, outrage, helplessness, conflicted desire, and deep grief that I would have to feel to be able to assist her. By becoming aware of my defensiveness, I was able to help Ms. B. recognize her indirect request for a fifth session and that, despite her many fears, she wished to bring more of herself and her difficulties into the analysis.

3 Be open to alternative understandings and meanings and not become enamored by my own ideas or interpretations

Hearing my consultant's understanding keeps me honest about an analyst's inherent limitations, particularly overvaluing my thinking. Becoming aware of alternative meanings, helps me remain alert to the danger of not fully appreciating the vastness and complexity of my patients' and my own unconscious.

As part of a consultation, I discussed Mr. C., a businessman with whom I've been working in order to help him with sexual inhibitions and relationship difficulties. In the six months since my last consultation about this case, I felt that Mr. C. and I had been steadily addressing his difficulties, both within and outside the transference, with finding a life partner and that the analysis was progressing well. In the last year, he had found a girlfriend and, I thought, they were working out their fears about being intimate. Yet, in the last four months, his girlfriend had begun a demanding new job, which required long work hours and interfered with their getting together. After presenting a recent session in which Mr. C. recounted that his girlfriend once again postponed a date by claiming she was too busy with work obligations, my consultant questioned my patient's overly optimistic accommodation. He suggested that Mr. C was kidding himself that this could be a committed relationship and that by finding another unavailable partner Mr. C. was once again enacting his difficulties with intimacy. Initially, I protested against my consultant's view. Then, I considered whether I was being self-justifying. As I thought about Mr. C.'s recent participation in the analysis, I realized that I, too, had been too accommodating with him and had been avoiding addressing his attempts to put me off. Refocusing on our interactions, I could see more clearly how his polite, edited way of speaking to me was continuing to keep me at a distance.

4 Sustain my optimism regarding the usefulness of analysis and a good-enough analytic frame

I have found that, as analysts, we need help from another to overcome our resistances to function as analysts, to be receptive to our unconscious, and to live with the wounds in others and in ourselves, without turning away or seeking premature closure. My experience of my consultant's psychoanalytic identity—belief in unconscious motivation, in fantasy and meaning, in transference-countertransference, in the past being alive in the present—fortifies my capacity to function analytically, adding to my confidence that the analytic journey is meaningful and that I can be of further help.

The emotional work that goes into preparing to present, presenting, and then reflecting on a helpful consultation results in the analyst's increased feeling of engagement in the analytic work and with the patient. I'm reminded that to sustain the best analytic version of myself, I must engage energetically and creatively on behalf of the patient and not rationalize going-through-the-motions participation.[6] In my own practice and in my role as a consultant, I've observed that analysts must refind their investment in psychological meaning in every hour, with each patient, and within each day of practice, which requires confronting resistances all the time. Doing so alone is a formidable and, I would argue, impossible task.

I'll provide another example of an analyst needing help to maintain an internal analytic frame. Dr. M., a senior analyst, consulted with me about a traumatized patient who experienced his feelings through his body. The analyst felt overwhelmed and doubted his capacity to help this patient. The patient remained convinced that he suffered an incurable disease, even though multiple medical tests disconfirmed it. Yet, Dr. M., a physician, felt pulled to continue to think about a possible medical diagnosis and overlooked his own feelings of impotence, inadequacy, urgency, guilt, and frustration. Under the sway of these powerful countertransferential feelings, he needed a reminder that his feelings and the patient's physical distress and fears of dying held psychological meanings. He and I were able to think about how his patient's recent career successes and his upcoming business trip, which would interfere with his analytic appointments, had mobilized his separation anxiety and guilt. In this patient's psychic reality, his success was equated with traumatic and premature separation from his mother and damaging further his mentally ill father and therefore called for punishment, even death. Refinding his footing, Dr. M. helped the patient recognize and begin to understand the emotional distress that underlay his physical symptoms and to begin to explore its many meanings.

5 Remain alert to my narcissistic vulnerability and the regressive pulls inherent in every analytic dyad

By seeking consultations, analysts can remain alert to their own inclinations to inadvertently and narcissistically misuse patients by imposing their own treatment agenda, fostering dependency, not examining or encouraging idealization, and sexually or aggressively overstimulating patients, among other possible misuses.

Receiving consultation assists me in maintaining my narcissistic equilibrium by helping me better tolerate the frustrations of the work and enjoy its pleasures more fully. In response to disturbing feelings in an analysis, I've observed in myself and my consultees the inclination to rationalize bending the frame (i.e. starting or ending late, not following one's billing or cancellation policy), daydreaming without reflecting, going along with patients' defenses, not addressing what is conflictual or traumatic in the transference, etc. A consultant's empathic understanding of the fears and pressures generated between a specific patient and me can allow me to better withstand these disturbing feelings. A consultant's empathy for the rigors and frustrations of the analytic process also supports my efforts to sustain the self-discipline, determination, and dedication that it takes to adhere to internal and external analytic frames that privilege the patient's treatment needs.[7]

I've observed that while helping analysts be more aware of their rationalizations and shortcuts, consultation can also help consultees not be unduly critical of their "mistakes" and, instead, utilize them analytically by considering their meanings. Consulting further contributes to an analyst's narcissistic equilibrium by providing an ethically acceptable containing space to share details of a case, which, of course, because of confidentiality cannot otherwise be shared.

6 Improve my supervisory capacities

Presenting my clinical work helps me in my effort to be a better consultant for others by enhancing my empathic contact with the emotional vulnerability inherent in being a supervisee. Regardless of many years of experience presenting, each time I present to a new consultant or group, I become reacquainted with my persecutory anxieties: anxiety of knowing I will inevitably reveal something I did not consciously intend and anxiety about my consultant's capacity to harness his or her supervisory countertransferences, to me or to my patient, and offer constructive feedback.

Staying in touch with the narcissistic vulnerability of being a consultee leads me to supervise with heightened awareness of the potential danger in consultation of the supervisor advancing some narcissistic aim of his or her own (showing off, self-aggrandizing, etc.) rather than addressing the consultee's needs. Encountering my own superego when I present my work also improves my capacity to recognize when my consultees' psychoanalytic superego interferes with their ability to practice with authenticity, make analytic use of enactments, and freely partake of the realistic pleasures of analyzing and of analytic intimacy.

When is consultation useful?

I have found that as imperative as it is not to idealize analysts' self-sufficiency, it's also necessary not to idealize consultation and to discuss its limitations. Like analyses, consultations vary in their usefulness. I've experienced some as extremely useful, others less so, and some even add to difficulties.

Consultation is only as beneficial as the degree of honesty between consultee and consultant. A good match in terms of level of psychological mindedness also matters. When my consultants can be open to their thoughts and feelings about the analytic process I present and share openly with me, I find myself freer and more productive in my participation. The same holds true when I function as a consultant. The more able I am to access my associations and articulate difficult feelings, the more likely my consultees will feel free to share their experiences of the analysis.

As I mentioned earlier, as a consultee, I present to individual analysts and two study groups. When I meet with a single consultant, I usually think more freely and access more difficult thoughts and feelings than I can in a group setting, even though I feel at ease with each group member of my long-standing groups equally. When I present individually, I focus more effectively on my own free associations than when in a group. On the other hand, when I present to one of my groups, I get the benefit of many voices at once. While difficult to integrate in real time, I find that considering in retrospect each contribution as representing aspects of myself or the patient disowned by either me or the patient, I eventually arrive at a richer integration of my experience in the analysis and a more complex understanding of the patient and our relationship.

In seeking individual consultation, I can be more open to myself and my consultant when the consultant sees the practice of consultation as ordinary and expectable. I find it disruptive when the consultant operates within an "I got you" frame of mind, which activates my own persecutory tendencies and defensiveness. Consultants' open, engaged participation brings me closer to the patient's experience and my experience of the patient. Conversely, when consultants stay far away or are critical of my patient, their input disrupts my capacity to use the process and interferes with my connection to and understanding of my patient.

Engaging in consultation honestly requires emotional work. As a consultee, I've observed that I often grapple with varying degrees of discomfort after realizing what I didn't know, perceive, contain, or process. Often after presenting, I also experience a sense of discontinuity and disruption before I can process emotionally and integrate the content and experience of the consultation and regain equilibrium.

As a consultant, I'm most useful when I can use my countertransferences to the material presented and my consultees speak freely enough so that I can help with the interferences that they don't consciously intend to bring. Of course, my consultee's trust in my capacity to function helpfully as a consultant develops over time, and time is required for consultees to feel free to speak openly and honestly.

As a consultant, I'm mindful of the potential of consultations to reinforce insecurities, harsh superego or regressive tendencies that interfere with learning. I try to be alert to the dangers of inadvertently participating in unproductive supervisory enactments that actualize regressive expectations that the consultant knows best, the consultee is a passive recipient of the consultant's knowledge, or the consultant is the one responsible for the patient's treatment.

My experience suggests that consultation alone does not help in certain instances. I've witnessed analysts who struggle with destructive identifications with past analysts or supervisors who have been hurtful to them. In their work, these analysts turn passive into active and inadvertently repeat the harshness, disengagement, blaming, seductiveness, and other mistreatments they suffered as analysands or supervisees. I found that in these cases, consultation was useful when the analyst has come to terms with his/her previous difficult analytic experiences. Otherwise, when the problems proved to be pervasive and persistent, I have recommended that they consider further reparative analytic work.

Resistances to consultation

As I mentioned earlier, although the need to seek consultation regularly has gradually been better accepted in the analytic literature, seeking periodic help for each patient isn't considered ordinary or imperative. If analysts participate in ways that we don't intend to or even recognize in each analysis, doesn't it follow that we should periodically seek consultation about each analysis? I've identified various obstacles that get in the way of analysts' seeking consultation for all their work.

Though we call analysis the "impossible profession," many of us haven't fully accepted the enormity of the emotional demands of analysis. As I started my career, I had to contend with my own unrealistic ideas about what's possible in analysis. It didn't help that in presentations, private talks, and publications, experienced analysts rarely spoke of difficulties and failures and more often presented sanitized, highly edited versions of analysis that I couldn't recognize in my everyday practice. To become more comfortable pursuing consultation, I had to more fully appreciate the enormous demands of analytic work and more fully accept the ongoing influence of my unconscious and my mind's propensity to constantly resist the most painful feelings and most disturbing fantasies and let myself know their meaning.

Consulting openly about one's work involves sharing shortcomings and vulnerabilities and is subject to the same resistances as being an analysand. I've observed, both in myself when I seek consultation for my work and in those who consult with me, that narcissistic vulnerability and shame about our limitations feature prominently as obstacles to seeking help. For instance, seeking consultation may evoke embarrassment about not being an idealized version of what an analyst is, the nature and intensity of our feelings, and losing the "as if" perspective and identifying with our countertransferences, among others.[8]

As ironic as it might seem, given that we are helpers, many analysts don't consider needing emotional help as ordinary or even register the need. In part, having grown up without much help with our emotional lives, many of us don't recognize as extraordinary the unbearable feelings and disturbing states of mind that we must contain and metabolize every day when we're able to work closely with our patients' most difficult feelings. Our notion of analytic self-sufficiency represents in part a repetition of our early experiences of having been left alone with intolerable feelings. We can reenact this experience by seeing a large number of patients back to back and getting little consultation, a recipe for demoralization and shortcuts that hurt patients and analysts alike.

Given the determining power of our unconscious, the notion of the analyst's self-sufficiency is an illusion. But what about the analyst's autonomy? My interest in exploring the usefulness of seeking consultation does not imply that I don't recognize the value of the analyst's independence. On the contrary, I think developing one's own unique analytic voice and identity is central to doing good analytic work. I've witnessed that the less analysts rely on formulaic knowledge and the more capable they become of using their own experience to understand the depth of feeling and the unconscious manifestations in the clinical encounter, the better they're able to help their patients. Seeking consultation, of course, can be used defensively—for example, as a retreat from acknowledging one's competence and skills and from genuine analytic thinking. An authoritarian consultant can promote destructive idealizations and feed into the consultee's personal insecurities.

Nonetheless, I have observed that a good-enough consultation enhances the analyst's capacity to function with relative freedom from authoritarian introjects, unrealistic ideals, and compulsively enacted unconscious fantasies. In consultation, as in analysis, the paradox of the human condition is that we can become more differentiated, integrated, and autonomous, more our unique selves, through our honest, caring connection to one another.

Concluding remarks

I've shared with you my experience that analysts' practice of consulting with other analysts about our work is an essential aspect of maintaining ourselves as effective analysts. I've found that frequent consultation with periodic presentation of every patient in one's practice is an important precondition for sustaining a generative engagement in practicing and teaching psychoanalysis. In the past when I offered my experience, some colleagues expressed concern that consulting frequently would add to analysts' already heavy load. I have found that frequent consultation isn't a burden. On the contrary, my experience as a consultant has led me to conclude that many analysts are already unduly burdened by their countertransferences and by preconscious guilt for participating in ways that they did not consciously intend to and that consulting regularly lessens that burden and frees them up to do more analytic work. Although not a panacea, I have found that regular, honest consulting on every case with a capable consultant can help tip the balance away from prolonged enactments and retraumatizations and toward more productive analytic collaborations.

Notes

1　It is one of the paradoxes of psychoanalytic training that candidates are given the message that a mature analyst is an analyst who works without supervisory help.
2　Supervisors repeatedly asked me when I would end my work with them and fellow graduates boasted that they had ended all supervision.
3　Part of analysts' best practices, continuing education, and ordinary self-care.
4　Shelley Orgel remembers that this was stated explicitly in the BOPS Standards when he was involved with the Board (personal communications).
5　It is of interest to note that the first papers devoted solely to consultation coincided with or shortly followed the publication of accounts framing the analyst's inadvertent participation, not as failures or evidence of the analyst's incomplete analysis, but as an inevitable and expectable, even desirable, aspect of every analysis.
6　Examples of going-through-the-motions participation include resting on or reaching for yesterday's understanding, listening but not participating emotionally, not making emotional use of my own thoughts and feelings in the moment, etc.
7　A consultant who enjoys his or her work also helps me remain in touch with the pleasures of being an analyst.
8　Shelly Orgel suggests that to seek consultation an analyst has "to get beyond idealized identifications with past generations of analysts who could not openly discuss their limitation, failures, disappointments" (personal communication).

References

Boesky, D. (1990). The psychoanalytic process and its components. *Psychoanalytic Quarterly*, 59: 550–584.
Gabbard, G.O. (2000). Consultation from the consultant's perspective. *Psychoanalytic Dialogues*, 10: 209–218.
Gill, M.M. (1982). Analysis of the Transference, Vol. I. *Psychological Issues, Monograph 53*. New York: Int. Univ. Press.
Jacobs, T. (1983). The analyst and the patient's object world: Notes on an aspect of countertransference. *Journal of the American Psychoanalytic Association*, 31: 619–642.
Kantrowitz, J.L. (2002). The external observer and the lens of the patient-analyst match. *International Journal of Psycho-Analysis*, 83: 339–350.

Kantrowitz, J.L. (2009). Privacy and disclosure in psychoanalysis. *Journal of the American Psychoanalytic Association*, 57: 787–806.

McLaughlin, J. (1981). Transference, psychic reality, and countertransference. *Psychoanalytic Quarterly*, 50: 639–664.

Mizen, R. (2013). On session frequency and analytic method. *British Journal of Psychotherapy*, 29: 57–74.

Muller, J.P. (1999). Consultation from the Position of the Third. *American Journal of Psychoanalysis*, 59: 113–118.

Ogden, T.H. (2005). On psychoanalytic supervision. *International Journal of Psycho-Analysis*, 86: 1265–1280.

Ogden, T.H. (2016). Destruction reconceived on Winnicott's "The use of an object and relating through identifications." *International Journal of Psycho-Analysis*, 97: 1243–1262.

Pizer, B. (2000). The therapist's routine consultations: A necessary window in the treatment frame. *Psychoanalytic Dialogues*, 10(2): 197–207.

Poland, W.S. (1984). On the analysts' neutrality. *Journal of the American Psychoanalytic Association*, 32: 283–299.

Sandler, J. (1976). Countertransference and role responsiveness. *International Review of Psycho-Analysis*, 3: 43–47.

Afterword

Looking inward and forward

I wrote this book in response to observations that clinical psychoanalysis is an endangered practice—threatened not only by its checkered past and the fast-paced demands of the modern world but also by analysts' daunting difficulties of functioning analytically, which can lead analysts to move away from disturbing feelings within ourselves and the suffering of our patients. Having experienced the pressures of functioning as an analyst firsthand and seen many other analysts struggle, I've wanted to share my thoughts about how I continue to maintain a strong psychoanalytic practice.

I based this book on my experiences and observations that psychoanalysis is a worthwhile endeavor. When things go well, psychoanalysis, more than any existing psychological treatment, fundamentally transforms a suffering person's life. It frees a patient from the shackles of her own mind and allows her to become more integrated and better able to love and be intimate.

I'd like in closing to highlight certain threads that run through this book and unite the chapters. These crystalize my understanding of the elements that contribute to analysts' good-enough participation in the analytic relationship.

- Practicing from the inside out by not externalizing difficulties but treating them as signals with psychoanalytic meaning.
- Acknowledging the power of the analyst's unconscious as it manifests itself in ambivalence about beginning and maintaining analytic relationships. Knowing that the analyst's reluctance and ambivalence constitute underappreciated parts of every analysis.
- Appreciating that difficulties, tensions, and paradoxes are inherent in psychoanalytic practice.
- Recognizing patients' wish for intensive help for integration and intimacy.
- Acknowledging the limitations of analysis without using them to rationalize one's fears of analysis.
- Recognizing that whether the analyst's professional identity functions primarily in the service of omnipotence and manic defences, or growth and creativity, rests on her own emotional work.

- Understanding that one is always becoming an analyst—continuously striving to access the parts of one's mind that allow one to be alive to one's experience and make use of that experience to understand patients and oneself more deeply and with greater precision.
- Appreciating that sustaining oneself as an analyst rests on ongoing internal work in the form of rigorous self-analysis, supervision, peer consultation and, often, reanalysis.
- Accepting the reality that, regardless of talent, experience or skills, analysts need help to maintain an analytic mind. The idea that analysts can practice autonomously belies the reality of our unconscious minds.
- Realizing that insight *and* the experience of being cared for and attended to in the context of a sturdy internal and external frame and genuine emotional contact between analyst and patient are essential for therapeutic change.
- Accepting that although psychoanalysis is widely criticized by the general public and other mental health professionals, its practice is more adversely affected by analysts' idealizations and unexamined disappointments with analysis and analysts.
- Recognizing that our pessimism about analysis is a symptom in need of analysis, as is unbridled optimism.

In a profession whose practice doesn't provide easy assurances about the value of one's work, how do we sustain our confidence, morale, and principles without idealizing or devaluing our training or practice? How do we sustain our capacity to practice optimistically and energetically and contribute to our analytic communities and the psychoanalytic field?

Although psychoanalysis isn't as prestigious or sought after by patients or trainees as it used to be in the 50s and 60s, I believe that our best days are still ahead of us. No longer tempted by prestige or popularity, those of us committed to practicing analysis can focus on practicing from the inside out and intimately and create a psychoanalytic internal and external holding environment to support us. Writing this book sustained me. I hope reading it sustains you.

Index

Abend, S.M. 18, 20, 77
abuse 51, 80–1, 85, 106, 147
abusive relationships 14, 81
additional sessions 34, 39–42, 52, 55, 81–4, 87, 95, 111, 129, 149
adults 3, 15, 18–19
advisors 55–6, 65
aggression 11–12, 20, 78–9, 135
agreement 1, 19, 40, 52, 104; analyst's unquestioning 104; lack of 1, 52; unspoken 40
allusions 34, 105, 135; to frequency in the patient's associations 34; repeated 105
aloofness 18, 36, 38, 42–3
amateur psychoanalysts 3
ambivalence 11, 16, 20, 30, 60, 62, 77–8, 89, 122, 137, 148, 156; about practicing analysis 68; exploring conflicts and traumas 60; inherent in every relationship and endeavor 53; managing 123; recognizing the omnipresence of 66; in recommending analysis to patients 11
American Psychoanalytic Association 9, 87
analysands 13, 19, 26, 28, 33, 66, 93, 123, 127–8, 143, 152–3
analysis 32, 95, 106, 125, 133; beginning 34, 45, 55, 66, 120; candidate's 54, 57; destructive 144; distant 95, 108, 111; five-times-a-week 15, 17, 106; four-times-a-week 49; helpful 25, 52, 67; hurtful 130; in-room 92, 95, 99, 106–10; incomplete 124; initiating 59, 62–5; intensive 87; long 102, 129; numbers of patients in 9–10, 12, 49–50; online 92; patients fear of 29; personal 19, 110, 133; post-graduation 123; practiced in the United States

9; productive 16; quitting 49; recommendation for 12–13, 20, 28, 77, 120; signals 26; training 11, 19, 50–1, 54, 65, 78, 124; trusting 137; useful 45, 53, 110
analyst-in-training 9, 52, 67
analysts 1–5, 9–14, 18–21, 24–36, 50–2, 54–6, 58–68, 77–9, 86–90, 92–9, 106–11, 119–37, 141–5, 148–54, 156–7; ambivalence 11, 77, 86, 89, 123; analyzing 19, 134; anticipation of the storm within 31; capacity to apply correct techniques 10, 28, 59, 62, 89, 97–9, 119, 122–3, 131, 153; contemporary 1, 125; and the emotional challenge of practicing 11, 121, 152; experienced 66, 78, 121, 128, 152; graduate 2, 5, 13, 50–4, 61, 65, 67, 121–2, 137, 141–2; helping 150; independence 153; male 1; mind 2, 5, 24–46, 60, 66–7, 79, 86, 98, 142; practice of 119, 130; reluctance to begin a new analysis 9–21, 77–8, 80, 88, 98, 106, 111, 156; senior 108, 149; and the sense of conviction about the usefulness of analysis 125; struggle to maintain their analytic identity. 78, 156; successful 120; training 11, 19, 50, 54, 65, 124; and the value of independence 153; zeal 87–8
analytic 28, 92, 110, 125; appointments 44, 129, 149; beginnings 12, 31; cases 9, 50, 54, 56, 119, 141; data 25, 30, 50, 94, 98; dyad 79, 143, 146, 150; endeavor 89, 125; engagement 18, 77, 79, 88, 94; frequency 29, 33, 37, 45, 58, 64, 79, 81, 88, 120, 130–2, 137; help 28, 110, 125; interaction 88;

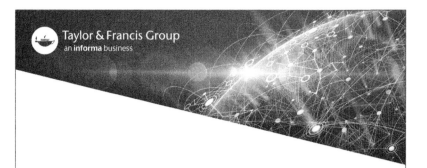

Printed in Great Britain
by Amazon

32178162R00104